MORAVIANS
IN TWO WORLDS

A STUDY OF
CHANGING COMMUNITIES

MORAVIANS
IN TWO WORLDS

A Study of Changing Communities

GILLIAN LINDT GOLLIN

COLUMBIA UNIVERSITY PRESS

NEW YORK AND LONDON 1967

This study, prepared under the Graduate Faculties of
Columbia University, was selected by a committee of
the Faculty of Political Science to receive the annual
Bancroft Award established by the Trustees of the
University.

For A.E.G.—my severest critic—with love

ACKNOWLEDGMENTS

THIS STUDY could not have been undertaken or completed had it not been for the support of a number of individuals and organizations. Sigmund Diamond was the first to bring the Archives of the Moravians in Bethlehem to my attention and provided invaluable stimulation and encouragement throughout my work on this study. Robert K. Merton criticized an earlier draft of this book and in his commentary demonstrated anew his rare ability to single out the sociologically significant from a vast array of historical data. My early attempts to formulate a comparative perspective profited greatly from the incisive criticism of Hans L. Zetterberg. As teachers, critics, and friends these three generated a spirit of intellectual challenge which transformed the often tedious processes of data-gathering and analysis into an exciting quest to comprehend the social dynamics of an earlier period.

I owe a very special debt to the Board of Elders of the Northern Province of the Church of the United Brethren in America for permission to examine and to quote from manuscripts and rare books in the collection of the Provincial Archives of the Moravian Church, North, in Bethlehem, Pennsylvania. I should like to thank in particular Bishop Kenneth G. Hamilton, who, as chairman of the Archives Committee in Bethlehem, gave me much valuable advice and direction in the early stages of research. His criticism of a draft of this manuscript gave witness to a quality I have found in many Moravians—an extraordinary willingness to see themselves as others see them, and to review the findings of an "outsider" with a degree of detachment we social scientists might well emulate. The late Brothers Görner and Fliegel spent many hours assisting me in the location of documents and deciphering of manuscripts;

Miss Martha Luckenbach gave me both hospitality and guidance during many of my visits to Bethlehem; and Mr. Vernon Nelson helped to locate and verify bibliographic references. In Germany, Dr. Erwin Förster, Director of the Unity of the Brethren in Herrnhut, and Mr. Richard Träger, Chief Archivist of the Moravian Archives in Herrnhut, supplied information on some of the documents in their collection and on some characteristics of the current population of Herrnhut. I acknowledge with gratitude their permission to quote from manuscript materials, the originals of which form part of the Herrnhut Collection.

To the Social Science Research Council I am indebted for a predoctoral fellowship which enabled me to spend fifteen months, free from academic duties, studying Moravian documents. The Graduate School of Howard University provided a grant for the final retyping of this manuscript. Beulah Harris displayed diligence and care in checking references and quotations; and Kathryn Schaeffer transformed a barely legible manuscript into clean and accurate copy with skill, promptness, and good humor. Frederick Nicklaus of the Columbia University Press saved me from many errors in grammar and style. Finally, I should like to express my appreciation to Virginia Dillon and Peggy Scott, who made it possible for me to combine the roles of scholar and mother by taking over, temporarily, many of a mother's responsibilities. My most personal debt is acknowledged elsewhere.

GILLIAN LINDT GOLLIN

February, 1967
Washington, D. C.

CONTENTS

All institutions exist for a purpose. When that purpose can no longer be attained, or falls away altogether, the social arrangement must be abandoned. That is how it has to be in a religious community, otherwise it becomes stale and moves only ex opere operato.

—HERRNHUT DIARIUM
December 31, 1734

INTRODUCTION

THE COMMUNITIES of Herrnhut, Saxony, and Bethlehem, Pennsylvania, separated by over 5,000 miles of land and ocean, constitute the focal points of this book. Herrnhut today is a small settlement in East Germany, close to the borders of Poland and Czechoslovakia, with a population of less than 2,000 and an economy in which crafts, handed down over generations, still predominate. For two centuries it has been united primarily by a common religious faith and a commitment to missionary goals. Contemporary Bethlehem is a sprawling industrial city in the eastern United States, with a population of over 75,000 and an economy tied to one of the corporation giants of the American steel industry. Its citizens, professing diverse religious beliefs, are for the most part bound together by a shared commitment to the values of American democracy and freedom of enterprise.

Both communities were founded in the first half of the eighteenth century by men and women who considered themselves members of the oldest Protestant church in the world—the *Unitas Fratrum.** They were established as exclusive religious settlements designed to further the missionary goals of the Moravian Brethren. In the early

---

* The terms "Moravian Brethren," "Moravian Church," "Unity of the Brethren," "*Unitas Fratrum,*" and "Herrnhuter" have often been used interchangeably to refer to one and the same religious group. The term "*Unitas Fratrum,*" commonly translated into English as "the Unity of the Brethren," remains to this day the formal designation of this ancient Protestant Episcopal Church. The term "Herrnhuter" has been used most often on the continent of Europe to identify not only the inhabitants of Herrnhut but all of the members of this religious group. The term "Moravian" refers to the geographical origins of many of the early members of the *Unitas Fratrum.* It has been generally used in English-speaking countries in order to avoid confusion with various other groups of self-styled "Brethren," with none of whom the Moravians have any connection whatsoever.

years the communities shared a common set of religious values. Their political, social, and economic institutions were also remarkably similar, and in each case differed radically from those of neighboring settlements.

A perusal of the literature on denominational and sectarian communities can help to define the focus of this inquiry more sharply. Although the comparative approach has been used in studies of changing religious communities, the comparisons have generally been made between the social institutions of different types of religious settlements.[1] Studies dealing with changes in the institutions of a single sect or denomination have generally ignored possible differences in the development of communities professing the same religious beliefs and goals.[2] They stress instead the characteristics which are common to all of the communities of that particular sect, ignoring for the most part intrasect differences in the structuring of the settlements. The most cursory reading of studies dealing with Moravian groups reveals significant differences in community development, notwithstanding the similarities of religious orientation. It reveals further that factors used to explain a given social change in one community often fail to explain why such a change did not occur in another settlement.

Even Max Weber, with his explicit commitment to the comparative study of the role of religious ideas as determinants of economic activity, appears to have ignored the possibility that the community of Herrnhut might not be representative of other Moravian settlements. His analysis, based on sources dealing only with the experiences of the Moravians in Herrnhut, led him to conclude that the emotional and nonrational elements of the Moravian religion tended to preclude the development of a rational attitude towards economic action, as exemplified in the capitalist spirit.[3] The history of Herrnhut does appear to confirm his hypothesis. The history of Bethlehem does not. But if the religious ideas of the two communities were the same, why then did the economic development of Bethlehem come to differ so radically from that of its sister community? How did it come to pass that the same religious ideas had different consequences in different social settings?

The central problem of this study, therefore, is to seek to identify underlying patterns of social change which enable us to explain observed differences in the nature and processes of change of the major institutions—religious, political, social, and economic—of Herrnhut and Bethlehem, between 1722 and 1850. The major objectives of the study are threefold: to describe specific changes in the value systems and social structures of the two settlements; to compare strategic differences in the dynamics of these social changes; and to analyze the principal determinants of such changes.

The decision to study only two Moravian communities was prompted by the fact that inclusion of additional communities would have proportionately reduced the detail and precision with which the changing institutions of each could be portrayed, without, I believe, significantly altering the patterns of social change observed. The communities of Herrnhut and Bethlehem represent the two most prominent centers of Moravian activity during the eighteenth and nineteenth centuries, and they survived longer than most as religiously exclusive settlements where membership in the Church of the Moravian Brethren was a condition of residence. The study is limited to a consideration of changes occurring in the first one hundred years of each community's existence. It incorporates a time span long enough to permit identification of the primary dimensions and determinants of change underlying the process of secularization yet short enough to allow a specification of this process in adequate detail.

The materials on which this book is based are historical. They include primary manuscript sources, notably those of the Moravian Archives in Bethlehem, Pennsylvania, and Herrnhut, Saxony, as well as a large number of secondary accounts of the two communities. The diligence of the Moravians in writing and preserving letters, personal and communal diaries, autobiographical sketches, statements of accounts, and deeds of property—almost all of which were written in eighteenth-century German script—provides an unusual opportunity to study in detail the changing character of their communities.[4]

The conceptual frame of reference of the study, however, is sociological. In the first place I am interested not in the delineation of historical events per se but in the reconstruction of the social systems of two Moravian communities in order to be able to analyze the processes of change which characterized the development of Herrnhut and Bethlehem during the eighteenth and nineteenth centuries.[5] Similarly the units of analysis of this study are also sociological. The communities are studied with reference to their dominant values, norms, ethics, and ideas, which taken as a whole may be said to constitute the value system of the community; their social structure, that is, the interrelationships of social statuses, roles, and organizations which together define the structural regularities of the community; and their major institutions.[6]

The early history of the Moravian Brethren may for our purposes be sketched in brief. The Moravians trace their religious origins to the fifteenth century, when followers of Jan Hus founded the *Jednota Bratrska,* later known as the *Unitas Fratrum,* and settled in Kunvald, east of Prague, to pursue a pietistic mode of life in which purity of morals and conduct was stressed over and above doctrinal uniqueness.[7] In 1467 the Brethren formally seceded from the Church of Rome, elected their own ministers, and through Stephen, a Bishop believed to have been a member of the Austrian Waldensers, secured for themselves the episcopacy. The Bible was accepted as the sole standard of religious doctrine and practice. By the beginning of the seventeenth century more than half of the Protestants of Bohemia and Moravia belonged to the Church of the Brethren. But with the outbreak of the Thirty Years' War, and the defeat of the Bohemian Protestants at the Battle of White Mountain in 1620, the Brethren were either driven underground or forced into exile. The church was kept alive largely through the efforts of their Bishop, Comenius (1592–1672), who publicized their history and

Early View of Herrnhut, the Moravian Community in Saxony

Courtesy the Archives of the Moravian Church, Bethlehem, Pa.

*Early View of Bethlehem, Pennsylvania, the Original
Moravian Community in North America*

Courtesy the Archives of the Moravian Church, Bethlehem, Pa.

doctrines in his *Ratio Disciplinae* and collected funds for the support of the "Hidden Seed" worshiping in secret in Moravia and Bohemia. Some of the Brethren sought refuge in Poland, where they were permitted to register as members of the Reformed Church while still retaining their own bishops and ritual. Others fled to Germany, crossing the border into Saxony, where many of them found asylum on the estate of an Austrian nobleman, Count Nickolas Ludwig von Zinzendorf.[8]

The Count, a fervent Protestant and follower of the German Pietists Spener and Francke, permitted the Brethren to settle on part of his estate of Berthelsdorf, in Saxony, hoping in time to convert them to his own particular brand of Pietism. On June 17, 1722, the emigrants from Moravia began to erect their first buildings at the foot of the Hutberg, and so laid the foundations of the settlement of Herrnhut (meaning literally "in the Lord's care"), a community which to this day bears the imprint of its religious origins. Zinzendorf, instead of converting the Brethren to his original beliefs, became a bishop of the Church of the Brethren, and he is revered by Moravians as the leader of the resuscitated Moravian Church.

The Moravians, spurred by missionary zeal, were not content to remain in Herrnhut indefinitely. Moreover, by 1736 relations with the government of Saxony had deteriorated to such an extent that Zinzendorf was forced into exile for a number of years. He used his exile to help create other sectarian communities, notably in America where the British had promised him the religious freedom he appeared to have forfeited on his own estates. An attempt to found a settlement in Georgia in the seventeen-thirties failed. The land the Moravians had purchased turned out to be a swamp, and sickness and death plagued the community from the start. The hostilities of the Spanish War compounded the difficulties of the Moravians still further. Their pacifist stand antagonized both the British and the Spanish. Undaunted, the surviving members of this first attempt to found a Moravian community on American soil traveled northward to Pennsylvania where George Whitefield, a Methodist and friend of Zinzendorf, had promised them land in Northampton County, in the forks of the Delaware. In 1741 they bought a tract of land from Whitefield and built their first log cabin. With their numbers reinforced by a group of Moravians from Herrnhut, they celebrated their first Christmas in Pennsylvania in the company of Zinzendorf himself, who decided to name the new community Bethlehem.[9]

This, then, is a study of two changing communities viewed from a dual perspective. On the one hand, the world of the Moravians in Herrnhut, living in the Old World of pre-industrial Europe, will be contrasted with that of the Moravians in Bethlehem, witnessing and ultimately participating in the emergence of a new nation. On the other, comparisons will be made over time, focussing within each community on the gradual secularization and consequent transformation of each settlement from religious enclave to worldly community.

PART ONE. RELIGION

I decree that there can be no
Christianity without community.
—ZINZENDORF
February 4, 1734

I. BELIEFS AND PRACTICES

THE KEY to understanding the nature of the communities of Herrnhut and Bethlehem during the eighteenth century is to be found in the Moravian religious institutions. Throughout this period the day-to-day activities of the Moravians were guided primarily by religious norms and sanctions. In order to comprehend more precisely the role of these sanctions in the development of the two settlements we need first to examine briefly the central doctrines, ethics, and rituals of the Moravians.[1]

Beliefs

The Moravians never developed a systematic theology. One is thus confronted not with a logically cohesive body of doctrine, but with isolated fragments of dogma held together by force of custom. Their members, lay and clergy, were bound to no creed.[2] In spite of this aversion to doctrine, part of which was due to Zinzendorf's personal distaste for theological dispute, the Moravians over the years acknowledged a number of canonical points.

When the immigrants from Moravia arrived in Herrnhut they brought with them a variety of religious traditions, dominant among which were those of the *Unitas Fratrum*. The *Unitas Fratrum* were themselves less concerned with doctrine than with conduct.[3] The Bible was regarded as the source of all religious truths; Christ, and not the Pope, was revered as the head of God's Church, and religious piety and ethical conduct were stressed far more than adherence to a specific set of beliefs.[4] In the seventeenth century under the guidance of Comenius these beliefs were formalized in a confession of faith.[5] The emphasis on the Bible as the sole source of religious doctrine was adopted by the resuscitated Moravian Church and has been upheld to this day.

Zinzendorf himself bequeathed to the religious heritage of the Moravians an assortment of beliefs and practices, some of which were derived from the writings of Comenius,[6] some from his early Pietist leanings, some from his dalliance with mysticism, and some from his partial reconciliation with Lutheranism in his later years. From the Pietists, under whose influence he had come through the ministrations of his grandmother, and especially his aunt, even before he became personally acquainted with Francke at the Pietist Pedagogium in Halle, the young Zinzendorf derived what came to be the central characteristic of his religion—the emphasis on the heart as the seat of religious experience: "Our Saviour has declared that the little ones, the children, believe in Him (Math. 18:6): From which we can well observe that faith has its seat not in speculation, not in thought, but in the heart. . . ."[7]

Underlying this conception of a religion based not on understanding but on feeling is Zinzendorf's view of God as infinite and absolute, defying man's attempts at apprehension through thought. It is this premise which leads Zinzendorf to devalue logical or rational thought processes, and to give pre-eminence to the emotions:

> There is nothing more dangerous or useless than a little brain, filled with thoughts about theology, trying to penetrate the godhead. . . . For if they [the angels] were able to penetrate the godhead and were to focus even briefly upon the progression of eternity, they would go mad in their own way. That is how infinite and endlessly beyond the comprehension of all living creatures is the divine.[8]

Since man cannot apprehend God through his thoughts, God must reveal himself in a manner comprehensible to mankind. This is accomplished in the person of Jesus, who is both God and man, and who becomes the central focus of Zinzendorfian and Moravian religious doctrine. It is the Saviour who has made God accessible to man, and it is through Christ's sufferings on the Cross that the ransom for men's sins has been paid.

In his insistence upon Christ as the sole means through which man could hope to understand God, Zinzendorf was in agreement with both Luther and Spener. But where he came to differ radically with the Pietists was in his conception of salvation. Zinzendorf believed that since Christ had atoned for the sins of man, man no longer was forced into eternal penitence but instead was free to love and adore God. To attain salvation it was not sufficient merely to believe in God and Christ; one had to learn to love Him: "Love thus becomes the fulfillment of the law, love institutes the very life and soul of belief, love is the *spiritus universalis* of a true religion." [9] Zinzendorf found it increasingly difficult to reconcile this emphasis upon love and adoration of Christ as essential to salvation with the Pietists' growing insistence upon the necessity of undergoing an exceedingly painful personal struggle for conversion and salvation. As Sawyer remarked: "To Zinzendorf salvation was not a process of guilt, pain, sin and distress, but a joyful apprehension of a loving Father, persistently yet gently leading his child into a new life of happy companionship with himself." [10] Here again the emphasis is upon experiencing a joyous reunion with Christ through one's emotions rather than with one's head. Salvation, Zinzendorf declared, depends less "on the truth in ideas than the truth in sensation." [11]

Since it was essential for the believer to keep the death and suffering of Christ on the Cross before his eyes at all times, the image of Christ became identified almost exclusively with His sufferings, His blood, and His wounds, a trend which reached its height during the extremes of the Sifting Period * in the seventeen-forties. [12] During these years the emphasis was placed upon visual contemplation of,

* This term, coined by the Moravians, and generally used to designate the years 1738–1752, derives from the following Biblical text: "And the Lord said, Simon, Simon, behold Satan hath desired to have you, that he may sift you as wheat [Luke 22:31]."

rather than verbal communion with, the Saviour. "Jesus in his
bloody condition stands before our eyes. That gives us such certainty
and infallibility, that even if we wanted to doubt, we would have to
feel ashamed. . . ." [13]

Although Zinzendorf had originally turned away from doctrinal
debate and speculation, he now made antirationalism an end in itself, declaring fervently that men "were not to use their own brains;
they were to wish they had no brains, they were to be like children
in arms; and thus they would overcome all their doubts and banish
all their cares." [14]

Societies of little fools, little worms, baby chicks, and even little
bees, "who feel at home in the Sidehole and crawl in deep" [15] were
formed not only in Herrnhaag,[16] the center of Moravian activity
during the time of the Sifting, but also in Herrnhut and Bethlehem.
The members of these societies were said to have no heads but only
hearts, and Zinzendorf came to be addressed as "Herzens Papa"
(Heart's Daddy).[17] All worldly cares were to be handed over to
the Saviour; concern about the future was taken as an indication of
lack of faith in God's ability to provide for those dearest to him.
This antirationalism was accompanied by an intense preoccupation
with the physical and emotional details of Christ's crucifixion. The
Litany of the Wounds became the central source of doctrinal
orthodoxy during these years.[18] The wounds of Jesus, including the
side wound and even "the unnamed and unknown wounds," were
characterized by a wealth of adjectives, such as "worthy, beloved,
miraculous, powerful, secret, clear, sparkling, holy, purple, juicy,
close, long-suffering, dainty, warm, soft, hot, and eternal." [19] Since it
is virtually impossible for an English translation to do justice to the
German original, many passages being almost unintelligible even in
German and full of grammatical and linguistic innovations, we
shall merely reproduce here a section of the original, to convey something of the sensual and emotional character implicit in the language of that period:

Vor aller eigenen gerechtigkeit,
Vor aller zucht-trokkenheit,
Vor der unblutigen gnade,   Behüt
Vor unbebluteten herzen,   uns
Vor aller schönheit ohne blut-strich,   lieber
Vor der gleichgültigkeit gegen deine Wunden,   Herre
Vor der entfremdung von deinem Creuze,   Gott!
Vor der entwehung von deiner Seite,
Vor ungesalbtem blut geschwätz,
Vor der ewigen tod-sünde.[20]

Religion thus came to center on a blood-sodden adoration of Jesus' wounds. To deviate from such adoration, according to Zinzendorf, was to manifest a lack of appreciation of the spiritual: "Fuga sanguinis hydrophobia spiritualis." (Aversion to blood is spiritual hydrophobia.) [21] Yet, as Sawyer has pointed out, this emphasis upon the wounds of Jesus was not peculiar to the Moravians. Luther himself consistently emphasized the wounds of Jesus as symbols of Christ's atonement, and many Protestant churches to this day use Toplady's hymnal, "Rock of ages, cleft for me,/let me hide myself in thee." [22] But the Moravians, unlike most other Protestants, developed for some time so exclusive a preoccupation with Christ's wounds that the symbols of Christ's atonement came to be revered as mystical entities deserving man's adoration in and of themselves, and not because they were symbolic expressions of the Saviour's sufferings for the salvation of mankind.

Just as the Sifting Period intensified antirational, emotional, and sensuous elements inherent in the early religious beliefs of the Moravians, so it brought to a climax the stress upon religious experience as a social rather than an individual act. Zinzendorf, although he admitted that everyone was ultimately alone in seeking and communing with God, insisted that since God had created man as a gregarious creature, He demanded that His followers be known by their "brotherly love for one another." [23] Under these circumstances religion became the basis not for a solitary, isolated experience but for an active communal life. The Church came to be thought of as the bride of Jesus, and the believers were referred to as the family of God. According to Zinzendorfian theology, it was not sufficient to believe in Christ and to love Him unless one also took an active part in communicating with His family of fellow-believers and came to practice brotherliness towards them: "A man therefore, who sees his goal in the Saviour, but who does not recognize His bride, and knows nothing of His family, is not the kind of person of whom I am speaking [i.e., a man who attains salvation]." [24]

During the Sifting Period kinship terminology was used extensively to characterize the relationships between God and man. What had once been only analogies now came to be regarded as mystical revelations of religious truths. The Holy Trinity was thought of as a family, with God as father, the Holy Ghost as mother, and Jesus as their only son. The Church of God on earth was pictured as Christ's bride who had been born in the Saviour's side wound, was betrothed to Christ on the Cross, and was finally married to Christ in the celebration of Holy Communion. The Church was thus not only Christ's bride and wife, but also the daughter-in-law of both God and the Holy Ghost.[25]

Finally, mention should be made of at least one other doctrine which came to the fore during this period—the doctrine of the elect. During the time of the Sifting the Moravians were so busy celebrating their exclusive relationship to God that they withdrew almost entirely from the world outside. Bethlehem managed to retain more contacts with non-Moravians during these years than either Herrnhut or Herrnhaag. This was due primarily to the fact that as long as the temperate Spangenberg, with his penchant for reasonableness, was in charge, the values so characteristic of the Sifting Period were restrained by his leadership.[26] Zinzendorf himself was convinced that his propagation of Spener's *ecclesiolae in ecclesia* was essentially a unifying measure under which all Protestant churches might once more be reunited under a single church.[27] Yet in fact it

is clear that Zinzendorf continued to believe that some churches
were a little more equal than others, and that the Moravians in
particular enjoyed an elect status because by virtue of their beliefs
and religious works they were a little closer to salvation than most.

This presumed superiority impeded efforts at unification in the
New World. The failure of the Pennsylvania Synods, convened by
Zinzendorf in 1742 in an attempt to merge various German Protestant groups in Pennsylvania, was due not, as the Count believed, to
the refusal of the various sects to join in a common "Church of God
in the Spirit" but to their rejection of a subordinate status in a
church in which the Moravians clearly were to be, if not the only
elect, then the most elect.[28] Although this tendency towards thinking of themselves as an aristocracy of the elect was most pronounced
during the Sifting Period, it lingered on wherever Moravian
missionaries espoused the belief that they had been especially chosen
by God to spread His gospel among the heathen. Personal humility
might reduce the saliency of this conviction but it could not eradicate it altogether.

Under the influence of Zinzendorf the religion of the Moravians
thus came to develop certain definite characteristics. It stressed religious feeling (*Gefühl*) and experience over and above dogma and
doctrinal uniqueness. It was Christocentric and adhered to a belief
in salvation based upon joyful and loving apprehension of Christ
whose sufferings upon the Cross had atoned for man's sins. It regarded religion as a social experience in which the faithful were
bound together in a community of brotherly love but at the same
time separated from the rest of mankind, who did not adhere to
their beliefs, and who, therefore, were not to be numbered among
God's chosen people.

During the next one hundred years the religious beliefs of the
Moravians changed remarkably little. Spangenberg, who was given
the task of writing a definitive biography of Zinzendorf and who
compiled the official doctrinal position of the Moravian Church in
his *Idea Fidei Fratrum*, modified some of Zinzendorf's ideas with-

out, however, adding any innovations of his own. Thus, the doctrine of the Trinity, which under Zinzendorf had been wrapped in complex and at times contradictory terminology, was simply deemphasized, the language became less flowery, and the sexual and sanguinary imagery was toned down. The Moravian Church, as Sessler has remarked, thus lost in originality what it gained in orthodoxy.[29] The Synod of Barby in 1775 was the only one throughout the remainder of the eighteenth century to devote any significant part of its deliberations to matters of doctrine. Yet all it did was to ratify the Zinzendorfian theology as interpreted by Spangenberg.[30] Not until 1818 did any doctrinal changes occur, and even these were in the form of clarifications of existing doctrine rather than innovation or abrogation. The doctrine of salvation, which previously stressed belief, obedience, and love of God, was now amended to indicate that the work of the spirit was furthermore made manifest in the fruits of a godly life.[31] Yet Zinzendorf himself had, as we have seen, laid considerable emphasis upon *praxis pietatis,* although he did not fully clarify the exact relationship between good works and the attainment of salvation. De Schweinitz, a Moravian Bishop of Bethlehem, summarized the doctrinal stand of the American Moravians in the eighteen-fifties in his *Moravian Manual.* Their position was almost identical to that of Herrnhut, the only difference being that the German Moravians acknowledged the Augsburg Confession, though this acknowledgment did not bind the conscience of any individual member, and the American Moravians did not. The overall similarity is no accident; it is to be attributed to the fact that both communities still adhered in all essentials to the doctrines adopted by the Church while Zinzendorf was still alive.

Ethics

The Moravians' doctrinal insistence upon the importance of *praxis pietatis* rather than orthodoxy of belief meant that their religion was concerned with the elaboration of religious ethics to a much greater degree than was the case in the traditional Lutheran Church. Yet in spite of the fact that the writings of their chief theologians, Zinzendorf and Spangenberg, abound with ethical maxims, these ethics, like the dogma from which they are derived, do not form a logical or coherent whole.

As an illustration, the Moravian doctrine of salvation, with its emphasis upon "Glückseligkeit" (heavenly bliss), could be interpreted in such a way as to lead men to devote all of their energies to the enjoyment of such bliss in the present world, thereby relieving them of the onerous necessity of struggling for a Calvinistic type of *certitudo salutatis*.[32] This interpretation of their doctrine has led historians like Knox to assert that the Moravians attained peace of mind through the conviction that they stood in God's favor.[33] Yet with the exception of the Sifting Period, it is clear that the Moravians themselves did not share this particular ethical interpretation of their doctrine. Instead they linked this doctrine to the belief that every good Christian who has found God must devote himself to his calling, his *Streiter Beruf,* if he is truly to serve his God.[34] This meant that the virtues of diligence, frugality, punctuality, and conscientious attention to detail came to be regarded not merely as desirable attributes in and of themselves, but as virtues essential to the way of life of a Christian.[35] Work, according to Zinzendorf, was an essential and indispensable part of every Christian's life. "One does not only work in order to live, but one lives for the sake of one's work."[36]

In this interpretation of the Moravian doctrine of salvation, work, though not causing or guaranteeing salvation, was nonetheless regarded as essential to the maintenance of a state of grace, which provided such a powerful ethical justification and impetus to the vast missionary enterprises of this group. The participation in "good works" was, according to the Count, so essential "that he who does not perform them is not really saved."[37] The Moravian doctrine of salvation did not, however, generate that ethical rationalization of conduct, with its emphasis upon accountability and methodical supervision of one's state of grace, which was found in Calvinism. Instead it emphasized the obligation of carrying out a task to the best of one's ability, a task to be accomplished in a spirit of loyalty, sincerity, and love.[38] But the Moravians tended to view each task independently of any other, for there was no ethic demanding, as in Calvinism, that actions must be evaluated within the larger context of one's life span and total accountability to God.

Another aspect of Moravian dogma which had repercussions for the development of their religious ethics is to be found in the emphasis placed upon the social character of religious experience. The belief that the true Christian who was part of the family of God and man must love not only his God but also his fellow men provided a powerful ethical basis for the development of a spirit of cooperation and a willingness to work together as one group. Without it one would be hard put to explain the success of the communal economy of Bethlehem, in which, as we shall see, the demands of the individual were so clearly subordinated to the requirements of the community as a whole.

This same emphasis upon the social aspects of religion largely counteracted the effects of the Moravian self-perception as an aristocracy of the elect, which might otherwise have given an ethical justification for alienation or total withdrawal from the rest of the world. One of the consequences of such alienation would have been the isolation and protection of the community from values or changes in values occurring in the world outside Herrnhut and Bethlehem. But since the pursuit of missionary work was a central goal of the Moravians, they could not sever their ties with the outside. Nor could they prevent their members from being exposed to the secular as well as sacred values and beliefs of the men and women with whom they came into contact in the pursuit of their missionary calling. Thus the very adherence to their religious goals, to the ethical precepts of brotherly love towards all mankind, and to cooperation, implicit in their dogma, forced them to expose themselves to the values of others.

Finally, mention should be made of the ethical precepts derived from the Moravians' belief in the need to keep the image of Christ constantly before their eyes. It was this emphasis upon the closeness of Christ's relation to man which enabled them to seek in His life ethical guidance for the conduct of their own lives. It provided moral precepts to guide the individual through all the stages of life, from infancy to old age. It stressed Christ's innocence, meekness, and obedience to His parents as appropriate for the children, His holy celibacy and life of dedicated work as appropriate to the single men and women, and it ingeniously emphasized His role as husband of all souls as providing ideal standards of conduct for both the married and the widowed.[39] During the time of the Sifting the exclusive preoccupation with Christ's sufferings and His wounds and blood upon the Cross tended to reduce the salience of the earlier emphasis upon the need for faithful and devoted executions of the tasks appropriate to one's status. It led instead to a stress on the purely sensual and emotional joys to be gained from the contemplation of the Saviour's wounds. Thus the use of Christ's life as a model for standards of ethical conduct could be used to justify two very different sets of values—a militant and dedicated pursuit of one's calling or a sensual contemplation and passive acceptance of one's status.

It becomes clear not only that the ethical precepts of the Moravians failed to constitute a logical and coherent whole but also that they could give no uniform and consistent direction to human conduct, since the same religious dogma could be and was indeed interpreted in such a way as to give rise to different and even opposing ethical maxims. The content of these ethics did not change significantly during the remainder of the eighteenth century, but what did alter was the saliency with which particular ethics were adhered to at different times. The place and influence of these religious ethics in the life of the Moravians of Bethlehem and Herrnhut will be a prominent theme of this study.

Ritual

In the early years of Herrnhut and Bethlehem the strong emphasis placed upon religious experience and emotion went hand-in-hand with an extensive and vital series of religious rituals that permeated every major institutional area. The Moravians engaged in many specifically religious devotions, including prayer meetings, hymn singings, recitation of litanies and liturgies, and participation in the Lord's Supper. The start or successful completion of most economic enterprises, whether the laying of a cornerstone for a new building, the bringing in of a new crop of wheat, or the clearing of a new field, was generally marked by a religious ritual known as a "love feast." This celebration, derived from the *Agapae* of the ancient Christian apostolic tradition, consisted of hymn singing or the chanting of a liturgy, in the course of which a simple meal of coffee and bread or rolls was consumed.[40]

So active was this participation in religious activities during the first half of the eighteenth century that, in Herrnhut in particular, it tended to overshadow all other activities, including the economic necessity of providing adequate self-support. During the time of the Sifting the Moravians came to spend so much time in religious devotions, the composition and recitation of liturgies and hymns, and the exchange of personal testimonies of belief that there was little time for participation in work of a more secular character which might have helped to sustain their economic livelihood.

Religious ritual was so interwoven with communal decision-making that it becomes almost impossible to make a clear-cut distinction between sacred and secular activity. The recourse to the lot, whereby God was expected to give his final verdict in a matter of communal policy,[41] was clearly indicative not merely of a specific type of political authority but also of the penetration of religious ritual into all major communal decisions.

The religious rituals associated with such activities represented an attempt to capture the sacred character of all human endeavor in a socially standardized form. Such rituals served not only to keep alive the individual's awareness of the sacred but also to provide a strong basis for the social cohesion and integration of the group.[42] The pervasiveness of religious ritual in all institutional areas of Herrnhut and Bethlehem during these early years gave a social cohesion to the communities at a time when formal social controls were largely absent and the division of labor within these institutions minimal.

Though the religious beliefs and ethics of the Moravians changed little during the next hundred years, the same cannot be said of religious practices. True, the character of the religious ritual was not significantly altered; the hymns, sermons, liturgies, and love feasts underwent no drastic innovations or modifications. Even the specifically religious rituals, such as the celebration of the festivals of Advent, Christmas, Epiphany, Lent, Easter, Ascension day, Whitsun, and Trinity Sunday, or the commemoration of historic "Memorial days" of the church continued to be celebrated in much the same manner as before.[43] To detect change one has to look beyond what would traditionally be regarded as the religious institutions of the society, and turn to the religious practices associated with the social, economic, and political life of the community. What changed was the definition of situations in which participation in religious ritual was considered to be appropriate. Whereas such rituals had once been associated with participation in every major institutional area, they were in mid-nineteenth-century Bethlehem restricted exclusively to the religious domain. Religious practices now belonged properly to one's church-going role and had no public place in one's economic, political, or social roles. In nineteenth-century Herrnhut the change was not as marked, although the direction was umistakable. Religious rituals which had once been part of every person's activities at work, in his family, or when deciding issues of communal policy now permeated the life of only a minority of its citizens. For the rest, such practices had, as in Bethlehem, become largely restricted to participation in church functions. Yet it is

significant that the minority in Herrnhut who continued to adhere
to the religious practices of old exerted considerable influence over
the community as a whole, so that activities in Herrnhut continued
to be largely subordinated to the religious norms of the Moravians.
Since the decline of these religious rituals is closely linked to
changes in the institutional life of both communities, the question of
how these changes in religious practices came about will be taken
up in our treatment of the historical development of these institutions.

PART TWO. THE POLITY

This form of government . . . suits
a monarchy because it has a Bishop,
an aristocracy because it has
a Board of Elders and
a democracy because it has a Synod.
      —COMENIUS,
          De Bono Unitatis
          (*1660*)

II. THE EMERGENCE OF
COMMUNAL GOVERNMENT

THE HISTORIES of the communities of Herrnhut and Bethlehem are marked by similarities as well as differences. Nowhere is this more apparent than in the development of their systems of government. In both communities Zinzendorf, through a combination of personal charisma and aristocratic status, played a key role in shaping the government of the two settlements. Strategic differences in the economic fortunes of Herrnhut and Bethlehem also vitally affected their patterns of political development. In order, however, to provide a better sense of continuity in the development of their political institutions, we shall take up each community in turn.

Leadership and Authority in Herrnhut

When the first refugees from Moravia and Bohemia arrived in the Oberlausitz in 1722 and were granted asylum on the marshes below the Hutberg, they had but one thing in common, a determination to establish themselves in a place in which they would be free to practice their religion and profess their beliefs. Most of these men and women expected ultimately to be able to return to their homeland; they were not, therefore, particularly interested in developing or participating in any form of local government. In these early days their common devotion to religious ideals and the intimacy which flowed from social interaction in so small a group of people made it possible for them to accomplish their daily tasks "in commune" without the guidance of any designated leader. No clear leadership emerged from their own ranks.

Although Zinzendorf, as lord of the manorial territory on which the Moravians had been given permission to settle, was outwardly the supreme power-holder in the community, he showed no particular interest in the welfare of the immigrants and spent most of his time away from Herrnhut and Berthelsdorf.[1] His authority, in short, was merely titular. He did, however, entrust the general supervision of the immigrants to Pastor Rothe, a Lutheran minister who was at the same time in charge of the congregation in Berthelsdorf.[2] Zinzendorf fully expected ultimately to merge the Moravians with this Lutheran congregation.

By 1725 it was becoming clear to the Moravians that their stay in Herrnhut was likely to be of some duration. Furthermore, Zinzendorf's implicit assumption that they would be assimilated to the Lutheran Church served merely to intensify the immigrants' preoccupation with their own religious heritage. There began to develop among them a gradual awareness of themselves as a group separate from the secular and religious communities of Zinzendorf. These immigrants constituted a motley assortment of individuals, all of whom had, it is true, fled their homes because of religious persecution, but who were by no means agreed upon the principles and beliefs of the particular religion they wished to uphold.[3] Even though those desiring to re-establish the Church of the ancient *Unitas Fratrum* were in a majority, their viewpoint was seriously challenged by a number of dissident elements.[4]

Zinzendorf, alarmed by the reports he received from Rothe, decided to return to Berthelsdorf to take a personal hand in subduing these separatist elements.[5] Discussions with Rothe and a number of the earliest and oldest immigrants convinced him that some form of communal organization and official government was badly needed. Christian David, one of the Moravians who participated in these discussions reported:

For although it is true that all children of God already share a common path, [symbolized] in Jesus the Crucified, it is also true that both the strong and the weak are in need of good support, if they are to be kept upon this path. And that is why we concerned ourselves with a review of our institutions so that we might develop statutes, boundaries, regulations and discipline in the spirit of Christ for the common good, in order to wrestle, walk and fight gallantly, and thus seize for ourselves the kingdom of God.[6]

From these meetings two major documents emerged, the Seigneurial Precepts and Prohibitions (*Herrschaftliche Gebote und Verbote*), which were binding upon every resident of Herrnhut, and the Statutes of the Brotherly Agreement (*Statuten des Brüderlichen Vereins und Willkür in Herrnhut*), which were binding only upon those who voluntarily subscribed to the rules and regulations of this association of Brethren in Christ.[7]

According to these constitutional documents the residents of Herrnhut, unlike those of Berthelsdorf, became free citizens under the seigneurial protection of the Count. Supreme authority rested in the hands of the Overseer, a position which Zinzendorf appropriated for himself, by virtue of his seigneurial status, and in which capacity he represented Herrnhut's interests to the world outside.[8] This position became the locus of de facto power in the community. At the same time a considerable amount of authority was delegated to a body of Elders, who were to be selected from the ranks of "honest common people to the exclusion of scholars and aristocrats."[9] It was the Elders who supposedly granted permission for immigrants to settle and to build houses in the community. Permission for Moravians to leave Herrnhut, to change one's occupational status, and to become engaged or get married similarly had to be secured from these Elders. They had the right to raise water and road taxes as well as to obtain the revenue necessary for the support of destitute orphans and widows of the community. In addition to exercising these powers they were also expected to take the steps necessary for the maintenance of law and order and proper decorum between the sexes.[10] The Elders had, however, only moral sanctions with which to enforce obedience. Where overt disobedience continued in spite of such sanctions, the culprits were referred to the judges of the local court of Berthelsdorf.[11] This represented an important restriction on the Elders' ability to regulate secular affairs.

According to an inventory taken in April, 1728, the "worldly authorities of the community of Herrnhut" included Zinzendorf as Overseer, de Watteville as his chief assistant, four Chief Elders who had been elected to office by means of the lot, and nine Elders.[12] In the hands of these fifteen men, who together constituted the Elders Conference, rested then the dominant power to regulate the affairs of the community of Herrnhut. The importance of the Elders Conference (which at first had met weekly) suffered a serious set-back in the seventeen-thirties for a number of reasons. With the growth of the community it had become increasingly difficult for the Elders Conference to handle all of the decisions that had to be made concerning the day-to-day affairs of the community. In order to re-lieve these men of some of their work a number of persons were asked to help them; they constituted what came to be known as the Helpers Conference, first established in 1729.[13] Gradually the power to legislate the secular affairs of the community was transferred from the Elders Conference to the Helpers Conference.

Two other organizations further reduced the importance of the Elders Conference as a decision-making body. One of these was the establishment of a Judiciary Council (Richter's Kolleg), which took over all of the judiciary powers previously exerted by the Elders Conference. The maintenance of law and order, the punish-ment of deviants, the legal enforcement of fixed wages and prices, all of these now became part of the work of the Judiciary Council.[14] Members of this Council appear to have had greater powers to en-force their decisions, including the right to expel members from the community, but the final law enforcement agency remained the Court of Berthelsdorf. Although the chairmanship of the Judiciary Council, unlike that of the Elders Conference and the Helpers Con-ference, was never directly in Zinzendorf's hands, he was able to exert considerable influence over its decisions because his deputy, de Watteville, was chairman, and a member of his personal household was secretary to the Council.[15] After de Watteville's resignation, the chairmanship of the Judiciary Council continued to be occupied only by members of the aristocracy.[16]

A separate Trades Conference, whose chairman was chosen from the members of the Judiciary Council, was established in 1735. At its inception, it consisted of seventeen master craftsmen and Zinzendorf's personal secretary.[17] The business of this Conference was to regulate day-to-day affairs concerning wages, employment contracts, and the maintenance of adequate standards of workmanship in the various trades. Much of the work of the Trades Conference seems nevertheless to have been shouldered not by master craftsmen (who, according to one report, "tended to be very sleepy in committee") but by the representative of the Judiciary Council.[18] The Trades Conference represents one of the first attempts to establish in Herrnhut an independent system for administering economic affairs; the authority granted to those who supervised economic matters was, however, very limited.[19]

Other elements of the authority once vested in the exclusive Elders Conference filtered down also to a newly established Communal Council (Gemeinrat) whose members numbered forty to seventy Brethren and Sisters.[20] Only members of "good character" were eligible for membership. In most cases they were nominated by senior officials of the community, but their acceptance often had to be further ratified by the lot.[21] It is not altogether clear just what the functions or powers of this Communal Council were. For the most part it appears to have provided a forum for discussion of matters of general communal concern, at the end of which the viewpoint of the group was summarized in a tally of votes.[22] Such expressions of opinion were then referred to the Helpers Conference and probably had some effect on actions taken by that conference. But as far as can be seen the Communal Council did not possess any executive powers of its own.

The status of Elder had been the major position of power to which the Moravian immigrants had access. With the gradual diversification of positions in Herrnhut in the seventeen-thirties this was decreasingly possible. The very success of the institutions of the Helpers Conference and the Judiciary Council reduced the need for

the appointment of new Elders. As a result of death and appointment for service abroad, the number of Elders declined rapidly,
until by the mid-thirties only Leonard Dober remained as Chief
Elder in Herrnhut, his role primarily that of providing spiritual
guidance in the community.[23] In addition the Chief Elder was
expected to play a major role in the direction and administration of
the missionary affairs of the community. Plitt, commenting on the
power exerted by the Chief Elder in those days, has noted "We
reverence him inwardly as much as the Roman Church does outwardly its Pope." [24]

The power and prestige attached to this position became so great
that Dober (who had occupied it for some years) felt compelled in
1741 to lay down his duties to make way for someone more
qualified for so eminent a position. But at that time the Synod of
Marienborn refused to ratify his decision. The same year, at the
Synodical Conference in London, pressure was again put upon
Dober not only to continue as Chief Elder but also to take over the
office of Overseer during Zinzendorf's proposed absence from
Herrnhut. Dober declined both positions, and this time his decision
was affirmed by the lot. After the lot had negated every other name
submitted, "all of a sudden the idea presented itself simultaneously
to every mind: The Saviour shall be our Chief Elder." [25] When this
proposal was submitted to the lot the answer was affirmative. As a
result of these proceedings Jesus came to be regarded as Chief Elder
and for many years was not only consulted in the personal prayers
of Moravians but was also asked for more direct guidance by means
of the lot.

One other position of influence stands out during those early years
of Herrnhut, that of Bishop. When the ancient *Unitas Fratrum*
broke away from the Roman Catholic Church in the fifteenth
century it took pains to include in its ranks an ordained Bishop so
that the principle of apostolic succession would be upheld and the
divine authority of the position be maintained.[26] Many of the early
immigrants who came to Herrnhut were fully aware of this his-

torical tradition; and as it became clear to them that they had no desire to be absorbed into the fold of the Lutheran Church to which Zinzendorf belonged, they decided that one of their members should be elected to the episcopate.[27] In 1735 David Nitschman was sent to be ordained by Jablonski, grandson of the revered Bishop Comenius of the *Unitas Fratrum*. According to Hamilton this step was prompted primarily by utilitarian considerations, since the Moravians felt that having an episcopate of their own would greatly facilitate their missionary activities.[28] The second Bishop to be ordained in the Moravian Church was Zinzendorf himself, in spite of the fact that he regarded himself as a member of the orthodox Lutheran clergy. But the Count declared that such a step was essential if he was effectively to represent the interests of the Moravian Church among the civil and ecclesiastical authorities of Germany and any other parts of the world with which the Church might wish to have connections.[29] By 1742 two more Bishops had been ordained. Hamilton aptly summarized the characteristics of the status of the early Moravian Bishops:

. . . the Bishop's office carried with it a considerable measure of administrative authority—though always over-shadowed by that of Zinzendorf, himself, and subject to modification effected by the frequent resort to the lot. Spiritual leadership, however, which the church later came to associate with this office was expressly committed to others.[30]

Finally, the Synod must also be regarded as an important decision-making body of the Moravians. In the early days of the *Unitas Fratrum* it provided a meeting place for all members of the faith. Doctrinal disputes could be aired, administrative matters of the church settled, and members could be nominated and elected to the episcopacy. The first Synod of the resuscitated Moravian Church met in Marienborn in 1736, and was largely concerned with a discussion of the functions of the episcopate.[31] Four other Synods which met during the next six years were also concerned primarily with matters of doctrine and missionary activity.

But at the Synod of 1741, held in London, at which Christ was elected Chief Elder, a number of organizational changes took place. This Synod had to provide for the administration of Herrnhut during the absence of Zinzendorf and a number of other leaders who were about to sail for America, where Spangenberg had recently found some land on which to settle in Pennsylvania. Although the Chief Eldership had been delegated to Jesus, it was felt necessary to appoint a special Elder for Herrnhut who would take over many of the day-to-day activities associated with the office of the Overseer. Grassmann was appointed to this post. In addition a so-called "General Conference" was formed, whose members included the two Moravian Bishops Müller and John Nitschmann, the assistant Overseer de Watteville, and a number of Moravians occupying prominent positions in the Helpers Conference and the Judiciary Council of Herrnhut.[32]

During the Count's absence this General Conference was able to secure from Frederick the Great, King of Prussia, a concession which gave full recognition to the Moravian Church as an independent episcopal institution and which guaranteed liberty of conscience to its members throughout Saxony.[33] When Zinzendorf heard of these negotiations he decided to return to Germany immediately. In the summer of 1743 he convened a Synod in Hirschberg, where he protested vigorously against the steps taken by the General Conference in securing recognition of the Moravian Church. (He still hoped that the Moravians would ultimately join the Lutheran fold.) [34] The Count insisted that since his office as Overseer had deliberately been left vacant, he should have been consulted in these matters. In a burst of anger he abrogated all the powers of the General Conference. According to Hamilton the members of the Conference "surrendered unconditionally, overcome as they were by the sense of what they owed to him and by a realization of his personal sacrifices." [35]

A few months later Zinzendorf was officially nominated to the position of *Advocatus et Ordinarius Fratrum,* thereby making him absolute ruler over Herrnhut, with unlimited powers, responsible to no one except presumably God. The gradually evolving administrative structure under which power was to be distributed among a number of reasonably autonomous committees crumbled the very first time it was threatened by what an unsympathetic outsider might call a dictator. The excesses of the time of the Sifting thus occurred in a period when power was concentrated in the hands of one man, who by virtue of his extraordinary charisma was able to command absolute obedience from the very men whose powers he had abrogated.

By 1750 even Zinzendorf could no longer close his eyes to the economic and political chaos wrought by the excesses of the time of the Sifting. Recognizing his personal failings, he appointed von Seidlitz, von Schrautenbach, Dober, and Waiblinger to a newly created Collegiate Board of Government.[36] Notwithstanding its grandiose title, this board acted in a purely advisory capacity and its decisions continued to be at the mercy of the Count's whims, which were, especially in economic and financial matters, erratic indeed. In 1754 at the Synod of Taubenheim a Board of Administrators was established whose main function was to supervise the estates and financial matters, not only of Herrnhut but of the Church as a whole.[37] This body was still responsible directly to Zinzendorf. Moreover, five out of its six members, including the chairman and vice chairman, came from the Count's social circle of the German aristocracy, and could be relied on to represent the Count's interests in most matters.[38]

A year later this Board of Administrators was, however, dissolved, and its place was taken by a Board of Directors which was to be responsible to the Church and not to Zinzendorf alone. The Count, saddened by the recent loss of his wife and of his son, Christian Renatus, was becoming aware of his own mortal constitution and is said to have remarked, "I shall also depart and—there will be improvement. For this the Conferences exist, and they will remain permanently." [39] The membership of the Board of Directors closely resembled that of the Board of Administrators it had replaced. Its

functions were still restricted primarily to economic affairs of the
Unity; this of course necessitated some involvement with the affairs
of the local communities, especially Herrnhut. During the remaining years of the Count's life no further organizational changes were
undertaken, although it is clear that with Zinzendorf's increased
preoccupation with spiritual and mystical affairs much of the responsibility for the day-to-day government of Herrnhut rested with
the Board. But theoretically the Count remained *Advocatus et
Ordinarius Fratrum* until May 9, 1760, the day of his death.[40]

Attempts to broaden the governmental structure of Herrnhut
beyond the immediate rule of Zinzendorf resulted in a proliferation
of various committees, boards, councils, and conferences. But these
organizational developments were not accompanied by a similar
broadening of the bases of power. On the contrary, with the establishment of every new major office the Count simply acquired for
himself a new position. Thus he became not only Count of Berthelsdorf and Herrnhut, but also Overseer of Herrnhut, Minister of
the Lutheran Church, Bishop of the Moravian Church, Chairman
of the Helpers Conference, and Chairman of the Communal
Council.[41] When the Chief Eldership was delegated to Christ in
1741, the spiritual leadership of the community was theoretically
placed in the hands of the Saviour. In practice, however, Zinzendorf
took over the administrative and organizational responsibilities
associated with that office.[42] Furthermore, since the office of the
Chief Elder had become endowed with a high degree of charisma,
its transfer from human to divine occupancy eliminated the only
remaining human threat to the Count's position of power in the
community. There was, however, one check to the autocratic rule of
Zinzendorf which at times overruled even the Count's desires—
recourse to the lot. But even here, as we shall see, the Count was
frequently able to use his influence in such a way as to be able to
manipulate this expression of God's will to coincide with his own
wishes.

The predominance of members of the aristocracy in all major

positions of authority, especially those concerned with the secular affairs of the community,[43] not only intensified the Count's control over the government of Herrnhut but also prevented an adequate representation and reflection of the views of the Moravian immigrants in the decisions taken by the government of the day. Max von Zinzendorf, an uncle of Nicholas, left the following description of this class:

> One finds there [i.e., in Herrnhut] a great many of the most agreeable, animated and learned persons of both sexes, who have come there from the far corners of the world. Many of them occupy positions of great prestige, others are simply using their lands and their riches in such a way that they may live in true peace in Herrnhut. . . .[44]

Small wonder that Uttendörfer was led to exclaim that Herrnhut had been transformed "from a meetingplace for heroic crusaders of Christ into a fashionable spiritual Spa for the nobility."[45]

The members of this class could be identified by the emotional and sensual character of their *Lebensgefühl*, their penchant for religious mysticism, and their belief in the sanctity of the values of feudal society.[46] Few of these values were shared by the Moravian immigrants who might well have given to the government of Herrnhut a very different direction had their role in the power structure of the community been more proportional to their numbers.

In spite of Zinzendorf's explicit emphasis upon the equality of the sexes, almost no women were appointed to positions of high authority. The Moravians, however, regarded their women above all as helpmeets, and since positions of influence were generally staffed by married men there was alongside almost every man of importance in the community a wife who could, if she so desired, exert considerable informal influence.[47]

The bases of legitimacy of authority appear to have been twofold. In the rule of Overseer, Elder, and Bishop tradition played an important role in ensuring obedience. Domination here rested largely upon piety and respect for the norms and values of the feudal order

and the ecclesiastic establishment of the ancient *Unitas Fratrum.*
Authority was derived from respect for "what actually, allegedly, or
presumably has always existed." [48]

The authority of the Chief Elder, as well as of Zinzendorf in his
role as Count and *Advocatus et Ordinarius,* was, however, legiti-
mated primarily by a belief in the charismatic qualities of the social
statuses in question. This emphasis upon charismatic authority
facilitated the emergence of the emotionalism and sensualism which
dominated so much of Moravian community life during the time of
the Sifting. It was this legitimation of the extraordinary, the irrational, and the revolutionary which made it relatively easy for
Zinzendorf to ignore so many of the traditional values of the society
during those years.

With Zinzendorf's death the period of autocratic rule over
Herrnhut came to an abrupt end. The Count had made no specific
provisions for a successor, believing that the existing committees
and Synods would be able to handle affairs adequately. Initially,
therefore, the members of what had been the Board of Directors
formed an Interim Conference to which de Watteville and Spangenberg were coopted.[49] In 1762 this conference was renamed the Inner
Conference but no changes in its membership took place. It remained in office as a kind of emergency council until the convening
of a General Synod in 1764.[50] From this point on, the government
of Herrnhut became intricately associated with the government of
the Unity as a whole. The majority of positions in the administration of the Unity were staffed by residents of Herrnhut. Throughout the remainder of the eighteenth century Herrnhut was essentially governed by these same men. In practice the government of
the Unity therefore became synonomous with that of Herrnhut.

The Synod of 1764 is generally referred to as the first Constitutional Synod, in that it was the first Synod to devote itself primarily
to matters of government. As a result of its deliberations a whole
series of departmental boards was formed, at the head of which
stood a "Directorium." The Directorium became the executive head

of the Moravians, its members being elected by the Synod and responsible to it.[51] Although some of the members of this Board were nonresidents of Herrnhut, they played an unimportant role in its deliberations; the Board met in Herrnhut, forcing them to make their views known by correspondence. Such letters frequently arrived too late to have any impact.[52] A board of Syndics, however, continued to hold separate control over the external affairs of the communities and especially their relations with civil authorities, while a Unity Wardens Board was placed in charge of financial affairs. Overlap in membership of these bodies and ambiguity concerning the real seat of executive power made this a most unwieldy form of government.[53]

At the meeting of the second Constitutional Synod in 1769, the Directorium, which had proved cumbersome and inefficient, was replaced by a Unity Elders Conference. It functioned as a single executive board, with members divided into three councils, Supervisory (Aufseher), Helper (Helfer), and Attendant (Diener).[54] All affairs of the Unity and of all the congregations, including Bethlehem and Herrnhut, were to be directed by this Conference. Herrnhut, partly because so many of the members of the Unity Elders Conference came from its ranks and partly because the Conference met nearby, became entirely subject to the decisions made by this body. The tendency towards centralization of power, which had been checked immediately after Zinzendorf's death, once more reasserted itself.

At the Synod at Barby, the third Constitutional Synod, held in 1775, centralization was increased still further. Ministers in charge of local Moravian communities were declared to be merely agents of the Unity Elders Conference, with no executive powers over local affairs. Even Bishops were from now on to be regarded as "Elders appointed by the Synod to ordain ministers of the Church." The selection of candidates for the ministry was to be the exclusive prerogative of the Unity Elders Conference.[55] These steps wrought few changes in the government of Herrnhut, for they merely gave official sanction to what had increasingly become the practice since the Count's death: the delegation of all power and authority to the leaders of the Unity as a whole, most of whom were residents of Herrnhut.

The remaining Synods of the eighteenth century left this governmental structure largely unchanged. As far as Herrnhut was concerned, the autocracy of one-man rule under Zinzendorf had been replaced by the virtual dictatorship of the Unity Elders Conference. Membership in the Synods had been restricted still further; thus the majority of the local population had no say in the government of Herrnhut. During this same period the holders of political office changed little. The men who had been Zinzendorf's major advisers, men like Köber, von Damnitz, von Gersdorf, de Watteville, von Seidlitz, Count Henry Reuss, and Spangenberg, continued to hold the reins of power until death finally put an end to their generation in the last few years of the century.[56]

So pervasive was this belief in the sanctity of the past that even after the death of these leaders their successors still clung defensively to the old ways. Herrnhut was at a standstill until almost the middle of the nineteenth century, when some attempt was finally made to put its missionary enterprises on a more dynamic footing. But the community never really recovered from the setback it had received as a result of the spirit of extreme conservatism which characterized Herrnhut's leadership for almost a hundred years.

Leadership and Authority in Bethlehem

Zinzendorf's idea in setting up a Moravian settlement in Pennsylvania had been to create a community whose institutions would mirror those of its sister community in Saxony. Moravians in America were to be subject to the same rules and regulations as their Brethren in Germany, all Moravians being ultimately controlled by one government and responsible to a central board.[57] Although this central authority was supposed to rest in the hands of the Unity as a whole, thus providing for representation of Moravians from all areas of Moravian settlement, it continued until long after Zinzendorf's death to be largely in the hands of the German Moravians, especially those of Herrnhut. Zinzendorf had himself gone to America in 1741 to supervise the organization of a Moravian community in Pennsylvania, but he became so engrossed in his attempt to unite the German Protestants of Pennsylvania in a single "Church of God in the Spirit" that many of the administrative details of the newly emerging community were in fact left to others.

In the early days of Bethlehem the conviction prevailed that there was no need for any establishment of a government; instead, "that which proves to be blessed and useful from week to week and month to month, that is what will be done." [58] Minutes of the Proceedings of a Communal Council of all communicant members held in June, 1742, make it clear, however, that it was nevertheless felt to be necessary to establish certain offices. The offices decided upon resemble very closely the apostolic positions introduced by Rothe into Herrnhut in 1725. They included those of Elder, Overseer, Teacher, and Monitor, as well as that of "Scharnier" (literally translated "hinge" or "joint"), which was reserved for the most respected member of the community and to which John Nitschmann was the first to be elected. [59] The community was divided into two groups, the congregation of pilgrims, which included Elders, missionaries, and others immediately concerned with the implementation of the religious goals of the community, and the local settlement congregation (Ortsgemeine), to which belonged all those Moravians working for the material support and welfare of Bethlehem and its extensive missionary undertakings. [60]

By 1744 the apostolic positions had either ceased to exist or, where they continued, had lost most of their governing authority in the community. Their place had by then been taken by various committees, similar in many respects to those of Herrnhut. Supervising all communal affairs was the task of the Elders Conference, sometimes referred to as the Conference of the Disciples. [61] Its membership was limited to the chief *Ordinarius* or leader of Bethlehem and a few others, mostly men who had already demonstrated their leadership capacities in other communities. Below this Conference, and with a much larger membership, stood the Judiciary or General Supervisory Council (Aufseher Kollegium), under whose charge were all economic and financial affairs of the community. It was headed by a general supervisor for "external affairs," and its members included the supervisors of all major branches of the economy as well as representatives from the Elders Conference. Its powers, especially in economic affairs were, however, much broader than those of its German counterpart.

Each major branch of the economy—agriculture, trade, commerce, and construction—had its own organization. Thus, for example, the branch conference of agriculture consisted of a chairman and the representatives of the following agricultural divisions: field tilling, gardening, forestry, vineyards, wood chopping, harvesting, cattle raising, and barn cleaning.[62] Similar conferences gave representation to the various occupational divisions within the trades, commerce, and construction branches. In addition a separate committee, the Diacony Conference, dealt with all financial transactions. A General Economic Conference which met once a month provided an opportunity for everyone to participate in the discussion of economic affairs, but the Conference had power only to make recommendations, not to implement proposals.[63]

A Communal Council (Gemeinrat), which included all adult male communicants as well as female "workers," provided an important forum for debate and discussion of impending changes or innovations in the community.[64] As in Herrnhut, the Communal Council had advisory powers only. Thus, although it could bring the weight of public opinion to bear upon a given issue, it did not itself have the authority to execute and implement its decisions. Bethlehem's Communal Council met far more often and was better attended than its counterpart in Herrnhut.[65]

Committee rule in general was practiced to a greater extent in Bethlehem than in Herrnhut. In addition to the above-mentioned conferences, there were many others, including those concerned specifically with the social welfare of the Moravians, the education of their children, the welfare and supervision of visitors, the maintenance of health standards, and the care of the sick.[66] Finally, mention should also be made of the Synods which originated in the seven Pennsylvania Synods of 1742, when Zinzendorf was diligently trying to foster Protestant Unity in Pennsylvania. Over the years these Synods took on an increasingly Moravian character; matters of doctrine as well as important economic, social, and political issues came to be aired.[67] After 1747 these Synods were referred to as Provincial Synods to distinguish them from the General Synods of the Unity as a whole. In the seventeen-forties and fifties such Provincial Synods were convened every few months, and all men and women working in Bethlehem were eligible to attend.

Theoretically Zinzendorf was supreme rule of Bethlehem as well as of Herrnhut. In practice, though, the men living in Bethlehem found it increasingly difficult to submit all decisions to Zinzendorf, who spent most of his time in Europe. By the time the Count got word of some proposed change that proposal had quite often already been implemented. Supreme authority over the affairs of Bethlehem rested thus not with the Count, but with the *Vicarius Generalis Episcoporum et per Americam in Presbyterio Vicarius.*[68] This office was first given to Spangenberg, although prior to his arrival in 1744 Peter Böhler had had nominal charge of the settlement, without, however, having any such episcopal or presbyterian honors conferred upon him.[69] Writing of this office, Peter Böhler comments on the qualities needed by its incumbent:

It cannot be denied that what is needed beyond any doubt is a Stephen. A man with an excellent mind as well as physical stamina who can supply both the necessary spiritual guidance for our cause and yet who also possesses the required understanding of economics to be able to supervise the agricultural pursuits of the old patriarchal enterprises and the administration of the newer trades, and commercial and construction activities.[70]

Erbe summarized the importance of Spangenberg as follows: "He is the soul behind all, he directs everything. Without his organizational talent and his gift for leadership the Economy could never have lasted long." [71] Among the local population he came to be known as "our Joseph." [72] In spite of his obvious talents he was replaced in 1749 by John Cammerhoff at the Count's insistence.[73] But by 1751 it had become clear that if Bethlehem was to survive Spangenberg must be permitted to take over the reins immediately. With the reappraisal of the time of the Sifting there remained little support for Cammerhoff, who died shortly thereafter. In December, 1751, Spangenberg returned to head the community, a post he was to hold until after Zinzendorf's death, when his leadership qualities became even more ugently needed by the Unity as a whole. But one aspect of his earlier office was not returned to him. In 1747 the Chief Eldership, following the example of Herrnhut some years earlier, had been delegated to Christ himself. Upon Spangenberg's return no attempt was made to abolish this element of theocratic government.[74]

After Spangenberg's return Peter Böhler became his chief assistant, although unlike Zinzendorf's deputy de Watteville, Böhler occupied no specific office per se, being active rather as a member of a number of important committees, including the General Supervisory Council.[75] The number of officeholders in the various committees entrusted with some specific aspect of government was large, partly because of the high degree of occupational mobility among the officeholders themselves. Although the quantity of official positions remained fairly constant throughout the years of the General Economy, power was dispersed to so many different hands at different times that, with the exception of Spangenberg and perhaps Cammerhoff, Böhler, and Antes, it is almost impossible to single out certain persons as the wielders of communal power.

Divergent Political Patterns in the Two Communities

A number of major differences in the organization and distribution of power in Herrnhut and Bethlehem during the pioneering years of the two communities thus emerge. In Herrnhut political power and authority were largely concentrated in the hands of one man—Zinzendorf—while government in Bethlehem was less auto-cratic, in part because the day-to-day activities of the community could not wait upon the decisions of a man five thousand miles away, and in part also because Spangenberg, who was the de facto leader of the community, was highly skilled in the delegation of power to others.

The government of Bethlehem involved many more Moravians in committee government than that of Herrnhut. In America the criteria of eligibility for membership in these Conferences were wider and actual participation was more diverse. Whereas Herrn-hut's leadership rested disproportionately in the hands of the aristocracy, Bethlehem's leadership rested primarily in the hands of skilled artisans and farmers. The number of aristocrats immigrating to Pennsylvania was negligible; their failure to play any role in the government of the community thus comes as no surprise. Women in Bethlehem appear to have held greater authority than in Herrn-hut, either as single persons holding official positions of their own or as helpmeets to their husbands. The names of women like Mary Spangenberg, Anna Nitschmann, Elisabeth Böhler, Anna Mack, and Anna Maria Lawatsch come readily to mind, but they appear to have had no counterpart in Herrnhut.

In both communities there were no clear-cut initial distinctions between secular and sacred authority, but by 1760 the Pennsylvania community gave evidence of a much greater degree of autonomy among the various branches of government than was the case in Herrnhut. The separation of secular authority from sacred authority was visible in Bethlehem at a date at which in Herrnhut no such distinction was yet evident.

Power appears to have received a different justification in Beth-lehem than in Herrnhut. In Herrnhut one finds a strong emphasis upon charisma as well as traditionalism as bases of legitimacy of authority. In Bethlehem charismatic authority played a minor part; Spangenberg clearly showed tendencies towards charismatic leader-ship but chose to suppress these instead of exploiting them as did

Zinzendorf. Traditionalism did play an important role in the legitimation of authority in the early years of Bethlehem. Most of the original positions of power were modeled on those of Herrnhut; it was assumed that what had worked in Herrnhut would also serve Bethlehem well.

Gradually, however, the Moravians in Bethlehem began to discover that a specifice communal organization could not be transplanted ready-made and still be expected to yield the same results five thousand miles away. Innovations were made, and the structure of the community which emerged no longer found a mirror image in Herrnhut. Many of the entries in the seventeen-fifties in the Bethlehem Diary, as well as the Choir Diaries and the records of the various conferences, are concerned with the elaboration of rules and regulations governing new statuses in the community. In this sense, therefore, the legitimation of authority in Bethlehem was beginning to break with traditionalism and move towards what Weber has termed "legal authority," in which submission is based upon "an *impersonal* bond to the generally defined and functional 'duty of office.'"[76] It was due in part to this difference in the bases of legitimation of authority between the two communities that the emotional excesses of the Sifting Period were unable to gain a strong foothold in Bethlehem. Indeed it was only during Cammerhoff's brief reign that the values associated with this period achieved any prominence in Bethlehem.

The Moravians in Herrnhut, however, viewed these innovations in the governmental structure of Bethlehem with increasing alarm. Many of the German Moravians were beginning to feel that the "American experiment" had grown too independent and that it was now necessary to impose a closer liaison with Herrnhut.[77] It had not gone unnoticed that it was invariably the American Moravians who were first to voice their criticism of existing arrangements. These fears of the gradual alienation of the Pennsylvania settlement might not have compelled the Germans to action had it not been for the fact that the Unity was in serious financial straits. Thus a further anxiety was added that the American Moravians might place their missionary goals ahead of their duty to the Unity as a whole; funds that could help liquidate the Unity's debt could instead be used for the support of American missionary enterprises.[78] In their enthusiasm to correct the errors of the Sifting Period the German Moravians were now only too willing to place the financial welfare of the Unity as a whole over and above the missionary functions of Bethlehem.

With Zinzendorf's death in 1760 it became imperative for Spangenberg to return to Herrnhut, where his talent for leadership was urgently needed; for the Count, like many charismatic leaders, had failed to clarify the problem of succession. The fact that Zinzendorf's own position within the Moravian Church had been unique merely aggravated the problem. It meant that not only was there no clear mandate as to who should succeed him but that ambiguity cloaked the very definition of leadership. Spangenberg was thus forced to leave Bethlehem at the very time when his leadership might have altered the history of this community in a crucial way. When, therefore, men like Köber and de Watteville pressed their plans for tighter organization of the Bethlehem community by Herrnhut, there was no effective local leadership to voice any clear opposition to such plans. True, Spangenberg did continue to plead the case for retention of the missionary character of the settlement and only minor modification of the General Economy, but he was at the same time so involved in the affairs of the Unity as a whole that he could not pursue this matter very far.

As a result of the deliberations of the Inner Conference, the interim governing body of the Unity established immediately after Zinzendorf's death, the government of Bethlehem was placed in the hands of a committee of four, including Mathäus Hehl, Peter Böhler, Nathaniel Seidel, and Friedrich Marschall, the so-called Interim Economic Conference (Interim Oekonomats Konferenz). Seidel was appointed Overseer for the missionary and spiritual affairs of the community while Marschall took over responsibility for the economic and financial reorganization of the community. Between them these men now shouldered the burdens of office which had once been Spangenberg's alone.[79] The predominance of German Moravians in the newly created executive board and the complete absence of any local communal participation in the government during these years attest to the power of the Inner Conference in successfully implementing its proposals.

In 1771 the Interim Economic Conference gave Bethlehem its new constitution, which the community was to retain for close to eighty years. Under the new system a Local Elders Conference, whose membership was restricted to ordained ministers of the church, their helpmeets, and representatives from the various choirs (major social groupings in the community), had oversight of the spiritual affairs of the settlement. Its chairmanship was given to the senior minister in charge of the local community.[80] Since all ordained persons were chosen by the Unity Elders Conference, this meant that control of the Local Elders Conference rested in effect in the hands of the Unity.

The secular affairs of the community were placed in the hands of a Supervisory Council, headed by a Warden whose members were elected by the Church Council. The Church Council in turn consisted initially of all adult communicants, but after 1775 its membership was restricted to a much smaller group and heavily weighted with ex officio representatives from the Local Elders Conference and the various choirs.[81] This meant that the Supervisory Council became more and more a body representative of the interests of the Local and Unity Elders Conference rather than the vox populi of Bethlehem. Some of the work of the Local Elders Conference was taken over by a Helpers Conference, whose membership was similarly restricted, and whose powers were advisory only.

The Moravians in Germany hoped that under this new government the American settlement would become a mirror image of Herrnhut, subject to the same centralized board of control in Europe. To this end the Synod of 1775 decreed further that the

Communal Helper, the supposed leader of the local community, was to be responsible not to his local community but solely to the Unity Elders Conference and the General Synods, and that he was to act merely as the local agent of the Unity. All missionary and educational activities were similarly placed in the hands of the Unity Elders Conference, which also gave final approval of all financial transactions.[82]

Yet even under this system of absentee government Bethlehem was not as devoid of local political power as might be supposed. The outline of government indicated above turned out to be a blueprint for the ideal distribution of power, a distribution which did not always correspond too closely to reality. Just as Zinzendorf's absentee government had failed, so now the absentee government of the Unity Elders Conference ran into trouble. The General Synods met only infrequently, generally once every ten years. In the interim the Moravians of Bethlehem were dependent upon couriers to convey policy decisions between Herrnhut and themselves. Nor was the general political unrest in America and Europe conducive to the maintenance of speedy communications. The Bethlehem Elders Conference became very reluctant to send any detailed, let alone verbatim, reports of its activities to Herrnhut for fear that they might fall into enemy hands and create trouble for the Moravians either in Bethlehem or in Herrnhut.[83]

During the time of the American Revolution, communications with Herrnhut broke down almost completely; for three years not a single word was heard from Herrnhut.[84] As a result, even those leaders who did not themselves wish to create any considerable degree of local autonomy for Bethlehem were forced into making decisions on their own. The former "agents" of the Unity Elders Conference increasingly identified themselves with the American scene. The privilege, initially thrust upon them in this period of crisis, of appointing men of their own choosing to office was never to be given up.

Finally, the War of Independence had another effect upon

Bethlehem which indirectly hastened the trend towards local autonomy still further. Finding themselves in the heat of conflict, the
Moravians were forced to re-examine their relationship to the
country on whose soil they had settled. Although initially their
impulse had been to side with the British—had not Zinzendorf been
granted the right for Moravians to settle in America by virtue of a
Royal decree?—the force of public opinion in Pennsylvania, fanned
by the presence of Washington's Army in the vicinity of Bethlehem,
soon brought the Moravians to the Yankees' side.[85] For better or
worse the Moravians were becoming not only Moravians but
Americans, thereby achieving a political position which was independent of their religious status. Unlike the Moravians in Herrnhut,
they had acquired their political status not by birth but by virtue of
having been forced to make a choice.

The governmental structure of Bethlehem was not officially
altered until the middle of the nineteenth century, although some
amendments were passed earlier. The American Moravians did not
find themselves particularly hampered by the increasing discrepancy
between their official powers and their actual authority in matters
of local government. The Unity Elders Conference was in no position to impose sanctions upon Bethlehem; what little energy it
manifested in the early decades of the nineteenth century was concentrated primarily upon the affairs of the German Moravians.
Moreover, once the Moravians in Bethlehem had made the decision
to obtain the necessary official ratification of their new powers, the
battle with the Unity proved long and arduous. Not only were the
Americans in a minority on most of the relevant decision-making
boards, but the Synods themselves were called at infrequent inter-
vals. Ultimately, however, the persistence of the American Moravians was rewarded. The "Act to incorporate the village of Bethlehem in the county of Northampton into a Borough," passed in
1845, severed all remaining political ties of Bethlehem's citizens to
the German Moravians. From this point on the local government of
Bethlehem was entrusted to a burgess and nine councilmen, all of

whom were elected by the voting citizens of the community, who had to be Americans but who need not necessarily adhere to the Moravian faith.[86]

Herrnhut remained too close to the seat of the Moravian Church's executive council to escape its oligarchic grasp. Local government for Herrnhut thus continued to rest in the hands of a religious elite whose length of office was determined solely by longevity and whose devotion to the ecclesiastic and feudal traditions of the past was unswerving.

III. THE USE OF THE LOT

NO DISCUSSION of the political organization of Moravian communities would be complete without some reference to the Moravian conception and practice of the lot, one of the most frequently misunderstood and misinterpreted of their social customs. All too often it has been regarded as a quaint folkway peculiar to the Moravians and unique in the history of mankind.[1] Yet the custom of submitting decisions to a lot is to be found in many societies both past and present,[2] and cannot, therefore, be regarded as a social innovation unique to the Moravian Brethren.[3]

Moravian treatises on the history of the use of the lot in their communities have generally regarded its practice simply as an act of faith, a realization of a theocratic government under which Christ's will could be manifested through the lot:

> We regard the lot as something divine, which the Saviour gave to His congregation and which is essential to a theocracy.[4]

The use of the lot in the Moravian Church, is neither a mysterious, theosophic appliance, nor an exclusive right and prerogative bestowed upon that particular communion, but simply a Scriptural act of faith, which any body of Christians may perform.[5]

But by focusing exclusively upon the religious aspects of the lot, Moravian historians tended to overlook the role of precedents established in the political practices of the *Unitas Fratrum* and in the personal habits of Zinzendorf, both of which played a significant part in promoting the use of the lot in communal decision-making in Herrnhut and Bethlehem. The history of the *Unitas Fratrum* provides an occasional reference to this custom, notably in the selection of candidates and the determination of policy issues at the Synod of Lhota;[6] yet it fails to establish a sufficient precedent for the

systematic employment of this practice in both private and public
affairs so characteristic of eighteenth-century Moravian settlements.

With Zinzendorf the practice of submitting decisions of an admittedly personal nature to the lot went back to his youth. Zinzendorf's earliest religious views presupposed a highly intimate contact
with God. Hutton, for example, claims that at the tender age of six
the Count "regarded Christ as his brother, would talk with him for
hours as with a familiar friend and was often found wrapped in
thought, like Socrates in the market place at Athens." [7] Zinzendorf
"was accustomed to carry lot papers in his pockets, by which he decided a multitude of questions in his own life." [8] The practice of
seeking divine guidance in personal affairs by means of the lot or by
resort to bibliomancy was not peculiar to Zinzendorf; many of the
Pietist followers of men like Spener and Francke, in whose ranks
could be found a good many of the Count's aristocratic friends who
subsequently moved to Herrnhut, also used the lot. [9]

Had it not been for the religious commitment of the Herrnhuters
and the authority which Zinzendorf wielded over the community, it
is unlikely that the personal practice of a few individuals could have
become an instrument for decision-making in the community as a
whole. [10] In this sense there was indeed an elective affinity between
the Moravians' faith in God and their usage of the lot as a means of
ascertaining His will.

The Occasions and Frequency of Its Use

The lot was employed by the Moravians for two major purposes:
to accept and allocate persons into various positions in the status
structure of the community and to determine issues of communal
policy. [11] The acceptance of an immigrant into the community was
made dependent not only upon his showing appropriate devotion
to the religious goals of the community, but also upon the verdict
of the lot. "Every week somebody arrives here with the intention of settling. We determine the application of each by lot, otherwise Herrnhut would soon be far too overcrowded." [12] The selec-

tion of new members for the community in Pennsylvania was similarly submitted to the lot, although it is not altogether clear whether the lot was resorted to only in cases which were considered to be marginal or whether it was used universally.

Once a person had been accepted as a member of a Moravian community the direction his life was to take had only just begun to be determined by the lot. In the religious sphere his acceptance for baptism as well as his admission to communion were dependent upon a positive response from the lot, even after all other criteria of eligibility had been met.[13] In the social sphere a person's initial acceptance into a choir—a type of Moravian family surrogate [14]—as well as his subsequent transfer from one choir to another, especially in the case of transfer from the Children's choirs to the choirs of unmarried adults, were all subject to confirmation by the lot.[15] Furthermore, should a Brother decide to marry, his initial decision and the name of the proposed spouse were submitted to the lot. Should the decision to marry be affirmed by the lot but not the spouse proposed, the name of another person could be substituted and similarly be submitted to the lot. In the economic realm the filling of occupational positions was also frequently determined by lot.[16] Finally, election to all the major political offices, with the exception of those held by Zinzendorf by right of birth, was determined by the lot. The selection of members of the Communal Council, the appointment of missionaries for posts overseas, the selection of ministers, the consecration of bishops, as well as the election of a Chief Elder, were all ultimately ratified by the Lord through recourse to the lot.[17]

Those whose nomination to positions of power in the community had been ratified by the lot soon found that the very power they had been given was in turn restricted by the lot. The community's decisions to establish new missionary outposts or to abandon old ones had generally to be ratified by the lot. In economic affairs, the buying of new land or selection of a site for a new community, the erection of a new building such as a new house for one of the choirs, or the establishment of a new industry or trade were all matters which had first to be approved by the lot. Even financial questions, such as whether to borrow money, and if so whether or not to accept a certain rate of interest or to inform members of the extent of the Unity's debts, were frequently submitted to the lot.[18] The ratification of rules and regulations governing social and moral conduct, or the type of punishment to be meted out to an offender, including the question of exile, were similarly submitted. Finally, political and administrative questions, such as when and where a Synod was to be held, or what items were to be included on the agenda for discussion at a Synod, were also often decided by recourse to the lot.[19]

Whereas there appear to have been no marked differences in the range of problems submitted to the lot in Herrnhut and in Bethlehem in the early years, the two communities did differ with respect to the relative frequency with which the lot was resorted to. Throughout the lifetime of Zinzendorf the use of the lot was supposedly voluntary, but with the Count himself resorting to the lot more and more frequently, the community of Herrnhut in turn was affected by his example. Until 1730 the instances of the lot's being employed for communal decisions were few. But the thirties witnessed a gradual increase in the frequency of its use, a movement which gained tremendous momentum during the time of the Sifting. The Moravians' self-perception as God's chosen people may be seen both as a cause and a consequence of the frequency with which they were employing the lot to consult God "as the umpire of all important questions."[20] Although the soul-searching which followed the excesses of the time of the Sifting was accompanied by some reduction in the use of the lot, especially in regard to marriages, it continued to be employed more and more often in the selection of persons for religious and political offices.[21]

In Bethlehem the lot was never used as frequently as in Herrnhut. This was primarily because Zinzendorf's personal example was of limited significance in Bethlehem, where Spangenberg resorted to the practice as infrequently in public as in his personal life. During

Cammerhoff's brief period of leadership the lot was used with much greater frequency, but upon Spangenberg's return it appears to have been employed primarily in the appointment of persons to missionary work and in marriages. Questions of economic policy were submitted to the lot very rarely indeed, and then only when there was a definite lack of consensus on the appropriate action to be taken.[22]

The Process of Drawing Lots

Up to this point it has been assumed implicitly that every use of the lot was qualitatively the same in that it involved the ascertainment of God's will on a given issue. But was the Moravian community truly a theocracy in which the Lord wielded sole power? Our study of the structure of political authority has already led us to suspect otherwise. To understand more precisely the importance of the lot as a tool of communal decision-making, the conditions under which the lot might be resorted to need now to be examined. One can establish whether the procedures adopted were invariable and, if not, whether there were opportunities for the human manipulation of a purported expression of divine will.

One could argue that faith in the efficacy of the employment of the lot as a means of reaching communal decisions is a precondition for its use. Yet, the very fact that this requirement was not made manifest until faith in its efficacy had begun to waver suggests that such a claim would represent an ex post facto rationalization. For practical purposes the precondition of faith can, therefore, be disregarded in the years prior to 1760. Another rule governing the employment of the lot stated that it was to be used only when there was a definite lack of consensus.[23] The problem with this rule was its vagueness. Did it mean, for instance, that if only a few persons disagreed the lot had to be consulted, or did it perhaps imply that the community had to be split almost fifty-fifty on a given issue before the lot could be used? Alternatively, did it refer not only to the existence of significant factions in the community but also to the absence of such factions, where no one had any clear notion as to what should be done? The very fact that the lot was used far more often in Herrnhut than in Bethlehem suggests that "lack of consensus" was interpreted differently in the two communities. Zinzendorf himself defined the occasions for its use with varying degrees of generality. For example, he insisted that "the lot will not be used unless no other reliable counsel can be found." [24] Yet elsewhere he also stated that if even one person "felt" that it should not be used, it would not be employed.[25]

Under these circumstances the very ambiguity in the criteria governing the use of the lot tended to play into the hands of the established authorities. The question of whether or not a given problem should be submitted to the lot was likely to be resolved by those individuals who had the necessary power to implement their own opinions. It is in this specific sense that men like Zinzendorf may be accused of manipulating, consciously or unconsciously, this purported expression of divine will in such a way as to further their own ends.[26] Thus the historical fact that the lot with rare exception tended to coincide with the viewpoint adopted by the Count or his aristocratic lieutenants should be interpreted not so much as an indication of the Count's favor in God's eyes, or of a simple reflection of the operation of a game of chance, but rather as evidence of human manipulation of divine will. It should not be overlooked that after Christ's election as Chief Elder the Lord in effect was generally granted no say in the matter of whether or not He should be consulted on a given issue.[27]

Such ambiguity was not peculiar to the specification of conditions under which the lot could be used. The very procedures governing the actual usage of the lot merely compounded existing obscurities. In the first place there was no uniform procedure governing the employment of the lot. Thus the formulation of questions to be submitted to the lot was entirely up to the powers that be. Since the definition of the problem was left entirely to the persons seeking an answer, there was room for those who held positions of importance to formulate a question in such a way that even a negative answer did not automatically threaten their own particular viewpoint. Furthermore, the wording of a given question could be left sufficiently vague so as to permit ample opportunity for personal interpretation of the Lord's will. Thus when Ettwein, a prominent leader of the Moravians in Bethlehem during the latter part of the eighteenth century, was trying to decide whether or not he should go on an extended missionary journey, the lot drawn, which according to his interpretation sanctioned such a step, merely read "Behold I am with you." [28] Had Ettwein's preference been to stay in Bethlehem he could presumably have interpreted the same text as an indication of God's approval for his remaining in Bethlehem and not going on a journey.

Even more crucial than the actual wording of a given question was the issue of the number of ballots to be submitted to the lot. Although the mean number was three, one affirmative, one negative, and one blank, the number was frequently altered to include more than one blank, or to eliminate a negative statement altogether and submit only an affirmative and one or more blanks.[29] Thus, although men could not coerce God's will into coinciding with their own, they could and sometimes did stack the odds of chance in the actual drawing of lots in their favor.[30]

If the ballot drawn was affirmative, the issue was closed, at least for the time being. But suppose the ballot drawn was negative, what then? At least three different paths of action were thereby opened up. In an election to a specified office involving a person whose name had been turned down by the lot, one could (1) elect no one to the office and let the matter rest there; (2) resubmit the name negatived by the lot, but when? tomorrow? in a month? in a year?; or (3) continue to submit other names until someone's candidacy had been approved and the relevant office filled.

Even if the slip drawn was a blank this did not offer an unequivocal reply. Take the case of a blank having been drawn when the name of a certain Sister had been proposed as wife for some Brother. This could be interpreted in at least five different ways: (1)

The Brother should first be consulted before the name of another Sister be submitted to the lot. (2) The Board was free to consider another name right away without first consulting the Brother in question. (3) The Brother was free to propose marriage to the Sister, whose name was not in fact negatived by the lot, but must do so on his own responsibility. (4) The Brother should himself select another spouse. (5) The Brother should shelve the question of marriage for the time being.[31] Thus, whenever the lot was negative or blank, persons were still able to interpret the reply according to their own judgment. In effect they were free to impose their own values in the implementation of a given action.

The most crucial aspects of the ambiguity surrounding the actual submission procedure of questions to the lot centered on the matter of resubmission of a given item. The drawing of a blank or a negative slip gave no indication of when or if this matter could be resubmitted. The matter of resubmission, therefore, tended to become a political issue in which the dominant political faction was ultimately able to impose its will. For example, by the beginning of the nineteenth century the leadership of the Unity and of Herrnhut had become so attached to the preservation of the status quo that when, following the Synod of 1801 the lot negatived the convening of a Synod in 1805, they were in no great hurry to resubmit the matter to the lot. At a time when the American and even the British settlements were beginning to clamor for some degree of home rule the leaders of Herrnhut were only too glad to shelve any convening of a Synod at which proposals for reform might be aired. God had expressed his will through the lot that a Synod was not to be held at this time, and the Herrnhuters were not inclined to give Him a chance to change His mind. The next Synod was finally convened seventeen years later, in 1818.

That the lot was used more than once or twice in cases where it had previously been negative or noncommittal on a given issue is attested to in the histories of a number of individuals. In Bethlehem Ettwein reported "Today Brother Philip finally received permission to partake of the communion again; the question has been put concerning him *very often before this."* [Italics mine.] [32] This procedure may also help to explain why none of Zinzendorf's aristocratic friends were ever refused admission to Herrnhut. Not only could the questions submitted to the lot be worded in terms sufficiently ambiguous as to permit ample opportunity for personal interpretation, but even if the lot was negative the matter could be resubmitted until a satisfactory answer was found.[33]

The verdict of the lot was binding only upon those who requested its use and participated in the procedures of its use and not upon those about whose fate the lot was being consulted.[34] Thus the Brother who asked the lot to help him find a mate was bound to abide by its decisions, but the Sister proposed by him was free to reject the offer of marriage. As long as the Moravians regarded the lot as an expression of God's will, its prescriptive power was considerable; few individuals dared to follow the dictates of their own heart or mind in preference to accepting divine guidance.[35]

Thus while the lot was regarded as the cornerstone of theocratic government in Moravian eighteenth-century communities, it in fact permitted a considerable degree of human manipulation of the expression of God's will. In providing for a divine legitimation of political actions which were often unpopular, the lot served to keep the existing social structure immune from criticism.[36] Yet in supplying such a mantle of divinity to cover human error, it tended to reduce the saliency of personal responsibility for actions taken by officeholders in the public interest. The absence of accountability to the public, which was especially marked in the Sifting Period, tended to enhance existing strains towards autocracy. The Moravians prided themselves on having found the perfect solution to communal government by ensuring the divine guidance of their affairs. Yet they failed to realize the extent to which they had merely changed the social structure without being able to eliminate the tendencies towards autocratic rule they so feared.[37]

The Drive toward Modification

With Zinzendorf's death and the imposition on Bethlehem of a type of government which, it was hoped, would bring the American Moravians into closer unity with their German Brethren, the lot came to be used with increased frequency in the American settlement.[38] While Spangenberg during his tenure in Bethlehem had never openly opposed the use of the lot he had kept its employment in communal decisions limited, compared to the extent to which it was being used in Herrnhut during the fifties. But with his departure von Marschall and Seidel saw to it that its use became more widespread, even though they never managed to enforce as mechanical a resort to it as had become the practice in Herrnhut after Zinzendorf's death.

The Brethren in Bethlehem did not accept this intensified usage with enthusiasm or even equanimity; indeed the growth of this practice merely intensified their opposition to its use, and so accelerated rather than retarded the long-run trend towards abrogation of the lot. They began to question how a divinely inspired instrument of decision could produce verdicts so clearly at variance with common sense. How, for instance, was one to explain away a marriage sanctioned by the lot being broken up by the unfaithfulness of one partner? Why was a missionary to be recalled home when he was clearly needed far more badly in the field? And why for that matter were other missionary outposts kept going long after their real work had been accomplished? Questions such as these were no longer being asked silently by an occasional doubting Thomas but were beginning to be aired openly.[39] It was becoming increasingly evident that the Moravians in Bethlehem were willing to accept the divine inspiration of the lot only as long as its verdict did not manifestly violate common sense. Yet once it was admitted that chance rather than God determined the outcome of the use of the lot, the very value premises of its employment in Moravian communities crumbled.

An American Moravian Bishop thus declared that "as soon as a majority of Moravian ministers and people declare that they no longer have confidence in this mode of determining the will of the Lord, it must necessarily be abolished." [40]

The same forces which had prompted the Moravians in Pennsylvania to rebel against absentee government under a system of exclusivism similarly made them oppose the indiscriminate use of the lot in communal affairs. The Brethren in Herrnhut had resorted to the use of the lot because of their belief in the absolute insufficiency of man; but the Brethren in Bethlehem, spurred on by their obvious economic successes and their increased awareness of the spirit of political freedom which surrounded them, were less and less inclined to entrust all important decisions automatically to God. Not that they had abandoned faith in God; far from it, for prayer was still regarded as a vital part of their activities. But what they wanted was for God to help them make their own decisions rather than for them to help God make His decisions.

The initial drive for modification in the communal use of the lot was directed at its use in connection with business and financial transactions, where it was felt to be an unwarranted intrusion of religious authority over purely economic matters. The General Synod of 1764 refused, however, even to permit the American Moravians to discuss the matter. At the Synod of Marienborn in 1769 the Moravians of Bethlehem made another attempt to press for modification of the use of the lot and did succeed in at least providing for a general discussion of the topic. It was generally agreed that this was not the only means whereby the Lord must rule over the Moravians, but that when it was used it represented a manifestation of His will. Most of the ensuing discussion focused not on the use of the lot in principle, for in principle its validity was upheld by the majority, but upon questions of method. All the shortcomings of the employment of the lot in the past were blamed upon methodological ambiguities concerning the number and type of ballots to be employed; and the overwhelming consensus of the meeting was that the adoption of definitive rules to regulate the manner in which the lot should be used would solve all problems.[41] The position of the American Moravians had been completely misunderstood: their opposition in principle was blanketed by the Synod's focus on methodology.

In Bethlehem, recourse to the lot in communal affairs was being criticized more and more frequently. In some cases its verdict was simply ignored. In 1769 the Moravians in Bethlehem had decided to appoint Sister Gammern to head the Single Sisters' choir, without first seeking the approval of the lot, for the simple reason that "no other suitable candidate could be found for this position." [42] Yet because the Elders Conference of the Unity subsequently reversed this decision she did not receive her official appointment until twenty years later. Another time the Moravians in Bethlehem simply refused to accept an appointment which had been made by the Unity Elders Conference and approved by the lot in Herrnhut because the appointment meant "advancing a comparatively young man over the heads of old and tried workers." [43] In yet another case the lot had been used by the Elders Conference in Bethlehem itself to approve the appointment of a certain Brother as leader of the Single Brethren's choir, but the members of the Single Brethren rebelled against the chosen candidate and the Brother in question was forced to withdraw his original acceptance of the call.[44]

The use of the lot came to be regarded with increasing disdain in other areas also. In matters of marriage it was felt that leaving the question of marriage or the selection of a spouse in the hands of God alone was incompatible with a striving for greater personal freedom. In connection with missionary enterprises it was felt that such questions as the resettlement of Indians in Christian settlements, the baptism of Indian converts, the naming of new missionary outposts, or the abandoning of old settlements could best be achieved without resort to the lot.[45] With the interruption of communications during the American Revolution the Moravians in Bethlehem had been forced to assume a greater share of responsibil-

ity for the government of their community. After the cessation of
hostilities they had petitioned the leaders of the Unity for official recognition of their increased local autonomy. Their demand had been
coupled with a request for permission to use the lot in the making
of appointments only when two-thirds of the Bethlehem Elders
Conference felt that such usage was "both necessary and useful to
the proposal."[46] Yet the petition, which concluded with the terse
comment "Need knows no law,"[47] was ignored and the request refused.

The lot had thus fallen into disrepute in Bethlehem long before it
was to be officially abrogated. The first triumph for the abolitionists
came in 1782 when the General Synod, meeting in Berthelsdorf,
agreed under pressure from the American Moravians to annul the
use of the lot in connection with questions of property.[48] Although
both the American and the British Moravians had pressed for abrogation of the use of the lot in marriages, they failed to secure the
necessary approval for such a step at the General Synods of 1782,
1789, or 1801.[49] The Moravians in Herrnhut were convinced that
their Brethren in North America "inspired by a love for national
freedom, manifested aversion towards all constitutional arrangements, and wished to abolish everything so as to be able to make
way for the new."[50] Their refusal to grant permission to discon-
tinue the use of the lot in marriages was based upon the hope, a
vain one as history proved, that the Unity could compel the Moravians of Bethlehem to conform to this practice. In 1818 the American
Moravians triumphed, and the use of the lot in connection with
marriages was abolished for all Moravians, except ministers and
missionaries residing outside Europe.[51]

In the case of the European congregations it was felt that since no
protest against this practice had been noticed at the grassroots level
there was no reason for abolition of this practice. Yet when communities like Herrnhut were informed of this decision their reaction
was uniform—a demand for the abolition of the use of the lot in
marriages. Their demand was granted in 1819.[52]

From this point on, the ultimate abrogation of the mandatory use
of the lot in all questions concerning communal affairs was but a
matter of time. In 1825 the use of the lot in marriages was made
obligatory only for missionaries, not ministers.[53] By 1767 it was
agreed that although the lot should still be continued in appointing
missionaries, the retention of uniformity in the methods of its usage
was no longer to be insisted upon.[54] In actual fact such uniformity
had never been attained. Moreover, it was agreed that even in cases
of missionary appointments the lot should only be used when those
making the appointment were "fully and unanimously convinced"
that they themselves needed such direction.[55] When an individual
asked for its use either in accepting the offer of an appointment or
in some other personal matter, the use had first to be approved by
the local authorities, usually the Provincial Elders Conference;
when approved and used, its verdict was, as before, absolutely binding upon the individual. The Synod of 1869 further modified the
use of the lot, making it obligatory only in the appointments of
bishops and the acceptance of candidates for missionary service.[56]
All other appointments to offices were to be made without the use of
the lot. Finally, the Synod of 1889 omitted all remaining references
to the lot as an element of communal decision-making in the
Moravian Church.[57]

The abolition of this practice marked the disappearance of the last
remnants of theocratic government. The Herrnhuters viewed the
practice of the lot as a God-given requisite for the attainment of
communal goals. They failed to realize that the American Moravians' demand for abrogation of this practice was an attempt to
achieve the religious ends of the community by means more suited
to the political and economic climate in which they found themselves, and was not an attempt to abolish the religious goals themselves.

PART THREE. THE FAMILY

> *The choir regulations, particularly
> those concerning the separation
> of the sexes . . . are* principia stantis
> et cadentis ecclesiae *upon which
> the persistence or decline of
> the community depends.*
> —*Synodal Verlasz, 1764*
> *Marienborn*

IV. THE DEVELOPMENT OF
THE CHOIR SYSTEM

TRADITIONALLY, through its regulation of procreation, the family has been the guarantor of a supply of new members to a community. In most societies the family has also been entrusted with the primary responsibility for the socialization and social control of the young. The preservation of social values and structures is thus typically determined by the extent to which the family is successful in performing these functions.

This allocation of rights and duties poses problems to a society or community which insists upon the total allegiance of its members to communal goals, for participation in the family inevitably detracts from participation in communal affairs, tending to generate particularistic loyalties which compete with the exclusive loyalty to the community as a whole. Most utopian communities, whether of a religious or political character, have therefore tried to abolish the family system and allocate the responsibility for the rearing of children to an institution less likely to threaten the exclusive allegiance of its members.[1] The Moravian solution to this problem was to develop a family surrogate in the form of the choir system which, by explicitly subordinating a Moravian's familial obligation to his religious duties, would maximize the individual's loyalty to the religious goals of the community.

Origins and Principles of the Choir System

The Moravian choir system, entailing a rigid stratification of the community according to age, sex, and marital status, emerged as a consequence of Zinzendorf's early attempts to enrich the spiritual life of the community by encouraging the formation of so-called bands or classes whose primary function was to satisfy the spiritual needs of their members.[2] References to the existence of such religious groupings are to be found in Herrnhut as early as 1727.[3] In these gatherings the emphasis was on the religious; members would meet for prayer, song, testimony, and special liturgical services. Since the primary objective of these bands was the deepening of the religious life of their members, a high degree of spiritual affinity was an important criterion of membership within such a group. But unlike the Waldensians or the ancient *Unitas Fratrum* in Kunvald, the Moravian bands were stratified not with reference to the degree of personal holiness of the individual, but according to the external criteria of age, sex, and social standing.[4] The religious content of these band meetings varied according to the social and demographic composition of their membership. Central to all was the theological premise that a study of the life and death of Christ was an essential precondition to man's salvation. Christ's passage through the stages of life from infancy to manhood provided an appropriate model of behavior for each of the bands.[5]

Although these bands constituted an important antecedent of the choirs, they were not synonymous with them. The degree of stratification was less rigid; moreover, membership in these bands was voluntary, whereas membership in the choir organizations became obligatory for every member of the community.[6]

Since the date of origin of the choir system cannot be pinned arbitrarily to a given year, we prefer to trace its beginnings to the development of the bands in the latter part of the seventeen-twenties, and to place the emergence of the choir system in the context of a gradual transformation of these bands over a period of at least ten years.

One other aspect of the stratification of both bands and choirs deserves elaboration: the requirement that all members within a given group be of the same sex. The considerable emphasis placed on the segregation of the sexes in Moravian settlements has to be understood in the light of Zinzendorf's personal views on this matter. The

Count was well aware of the danger that the emotionalism associated with a religious awakening could be directed toward sexual rather than religious objects. "We know from experience that in times of religious agitation, sensual relationships, with their attendant evil consequences, may develop all too easily out of the spiritual influences of the time. . . ."[7]

Zinzendorf sought to prevent such outbreaks through the imposition of rigid disciplinary order and social control. The "Brotherly Agreement" of May 12, 1727, stated: "Familiar or intimate relations between single men and women are to be positively forbidden; moreover the Elders have the power to prohibit social intercourse as soon as they have even the slightest suspicion, no matter how worthy its purported goal."[8] Segregation of the sexes was considered to be mandatory in the bands where religious enthusiasm and emotionalism were likely to be particularly prominent. When the bands were gradually transformed into choirs and the choir members took on not only religious, but also economic and social roles within the framework of the choir, the principle of sexual segregation was transferred from band to choir, and its mandate extended to economic and social activities.

Such segregation of the sexes was not unique to Herrnhut. In Bethlehem in the seventeen-forties an ordinance detailing separate walks for Single Brethren, Single Sisters, and the Married People's choir was designed to ensure against their meeting.[9] Twenty years later the Moravian congregation in Bethlehem was still adamant that:

As far as the choir regulations and especially the segregation of the sexes are concerned, we must needs remain immutable on that point, if we are to remain a people of God. . . . The most prudent segregation of both sexes from childhood to old age is a basic principle of our closed community.[10]

The extremes to which this principle of segregation was carried is graphically illustrated in a memorandum from Zinzendorf to Cap-

tain Garrison, the commander of a ship chartered by the Moravians
for the transatlantic transportation of their missionaries, in which
the Count wrote: [11]

I would like to see to it that the seating [on the *Irene*] could be so ar-
ranged, that the Single Brethren do not have to look the Single Sisters
straight in the face. On shipboard of course, it is not possible to be too
particular about these matters, but whenever possible could they be
seated as follows:

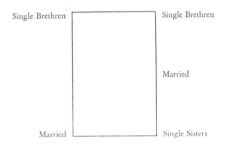

The Dominance of Religious Functions

The early development of the choir system, although primarily
the outgrowth of religious enthusiasm, can also be seen as an organizational response to Zinzendorf's insistence on the segregation of
the sexes. This motive is clearly an important one in the formation
of the first choir, that of the Single Brethren. The Diary of Herrnhut notes that on February 11, 1728, young men, living in houses
whose occupants included single women or married women whose
husbands were absent, were forming a household of their own in
order to be able to further their "growth in spiritual grace." [12] At
first these Single Brethren were housed in a wing of the orphanage,
but as their number grew, they were moved to the inn, which from
1731 to 1733 was managed by the Single Brethren's choir. [13]

The official records of this period contain little information about
the religious and communal life of these early days of choir living.
A list of rules and regulations drawn up by the Single Brethren in
1736 attests to the religious emphasis of their way of life: "No one is
permitted to live here, who is not primarily concerned with the wel-

fare of his soul." [14] The remainder of the rules and regulations deal with less profound matters, detailing responsibilities for the cleaning of the house and placing restrictions on gossiping and the telling of tales.

With the growth of the community and the increasing emphasis placed on a total segregation of the unmarried men and women, even the inn became too small to hold all the Brethren. A new building was erected in 1739 for the specific purpose of housing all the Brethren under one roof. But only a year later another building had to be added to accommodate additional increases. [15]

The population statistics of the Herrnhut community similarly attest to the growth of the Single Brethren's choir. In 1728, the year of the formation of the choir, its members numbered twenty-six, comprising approximately eight per cent of the total population of Herrnhut. By 1733 there were ninety single men, constituting about fifteen per cent of the community's total population, but no figures are available as to how many of these single men were members of the Single Brethren's choir. By 1740, twelve years after the founding of the Single Brethren's choir, their members constituted seventeen per cent of the total population. [16] Assuming that the proportion of single men in the community remained relatively constant throughout this period, one is led to the conclusion that by the end of the decade the number of single men not living in the Single Brethren's choir was negligible. The striking decline in private home ownership throughout this period would seem to lend further credence to this conclusion. [17]

Although the young men of Herrnhut were the first to band together as a choir, the young women followed soon thereafter and formed a choir of their own in the spring of 1730. The young women vowed to dedicate their lives completely to the Saviour, and to this end, to leave all decisions to Christ and the Elders of the community, and to "retain no will or choice of their own." [18] Notwithstanding this rigid dedication to a religious life, the Moravian Sisters explicitly renounced the taking of a vow of celibacy. The choirs should not, therefore, be confused with any attempt to develop forms of Protestant monasticism.

The chronic housing shortage of Herrnhut prevented the Single Sisters from living under one roof, but in spite of this difficulty fourteen of them had managed to find a common home by 1733. By 1734 their number had grown from the original eighteen to sixty-two, constituting approximately ten per cent of the total population. By 1742 there were approximately 120 Single Sisters, of whom about one-third were still living with their families.[19] As their number grew, the demand for more adequate accommodations increased. In this respect they were, however, less fortunate than the Single Brethren, for as late as 1743 a decision to build a separate Single Sisters' choir was still being negated by the lot.[20]

Religious services, prayer meetings, and individual religious testimonies appear to have taken up a large part of the day, although some time was also devoted to writing and spelling lessons. During these early years of the choir system all economic activities were subordinated to religious pursuits. Opportunities for work were often turned down because they might expose the employee to "unfavorable influences" of the secular world. The economic situation of the choirs was precarious, but the extraordinary religious enthusiasm of this period enabled the Sisters to accept the shortcomings of their economic position. The happiness of living together in a religious community in many ways compensated for the poverty of their material lives.[21]

During the seventeen-thirties and forties the principles of choir organization extended only in a limited degree to the married, the widowed, and the children of the community. For both the married and the children band meetings continued to provide the major opportunities for spiritual edification throughout this period. Although in 1736 a number of children had been organized into a Children's choir in Zinzendorf's orphanage,[22] most of these youngsters were the offspring either of very poor members of the community or of missionaries working abroad whose parents clearly were not in a position to be able to support them.

As to the widows of Herrnhut, economic rather than religious considerations appear to have been instrumental in forcing a transition from band to choir. Underlying Zinzendorf's initial gathering of a few destitute widows in Herrnhut's orphanage and poorhouse in 1727 was an obvious concern for the material welfare of these elderly ladies in a community where both opportunities for work and housing facilities were severely limited.[23] The early history of this choir is depicted in the official records as a series of moves from one house to another as their numbers increased. Not until 1743 did they finally manage to get a whole house of their own.[24] Even after the acquisition of a choir house their numbers remained relatively small. Of the forty-four widows living in Herrnhut in 1744, only twenty-nine were actually living within the four walls of the choir house.[25] That economic and social considerations, rather than religious ones, were similarly instrumental in the formation of the Widowers' choir is suggested by the fact that a choir of the Widowers was not formed until 1746. Its emergence thus coincided with a very considerable tightening of the community's regulation with regard to the segregation of the sexes, which resulted in widowers no longer being permitted to keep their unmarried daughters in their own homes.[26]

The archives are silent about any choir development in the ranks of the married persons during this period. The numerous accounts attesting to the very active participation of married men and women in religious activities both at home and abroad and their disproportionate share of the burden of community leadership suggest that they would have been less likely to have had time and inclination for extended religious meetings devoted to thought and meditation rather than to action. Although bands which conducted meetings were formed among the married, these meetings were held less frequently than those of the single persons, and the impetus for an ex-

pansion of such religious gatherings and for the possible transformation of band to choir was therefore lacking.

In Bethlehem as in Herrnhut, the first attempts to organize the
new settlement were directed to the formation of bands whose functions paralleled those of their German counterparts. But the development of separate choir institutions did not lag far behind.[27] A
house for the Single Brethren was erected as early as 1742, and segregation of the married, the single men, and the single women was
practiced even during the very first days of the community's settlement. This system of stratification was above all a matter of economic convenience, if not necessity, during the first months and
years of settlement on the frontier. The choirs did not even have the
time to develop a religious program of their own, and the bands
continued to fulfill this function until about 1744.[28]

The principle of choir segregation was formally incorporated into
Spangenberg's first plan for the community: "A house for the single
women and one for the single men, and the organization of the
older boys and girls into choir divisions are proposed." [29] Pursuant
to this plan a second choir house was begun in 1746 and completed
in 1748. When the Single Brethren moved into the new building the
Single Sisters took over the house formerly occupied by the men.
The first Bethlehem choir diary, that of the Single Brethren, was begun in 1744, though it does contain some information on the two
preceding years. The choir diary of the Single Sisters was not begun
until 1748, but we know from the Bethlehem Congregational Diary
that shortly after the foundation of Bethlehem the single women
were not only being housed together but were also holding their
own religious services. By 1748 the choir diaries of the Single Sisters
record a membership of twenty-one Sisters and twenty-nine "young
Maidens," giving a total of fifty, whereas in 1740 they had numbered
only seven Sisters and six Maidens.[30] All children were placed in
the nursery or Children's choir at an early age. Although this action
was prompted by religious considerations, namely the freeing of the
parents for greater service in the name of the Lord, there were also

important economic considerations which made it difficult, if not impossible, for persons actively engaged in the rapid building of a new community or in missionary pursuits to have their children with them all the time.

The Moravians' original decision to immigrate to Bethlehem had been prompted by religious motives: "The purpose of our coming into this region was not to seek economic support nor to gain freedom of conscience—we did not lack either—but rather the desire to inform others also of that which we know to be conducive to the eternal salvation of mankind." [31] Their profound dedication to spiritual goals found ample expression in the choirs of that period. The choir diaries of the seventeen-forties are filled with entries documenting the number and variety of religious meetings taking place on any given day of the week. Every day was marked by religious devotions, for each of which a time and a place were clearly set aside. At daybreak the awakening by a night watchman was followed by morning grace of the Elders. At eight o'clock, sermons of Zinzendorf were read and studied, and a Biblical watchword for the day was announced. At sundown this watchword was subjected to discussion and explication. After supper half an hour was devoted to the study of the Bible, then smaller groups met for personal testimony and religious fellowship until 8:30 P.M. Then an hour would be devoted to the singing of hymns related to a specific text, and at ten o'clock a quarter of an hour was set aside for special prayers on each day of the week. Finally at eleven o'clock the night watchmen would begin their rounds. [32] Bishop Levering noted, with a touch of humor, that the extreme brevity of most of these religious services "caused such programs to be less burdensome to the flesh than might be supposed." [33] If we bear in mind that this list includes only daily religious activities of the choirs and omits the additional services, litanies, and homilies held for the whole congregation on the Sabbath, one gains an idea of the profound extent to which religion permeated the life of the community.

In sum, the origin of the choir system, both in Herrnhut and

Bethlehem, was deeply rooted in the religious goals and activities of the communities. The choirs emerged in response to a demand for greater spiritual fellowship and provided a socioreligious framework within which the needs of the individual could be met more readily than in the larger congregation of the community. Through the provision of a common place of residence, the choirs were able to offer their members a much fuller and more extensive participation in religious activities than had been possible in the weekly or even bi-weekly meetings of the bands. In introducing a rigid ecclesiasticism into the social structure of Moravian communities, Zinzendorf had hoped both to deepen and to broaden the religious life of the members of these settlements. But he failed to foresee the extent to which the very success of the choir system carried within it the seeds of destruction of its original principle.

The Development of Economic Functions

The history of the choirs may be portrayed not only in terms of a growing concern with the spiritual, but also as a history of house moving, rental negotiations, and building developments. The building program was extensive, but the steady influx of new immigrants continued to place heavy demands on an already overcrowded community. The communal living arrangements of the choirs, though originally motivated by religious considerations, offered an ingenious solution to the housing problem by reducing very considerably the number of separate dwelling units which would otherwise have had to be built.

Herrnhut was in the seventeen-twenties and thirties being invaded by a large number of single persons, many of whom had no kinship affiliations in the new community. The cost of constructing separate housing facilities for each of these bachelors and spinsters would have been prohibitive. As it was, the choirs of the Single Brethren and Single Sisters provided an ideological and religious rationale for the sharing of quarters that were generally crowded and frequently devoid of privacy,

Bethlehem was faced with housing problems very similar to those of Herrnhut and it resolved them in the same manner—by minimizing the cost of housing through the substitution of large choir houses for private family dwellings. But since the choir principle was introduced into the American community at the outset, Bethlehem did not have to go through a phase of converting existing single family houses into institutional living quarters. The building plans of Bethlehem were initially predicated on the assumption that the choirs and not individual families were the social units determining the size of any given home. A visitor to Bethlehem in 1754 has left a graphic account of the living quarters of the Single Brethren's choir:

It is similar to a castle; is built of sandstone, has five stories and contains over 70 large and small rooms. In the basement there are several carpenter's shops. On the first and second floors there are two dining halls, five tables in each, at which twenty people can be seated per table. The whole of the third floor is taken up by sleeping quarters with its 200 beds. On the fourth floor is the silkworm industry, and on the fifth hang the clothes of the Brethren. The roof is flat, in the Italian style, so that one could actually walk on it.[84]

This description sheds light on a number of other economic functions which the choirs gradually took over. Thus the provision of clothing and of food became the responsibility not of any one individual or even of the head of a family, but of each choir. As a result, both food and clothing were purchased in large quantities. Time and money were further saved through the communal preparation of meals and the allocation of choir personnel to the tasks of making and repairing clothing.

The choir principle of shared living quarters provided a partial solution to another problem facing both Herrnhut and Bethlehem in their early years, namely, that of unemployment. By providing opportunities for the development of home industries within the choir houses rather than the families, it increased the size of the working unit and not only spread the cost of overhead, but enabled the introduction of machinery that no one family could possibly have afforded on its own.[35] In addition, by relegating the place of work to the choir rather than the family abode, the choir system did away with the necessity of building separate workshops for large numbers of single men and women who had no family connections in the Herrnhut community.

In Bethlehem everyone worked in his or her respective choir division—the single, the married, the children, and the widowed— all toiling for the community as a whole. The choir delivered the proceeds of this labor to the central administration and in turn was regularly assigned its share of necessary foodstuffs, clothing, and linen. Everyone ate, slept, prayed, and worked within the choir organization. The Single Brethren built their own house, and together they would go out to till the land, while the Single Sisters reaped the harvest and the widows spun the cotton.[36]

So far the gradual accretion of economic functions by the choirs has been portrayed as advantageous to the community, not only from the point of view of furthering the spiritual life of its members, but also coincidentally and conveniently furthering their economic position. This was not always the case. For example, the choirs' exclusive employment practices did offer certain economies by enlarging the size of the basic work unit. But by insisting on the strict separation of the sexes as a cardinal principle of social order, they sacrificed many advantages that would have accrued from a more rational division of labor. Minutes of the Elders Conference for this early period in Herrnhut are filled with directives designed to maintain such segregation of the sexes, no matter how disruptive this might be for the economic development of the community as a whole. Thus we are told, "David Christopher is taking two Sisters to work for him and the Brethren must leave."[37] And "Göbel had to get rid of his spinning girl because Berndt's two boys lived in the same house."[38] Even more serious for the Single Brethren was the following mandate: "No unmarried tailor may measure or fit young girls or any other womenfolk, this work is to be left to the married tailors exclusively." [39]

The early years of Bethlehem were characterized by a similar insistence on the segregation of the sexes with regard to all occupational duties, often leading to an inefficient duplication of services. Furthermore, once the choirs had established their own work unit, any employment outside the community was not only discouraged but forbidden. These factors seriously limited the potential economic development of the community. The accretion of employment functions by the choir was thus, from the point of view of the economy, something of a mixed blessing.

By interpreting their responsibilities for the spiritual welfare of their members in so broad a manner as to include a concern for the economic welfare of the individuals under their care, the choirs were brought face to face with the problem of having to create an economically self-sufficient and independent working unit. In Herrnhut as early as 1733 the Single Sisters' choir attempted to solve its economic problems by insisting on a sharing of all the economic goods of the members of the choir. Unfortunately we have little information on the extent to which such communistic practices were carried through. Anna Nitschmann, the leader of the Single Sisters' choir at the time, devotes only a cryptic reference to it in her autobiographical sketch: "We lived in the beginning in a community of goods, but then suspicion and mistrust began to spread among a few, and love was disturbed." [40] Whatever the character of this early attempt at communal living, its duration was short. No other attempt at a similar community of goods appears to have been made in Herrnhut. Their choirs did, however, take over many of the responsibilities for the care of the sick and the poor. [41]

In Bethlehem, on the other hand, the early years were marked by an admittedly loose but effective community of goods, the sharing of property occurring not within the choir unit but within the whole community—the Elders of the community acting as administrators of these funds.[42] The care of the sick was for many years the responsibility of the individual choir; poor relief, however, was from the beginning provided by the community as a whole.[43]

Both in Herrnhut and in Bethlehem the choirs thus developed more and more into self-contained economic units, while still retaining their religious basis and pedagogic purpose. Although the economic functions served by the choirs were neither anticipated nor intended in the original development of this institution, they provided an effective solution for some of the more serious economic problems of the two communities. In time, fulfillment of a purely economic function became in itself a raison d'être for the continuation and expansion of the choir system.[44] At the same time one should not blind oneself to the fact that the choirs, while solving certain pressing economic problems, also created new ones for the community as a whole.

The Acquisition of Social Functions

Once the choirs had become established as independent socioeconomic units with their own living, sleeping, and eating quarters, it was inevitable that the socialization functions of the choirs should be similarly broadened.[45] Originally they concerned themselves with such purely religious matters as the promotion of the spiritual growth and development of their members. As the choirs came to control a larger and larger share of an individual's daily activities the definition of their social functions broadened considerably. The nature and consequences of this extension of responsibilities varied among the different choirs.

According to Zinzendorf, choir socialization began even before the child was born: "When the marriage has been consecrated to the Lord and the mother lives in continuous interaction with the Saviour, one may expect that already in the mother's womb the children form a choir, that is, a grouping of the community consecrated to the Lord's work." [46] To this end pregnant women were expected to be particularly painstaking in their religious devotions. In their choir meetings they would discuss with their supervisors many of the issues, both religious and social, associated with the birth of a child. To the secular mind of the twentieth century such spiritual preoccupation with the embryo may seem a trifle ludicrous, but the fact that in these meetings women were receiving specific preparation for the distinctive social roles they and their children would soon be playing in the community should not be overlooked.

Such indoctrination as to the place of the child in the community helped make it possible to take infants away from their mothers at a very early age. Since the mothers were so thoroughly socialized, the idea of handing over their children to the nursery caused little apparent friction. In Bethlehem the chief supervisor of the children's nursery wrote to Zinzendorf that "the mothers plead almost with tears in their eyes, that they [their children] may be placed in the nursery, as soon as they have been weaned." [47] Generally the children were taken away from their parents and put under institutional care at the age of one or one and a half, although in Herrnhut they were often somewhat older. The christening ceremony marked the transfer of responsibility for the child from parent to the community.

All children received religious instruction at meetings with their choir Brothers and Sisters at a very early age in accordance with Zinzendorf's notion that children should be acquainted with the nature of salvation as soon as they could think for themselves. That this was assumed to be fairly early is attested to by the fact that in 1723 Zinzendorf composed a catechism for children aged one and a half.[48] Although these educational meetings, often conducted by Zinzendorf himself, initially achieved great popularity and success, the Count came in time to be disappointed, feeling that the sense of devotion among the children had waned. On occasion he was so appalled by the "unliturgical" behavior of the small children that he would dismiss the whole meeting.[49]

Zinzendorf was convinced that the supervisors in the choirs could be trained more systematically than natural parents to instill in their charges a devotion to the religious goals of the Moravians. He regarded these foster parents as "visible imprints [*Abdrücke*] of the Father, the Saviour and the Holy Ghost." [50] In practice the children's foster parents were not always successful in living up to these demanding ideals. Towards the end of his life Zinzendorf, influenced largely by the failure of these children's educational institutions to produce the diversity of personnel necessary for the filling of new posts in the community, reversed his stand and insisted that parents should "raise their own children, in order that they [the children] may savor the toils of life from childhood on and learn to work. Otherwise we get nothing but princes, priests and officers, and no common soldiers." [51] Zinzendorf had failed to foresee that the type of education provided by the children's choirs, though eminently suitable for persons contemplating a career in the professions, was unlikely to motivate the children to pursue humbler careers. As a result the choirs failed to produce suitable replacements for the majority of unskilled and semi-skilled positions that needed to be filled. A child raised in his own family was more likely to choose his father's occupation than any other, and so help to maintain occupational diversity. The same was not true of the choirs, who by virtue of their religious egalitarianism were bound to educate all of their charges to the same level.

In Bethlehem, owing to the housing shortage in the early years, a separate nursery was not founded until 1746. Maria Spangenberg, in a letter to Zinzendorf, noted "we have not less than one hundred and fifty children and of these at least half can barely walk or not at all . . . but because many of them cannot walk yet, each choir has its baby carriage. When they go for a walk one Brother or Sister goes ahead, and the bigger children help with the pulling." [52] Every evening the children of the nursery choir would have their singing lessons where they were taught to carry a tune and memorize the verses of hymns. At the age of five or six the children were segregated according to sex; the little girls and little boys aged six to twelve thus forming separate children's choirs. It was in these choirs that the children received their formal schooling, which for colonial times was considerable.[53]

The contemporary distinction between secular and religious education was alien to Moravian thought. Thus Nazareth Hall, an important educational institution in the Bethlehem area, had from its inception the dual purpose "to educate not only skillful mechanics, but also assist in the work of the Lord." [54] Barely fifty years after the founding of the Bethlehem community in a complete wilderness, the Moravian educational institutions were giving instruction in Latin, Greek, Hebrew, French, German, English, mathematics, general history, ecclesiastical history, geography, and drawing.[55] Already in the early years the Moravian children were being taught to read and write not only German and English but also the languages of the Mohawk, to fit them for their missionary activities. Even in the turmoil of Indian uprisings in the seventeen-fifties there were examinations conducted in reading, writing, arithmetic, sewing, knitting, spinning, and music.[56]

The Older Boys' and Older Girls' choirs consisted of those aged twelve to seventeen. These choirs were considered particularly important in preparing adolescents to take their places as adults in the community. It was here that both boys and girls were apprenticed to specific trades and taught the skills necessary for a certain occupation. Their training was not restricted to the acquisition of trade skills alone; the choir supervisors were expected to help them also in solving "the social problems so pressing among youths of that age." [57] Finally at the age of seventeen the children would be initiated into the Single choirs to carry out their vocation. The transfer from one choir to another was regarded as an important rite of passage and accompanied by appropriate ceremonial activities. The choirs of the Single Brethren and Sisters proved to be effective agents of socialization and control for individuals who might otherwise have retained a marginal status within the traditional kinship system of the society of that time. This is true particularly of Herrnhut: a majority of immigrants to the community were single persons who would otherwise have had few or no intimate social ties during the first few months or years of their stay.[58]

In Bethlehem the problem of developing social roots for the single man or woman was resolved in a similar manner. The newcomer was granted membership in a ready-made primary group in which a variety of religious and social activities went hand in hand with a heavy work load; little time was left in which to develop a sense of loneliness.[59]

During the forties, the principle of choir segregation was extended to the married people in both Herrnhut and Bethlehem, although for somewhat different reasons. In Herrnhut, Zinzendorf had discovered on his return from exile that discipline and social control, particularly with regard to the matter of segregation of the sexes, had become rather lax. In an attempt to put an end to any possibility of sexual misdemeanors, he insisted on a very rigid enforcement of sexual segregation, and to this end extended the principle of choir segregation to all members of the community. As a result, married couples were assigned to their respective choirs, one for the married men and one for the married women.[60] Documents relating to the history of these choirs lack the detail to be found in the diaries of the Single choirs. The very absence of such literature, in the face of the overall conscientiousness of the Moravians in keeping records, would suggest that the choirs of the Married People never flourished to the same extent as did those of single persons. Indeed, a good many of the married men and women continued to live in their own homes, or shared a home with a small number of other couples. It would thus appear that, although the choir principle was extended to cover married persons, it retained with them its religious function of providing institutionalized opportunities for the spiritual growth and education of its members.

In Herrnhut the Married Person's choir never attained the degree of socioeconomic independence secured by the Single Sisters and the Single Brethren. But to assume that because these married choirs did not branch out so readily into the economic and social field they therefore did not have important consequences for the community would be to ignore some strategic repercussions of their development. The very existence of choirs for married persons, irrespective of the degree to which segregation of the spouses was actually attained, posed a very real threat to the traditional family system. It was made quite clear that the survival of the family system, even in modified form, was dependent on the subordination of family to choir. In more personal terms, this meant that the individual's duty to the welfare of his soul and to the religious development of his choir was placed above and beyond his duty to his family. For several decades the choir and not the family socialized individuals to their new roles. Newlyweds, for example, immediately following their marriage were expected to, and in most cases did, live within their separate choir institutions, so as to receive full instruction in "Christian behavior and the conduct of their marriage in a manner well pleasing to God. . . ." [61]

In Bethlehem the Married People's choirs developed side by side with those of the single men and women. Provisions were made to give this choir a house of its own, and couples, especially in the early years, did not generally live together. Detailed information on the extent to which such segregation of married spouses was carried out is unfortunately lacking, although a number of entries in the Bethlehem Congregational Diary indicate that arrangements were made to set aside a time and place for each couple to meet in privacy once a week.[62] Bethlehem thus went further than Herrnhut in its early practice of choir segregation, and in the early years there appears to have been relatively little antagonism toward such living arrangements for the married persons.

Documents relating to the histories of the Widows' and Widowers' choirs, both in Herrnhut and Bethlehem, are sketchy. Bethlehem in its early years had a disproportionate share of young people and it was thus not until 1760, the end of the General Economy and a time when the choir institutions as a whole were already beginning to decline, that the Widows' and Widowers' choirs began to come into their own.[63] In Herrnhut by the late forties the majority of widows and widowers had, however, joined a choir.[64]

A number of nineteenth-century commentators on Moravian developments, imbued with their own notions about the importance of freedom of the individual, focused only on the choir's negative functions of severely depriving the married of privacy.[65] They ignored the very important positive role played by the choirs in the integration and resocialization of many individuals, particularly the single and the widowed. The choir system not only strengthened the integration of these people into the life of the community, but also provided for a much greater utilization of their social and economic skills.

Conformity to a group's norms and values is achieved not only through an effective process of socialization but also by means of social controls which limit the disruptive consequences of deviant activities for the group as a whole. In the early years of Herrnhut the emphasis placed upon social control often outweighed the concern for effective means of socialization. Zinzendorf himself believed that one of the great advantages of the choir system rested in its ability to administer discipline within a small group context, thus combining the advantages of the intimacy of a familial setting with the supposed greater degree of objectivity of a large-scale organization.[66] Although some form of regulation was exerted not through the choirs but by the Helpers Conference and the Judiciary Council, these boards acted as final arbiters to whom only the unrelenting culprit was sent. The majority of deviants never came before them; in their cases the types of sanctions employed by the choirs were usually all that was required.

The weekly choir "speakings" (*Sprechen*) required every individual to discuss and review his past actions with a choir supervisor, who in turn gave advice and admonition where necessary. The eighteenth-century Moravian, living under the choir system in a closed community, could not readily avoid such confessionals: he could not sleep, eat, or work without coming face to face with his supervisor. The authority vested in the status of choir supervisor was considerable. Not only could the choir supervisors deprive individuals of their right to attend religious and social gatherings of the choir, reduce an individual's weekly pay, or force him to retire to solitary quarters, but they could also hand over such deviants to the community Helpers Conference and Judiciary Council, who in turn had powers to arrest, beat, or even expel members from the community.[67]

The range of deviant acts subjected to such control varied from choir to choir. Several boys, for example, were beaten for having secretly tried to make some money by selling their food.[68] A young apprentice was imprisoned for having disobeyed his master. Two young men who spoke lightly of marriage and courtship while following a Sister on the street were each assigned six days of street cleaning.[69] Three Single Sisters were asked to leave their choir after exhibiting "vulgar and unbecoming behavior in the company of three men" in the local store.[70]

Sexual misdemeanors constituted a recurrent problem for the choir supervisors. Even in the pioneering years in Herrnhut the Moravians were never entirely successful in enforcing a strict segregation of the sexes. Notwithstanding very strict punishment of the offenders, such misdemeanors continued to occur even in the seventeen-forties when choir segregation was at its height. The severity of the punishment of offenders was at times so extreme as to attract the attention of the neighboring communities, and at one point even led to a governmental investigation.[71] But the Moravians successfully defended their methods against such attacks and, what is more significant, were never faced with any open revolts from within as long as these rigid measures were enforced.

Although Bethlehem never adopted quite such punitive methods, the amount of social control exerted by the choir supervisors was considerable. They firmly believed that "where subordination is absent no kingdom of angels can be established." [72] A list of rules and regulations of the Single Brethren's choir in 1744 includes the following prescriptions:

All Brethren must rise with the first bell in the morning; they must be punctual, orderly and clean; they may not smoke tobacco in the house, and must not be in any of the rooms without lights being on. Nor may they participate in any community affair without "good reasons." They must all retire at the usual time (10:30 P.M.) unless special permission has been granted.[73]

What is striking is not the detail of these rules or the way in which they affect all aspects of a Brother's day-to-day activities, but the fact that such regulations were rarely disobeyed, especially in these early years. Indeed, in the seventeen-forties and fifties the choirs in Bethlehem seem to have been more successful than their counterparts in Herrnhut in controlling their members and so had to resort less frequently to higher tribunals of arbitration.

Twenty years after the creation of the choirs for the promotion of religious fellowship and spiritual growth, these same institutions had become largely independent socioeconomic institutions under whose care the Moravian was nurtured and guided literally from cradle to grave. But just as the expansion of the choirs' economic activities created a potential threat to private business, so the expansion of the choirs' social role jeopardized the continued existence of the traditional family system. The choir rather than the family had become the formal agent of socialization. As the choirs came to exert more and more control over the actions of their members, the authority formerly vested in the head of the family waned. Since the choirs made it quite clear that children belonged more to the church than to their parents, for several decades parental authority was almost nonexistent.

As the number of choir members in any given choir increased, the choir was faced with a dilemma. On the one hand its expansion attested to the success of its undertakings and confirmed its ability to attract new members. On the other, this very increase in numbers was jeopardizing the effectiveness of its socializing function by destroying the intimate character of the primary group. For a while the problem was resolved, both in Herrnhut and in Bethlehem, through the creation of further subdivisions within any one choir. For example, in Bethlehem the Married Sisters' choir was further subdivided into the following classes: the newlyweds, those who had been married for a number of years, the older generation, the nursing mothers, and the pregnant Sisters.[74] Similarly, the Children's choir was subdivided into the little boys, the little girls, the toddlers, the infants, and the "embryos." [75] This subdivision maintained for a time the degree of social intimacy essential to the choir's socialization functions. Ultimately, however, even these smaller choir units grew too large to socialize new members adequately.

The gradual emergence of the choir as a family surrogate was neither intended nor anticipated by the vast majority of eighteenth-century Moravians. Documents of the period are filled with memoranda and discussions of a host of pressing social problems, but none of these shows any awareness of the possible implications of choir development for the structure of the traditional family.[76] The Moravian choir system, with its explicit subordination of family loyalties to those of the choir, bears ample testimony to the degree to which in the early years the concern for the sacred dominated and overruled all other considerations. In this overriding concern for the spiritual welfare of the community, all considerations with respect to the possible economic disadvantages of separate choir industries or the social penalties of the abolition of the family as a primary socialization agent were ignored.

V. MODIFICATION AND DECLINE
OF THE CHOIRS

DURING THE YEARS in which the choirs had gradually taken over most of the economic and social responsibilities of the family, the religious values which had originally led to the establishment of the choirs had also been subjected to change. The earnest and diligent religious enthusiasm of the early years gave way during the time of the Sifting to a more fanatical, emotional, and sentimental concern with the sacred. This shift in the religious values of the Moravians affected the choirs in a number of ways. In the first place, hymns and litanies celebrating the wounds of the Saviour were widely adopted in Herrnhut. The Single Sisters appear to have taken quite literally Zinzendorf's admonition that as virgins they were to enjoy themselves in the wounds of Jesus. Jesus was now regarded as the spouse and bridegroom of all virgins; a number of hymns dating from this period attest to the vivid imagery in which this new marriage of body and soul was depicted.[1] Most of the Sisters were too busy rejoicing in the knowledge of their newly defined relationship to Christ to be troubled by mundane matters. More time was devoted to religious assemblies and less time to work, as a result of which the already precarious economic situation of the Single Sisters' choir became even more difficult.[2] Among the Single Brethren the hymns and liturgies emphasized a marriage of chastity as portrayed in Jesus' life on earth.[3]

But the Married People's choirs, by no means perturbed by the fact that for them chastity and virginity could no longer remain their personal ideals, focused on Jesus' role as the husband of the soul. Since all souls were considered to be female, Christ became the husband of both the married men and women.[4] The members of the Widows' choir were regarded as the favorite brides of Jesus. The Widowers, however, had to console themselves with the thought that their departed wives, depicted as doves, had found a safe haven of rest in the side wound of Jesus. In the Children's choir the emphasis on childlike simplicity, on feeling one's way to God rather than trying to comprehend the complexity of the Trinity with one's mind, became paramount. The choir members thus came to spend more and more time in religious devotions, the composing and recitation of liturgies, and the exchange of vivid testimonies of belief. From 1745 to 1749 most of the entries in the choir and congregational diaries pertain to religious matters, and little mention is made of the economic affairs of the choirs of the community.[5] Not until the collapse of the Moravian settlement in Herrnhaag, in Wetteravia, plunged the whole of the Unity into financial straits did the choirs in Herrnhut begin to take stock of their own financial and economic situation.

Another consequence of the Sifting Period is to be found in the increasing number of the aristocracy residing in Herrnhut. A few persons of nobility had lived on Zinzendorf's estate in the period prior to his exile, but their number was greatly increased following the Herrnhaag incident.[6] Ritschl's characterization of Moravianism as a "religious dilettantism of the leisure classes," [7] although exaggerated, bears some truth when applied to the Moravian aristocracy of Herrnhut, for many of whom the pursuit of religion was little more than a fashionable pastime. The aristocracy subscribed, as we have seen, to the view that man's salvation could best be enhanced by an emotional preoccupation with Christ's crucifixion. They ignored, particularly during the time of the Sifting, all problems of a material nature, and encouraged their fellow choir members to do likewise.

For the first time in the community's history outsiders had to be hired as servants for the aristocracy and for Zinzendorf's family, since Moravians could no longer be found who were willing to fill these places.[8] The clothes of the choir Sisters underwent some radi-

cal changes. In the seventeen-twenties and thirties the choir supervisors had occasionally had some trouble in enforcing rigid simplicity of dress. During the Sifting Period, however, all pretentions
to simplicity were abandoned: silk came to take the place of cotton
and the choir Sisters flaunted gay ribbons and ornate bonnets and
vied with their aristocratic members for elegance of dress.[9]

Throughout this period Bethlehem was in continuous communi-
cation with the Moravians on the European continent. Not only
were reports of all activities sent weekly to Herrnhut but a considerable exchange of personnel took place as missionaries crossed and
recrossed the Atlantic. A number of Moravians thus came directly
from Herrnhaag to Bethlehem, bringing with them tales of the new
life.[10] Their socioeconomic standing differed markedly from that of
the Herrnhaag emigrants to Herrnhut, the former comprising a
much larger proportion of skilled artisans and apprentices.[11] The
consequent encouragement of leisure and idleness which followed
the infiltration of the aristocracy in Herrnhut was lacking in Bethlehem.

Spangenberg, the leader of the Bethlehem congregation, had re-
peatedly requested an assistant, and finally in 1747 John Frederick
Cammerhoff, a former resident of Herrnhaag, was sent by Zinzendorf to help guide the affairs of the American community.[12]
Cammerhoff was representative of the sensual and sentimental ex-
tremists of the Sifting Period and gained some following in Bethlehem. But unlike Zinzendorf in Herrnhut, Cammerhoff's leadership
lacked charisma. His influence was limited, moreover, by Spangenberg and Peter Böhler, who strongly opposed the values he sought
to encourage.

Nevertheless, the choir diaries from 1743 to 1754 contain many
"bloody" references to Christ and His treasured side wounds.
Cammerhoff's letters to Zinzendorf were filled with joyful reports
that "among them [the Moravians in Bethlehem] you hear nothing
but wounds and wounds and wounds."[13] Litanies of the wounds
and choir hymnals, often identical to those used in Herrnhut and

Herrnhaag, became the vogue in the choir and congregational gatherings.

Nor were these religious sentiments, characteristic of the time of Sifting, confined to the adult choirs. We are told that in the Bethlehem nursery "the little lambs know of nothing but the Lamb of Wounds and they don't even want to hear about anything else. They think and speak and sing and play and dream of Him." [14] Although the choir rituals of Bethlehem were significantly affected by the religious enthusiasm of the period, they failed in America to engender as exclusive a preoccupation with religion and consequent disregard for the day-to-day affairs of the world as had been the case in Herrnhut.

The Decline of the Choir System in America

The choirs of Bethlehem, having successfully weathered the emotional excesses of the Sifting Period, continued for a number of years to fulfill the religious, economic, and social functions which they had acquired during the preceding decades. Between 1745 and 1760 the choirs not only increased their membership but they improved their economic position considerably. [15] At the same time there were already undertones of discontent. True, these were for the most part not to be found in any of the official choir and congregational diaries, but some of the correspondence between Bethlehem and Herrnhut dating from this period already suggested that a decline in religious enthusiasm was taking place and that traditionally accepted beliefs were beginning to give way. [16]

By 1761 discontent with the existing communal system had reached such proportions that the Unity attempted, as we have seen in our analysis of political institutions, to prevent a potential secession of the American community from the Moravian Church by enforcing upon Bethlehem a socioeconomic system whose arrangements mirrored more closely those of Herrnhut. The choirs were ordered to abandon their communistic enterprises, and every choir member now received a wage for his work, and in return paid the choir for his bed, board, and clothing.[17] The Elders overseas failed, however, to realize that the choir institutions could not possibly compete with wage scales in the rest of Pennsylvania. Thus what was originally construed as a wage came to represent a mere pittance.[18] Since Bethlehem remained a closed community throughout the eighteenth and early nineteenth centuries, non-Moravians were refused permission to reside in Bethlehem; alternative sources of employment by outsiders within the settlement were thus non-existent.

If, therefore, a Moravian chose to make a decent living he had to abandon not only his choir but also his community and seek a living in the outside world. Although we have no reliable statistics on emigration to other American communities, the overall decline in the population of Moravians in Bethlehem throughout the remainder of the eighteenth century, and especially the decrease in the proportion of single adults, when coupled with the continued rise in the number of children being born, suggests that quite a number of young people did in fact leave Bethlehem for other, economically more lucrative pastures. Such emigration does not, however, appear to have occurred on any large scale until after the Revolution.

The majority of Moravians had to try to make ends meet with the choir wages being offered in Bethlehem. Yet here the choir institutions were beset by another problem. It became obvious that no matter how well intentioned the Brethren were about "managing" to live within their means, very few were able to do so. Since their wages were for the most part destined to return to the choirs in the form of payments for bed and board, it was the choirs rather than the individuals who were faced ultimately with an accumulation of debts and economic ruin.[19] The absence of any sizable class of wealthy choir members, in contrast to Herrnhut, prevented the choirs from ameliorating their position through the acquisition of endowments and bequests.

The decline of the choir system in Bethlehem cannot, though, be attributed solely to the rigid exclusivism enforced upon it by the

German Elders of the Unity. Even without interference from abroad it is extremely unlikely that the choirs in Bethlehem would have continued for very much longer. The religious enthusiasm and militant spirit of the forties, which had in a very real sense wrought economic miracles in the wilderness of Pennsylvania, had also helped to bring forth certain unanticipated changes. The very economic success the choirs had fostered brought with it changes in the Moravians' orientation to the world in which they lived.

More specifically, the necessity for pooling all economic and social resources became less obvious as the community's rapid rise to prosperity attracted the attention not only of outsiders but of the Moravians themselves. Moreover, the Moravians' contacts with the outside world brought many of their more business-minded members under the influence of the ethics of another economic system. The Moravians who engaged in commerce had begun in the seventeen-fifties to clamor for a greater degree of economic independence and a system under which profits would accrue to the individuals engaged in a given business enterprise, rather than to the choirs or the community as a whole. To these people, therefore, the choirs came to represent an obstacle to the realization of the economic potential of the community as well as their own.

It was this fundamental change in the outlook of many of the American Moravians that was instrumental in bringing about the decline of the choir system. As the worldly ethics of the newly emerging middle class came to take the place of the militant spirit of the early Moravians, not only did individuals become more interested in making their own profits, but the choirs themselves came to think largely in terms of economic gains rather than spiritual development.[20] By 1769 a leading Moravian in Bethlehem was complaining that "the Single Brethren accept no one who is not useful to them or whom they do not need in one of their trades." [21] And the Single Sisters appear to have been equally insistent that even among those members already admitted to the choir each person receive only what she can herself pay for.[22] The preoccupation of the choirs with their own material welfare failed, however, to stem the tide of economic decline. Without going into the details of their financial situation, it may be noted that even the Single Brethren's choir, which from an economic standpoint had always been the most prosperous, was faced with mounting debts.[23]

But now that the Moravians in Bethlehem were no longer willing to pledge their labor, their time, or their worldly goods exclusively to the choirs or the community, there was also much less reason for the choirs to fulfill their side of the bargain and continue to socialize new members to the dominant values of the community. The married people, moreover, were beginning to regard the living arrangements of the choirs as an unwarranted encumbrance and to demand a greater share in the upbringing of their own children. Until 1759 the married persons' living quarters had been segregated according to their choir classification. But with the successful elimination of the harshness of early pioneer conditions in Pennsylvania, the Moravians were now less willing to abide by a code of rules whose regulations made such inroads into their private lives. The increase in the proportion of married couples with children in the community, a consequence, in part, of the usual demographic over-representation of young persons of marriageable age in an immigrant population, merely aggravated discontent with the choir system.

By 1760 a large number of Moravians in Bethlehem were demanding that they be given the rights and privileges to set up their own homes and to raise their own children.[24] With the growth of economic prosperity the economic advantages accruing to choir living arrangements and mass education of the young had become less meaningful to the individuals concerned; many could now afford financially to take care of their own children and to provide them with a home of their own. At the same time, one wonders whether the willingness of parents to raise their own children was enhanced only, or even primarily, by the rise in the standard of living. If we remember that one of the supposed advantages of the original choir system was that it left the parents free to engage in missionary activities and to travel when and wherever commanded, the resurgence of the traditional family would seem to indicate that here also religious enthusiasm was declining and spiritual concerns were being relegated to a secondary place. Their demands were met when, following the breakup of the General Economy, a start was made on the construction of individual family housing. Children's choir institutions were gradually abrogated, and the nursery closed.[25] The actual transition from institutional households to private family life took a good many years. Since Bethlehem's original building program had been shaped by the demands of choir segregation, its large houses could not readily be converted into individual family units.

The success of the choirs in meeting their social responsibilities was further impeded by the fact that very often the most devout and charismatically most gifted were also more likely to be selected for important missionary posts; the best qualified were thus rarely available as teachers and instructors of the young. A religious community which cherishes its missionary commitment is inevitably faced with the dilemma of having to decide whether to send its religious elite among the heathen of other lands or to place such leaders among the potential heathen of its own ranks. The Moravians chose the former, without perhaps fully recognizing the risks such a choice entailed.

With the growing interest in family life came a corresponding decline in the extent of involvement in the day-to-day life of the choirs. This was particularly so for the married people, whose choirs were never revived after the abrogation of the Economy. But even for the unmarried the choirs had by the seventeen-seventies degenerated into respectable boarding houses for lodgers who paid rent and whose religious activities had become in many cases the habitual reflexes of past religious enthusiasms.[26]

With the general material and spiritual decline of the Single Sisters' choir, its members were increasingly handicapped in their attempts to force demands and complaints upon the Elders of the community. As a result, their discontent with such matters as prospects of marriage was largely hushed. The Single Brethren seem to have been somewhat more successful in bringing their wishes to the attention of the authorities. Here too, however, the radical changes in the socioreligious ethos permeating their institution were reflected in the striking decrease of missionaries recruited from the Single Brethren's choir, a choir which in the early years had been a major supplier of such manpower. The decline in missionary candidates was due in part to the overall decrease in the numbers of the Single Brethren's choir, but in part also to the reluctance of members of the choir to leave the shelter of the choir house for the uncertainty and precariousness of missionary work in the field.[27]

During the years following the breakup of the Economy, the character of the Widows' and Widowers' choirs was gradually transformed. After ceasing to provide living quarters for their members, they became pension societies.[28] The very fact that these choirs were not simply left to die out, but were transformed into institutions whose utilitarian goals were undeniable, may be taken as a further indication of the extent to which a materialistic ethic had come to permeate the Pennsylvania settlement even though Bethlehem remained for some years to come nominally an exclusive community.

With the outbreak of the American Revolution, and as new ideas undermining the official policy of exclusivism permeated the settlement of Bethlehem, the choirs of the Single Sisters and the Single Brethren received a further setback. But even if all the American Moravians had desired to stay clear of the affairs of Pennsylvania and the events of the War of Independence they would not have been able to do so. The enforced encampment of Washington's army hospital within the very walls of the Moravian choirs in Bethlehem forced them to take note of what was going on around them.[29] The Moravians' refusal to bear arms, their friendship with the Indians, and their ties with settlements of the Brethren in England and Germany were viewed with suspicion by supporters of

American independence. As a result, the Moravians were forced time and time again to explain their position and placate those hostile to their settlements in Pennsylvania.[30] In short, they could no longer ignore the world around them and were forced to come to terms with it.

The trend toward accommodation was subtle but unmistakable. The absence of any movement to rally to the old policy of exclusivism may be taken as an additional indicator of the demise of the religious ethos so characteristic of the pioneering years of the settlement. The American Moravians tried as best they could to reconcile their German Brethren to the changes that were taking place. But the leadership of the Unity of Herrnhut, few of whom had had any direct contacts with the events of the American Revolution, tended, as we have seen, to turn a deaf ear to the American Moravians' demand for change.

Though the leaders of the Unity in Europe were able to force the retention of the exclusive status of Bethlehem for some years to come, they could do little to stem the decay of the choir system of the community. The financial and social plight of the choirs had reached such proportions that the Single Brethren's choir was formally disbanded in 1817.[31] The Single Sisters' choir managed to eke out an existence until 1841, though its membership was dwindling throughout this period.[32] The choir diaries for the last few years yield very little information that could provide a clear insight into the nature of the decline of these institutions. They confine themselves to reporting only highly ritualized events: who partook of Communion, or who left for other settlements; who died, and who arrived from overseas. The last diary of the Single Sisters' choir, covering the years 1805 to 1841, constitutes in itself a testimony to the changing times, for not only do its entries become more and more sparse, but during the eighteen-thirties even the handwriting of the recorder degenerates into a careless and untidy scrawl, contrasting graphically with the elaborate artistic embellishments and orderly handwriting found in the earlier diaries. The vacant whiteness of the folio's remaining pages stands to this day as a silent but telling testimony to the decay of a once flourishing social institution.

Modification of the Choir System in Herrnhut

The choir system in Herrnhut was, as we have seen, much more severely affected by the religious excesses of the Sifting Period than it had been in Bethlehem. Yet, paradoxically, it was the German choir system that was to outlive its American counterpart. In order to understand the reasons for the perpetuation of the choir system in Herrnhut, the development of these choirs in the second half of the eighteenth century needs to be sketched in brief.

With the fall of Herrnhaag and the subsequent gradual decline of religious emotionalism in Herrnhut, the seriousness of economic and social problems besetting the choir institutions could no longer be ignored. After the rigid reinforcement of choir segregation by Zinzendorf in 1744, the economic welfare of individuals and of the community as a whole had come to rest exclusively in the hands of the choirs.[33] This total subordination of economic matters to religious principles of action failed, however, to guarantee the economic self-sufficiency of the choirs.

The Single Brethren's choir alone had managed to stay clear of debts,[34] but it could do so only by providing for the sole support of its own members and ignoring the plight of the other choirs. Thus, one of the Elders of Herrnhut noted in 1769:

The Single Brethren's houses have developed and continued to exist because of their own initiative; they can therefore not be regarded as branches of the community, but must be considered as separate families . . . these choir houses must not be viewed as business enterprises of the Unity.[35]

But even among the Single Brethren, income was frequently insufficient to meet their needs. The very low marriage rate of this period is largely attributable to the inability of the majority of these Brethren to shoulder the additional financial burdens of marriage.

The economic stability of the Single Brethren's choir was further threatened when extensive missionary activities and exchange of personnel from different Moravian communities gave rise to a very high rate of geographic mobility and labor turnover.[36] Everyone had to be prepared at a day's notice to lay down his work in the choir and go out into the world to help spread the word of the Gospel. Over the years the willingness of the Single Brethren to serve abroad had diminished somewhat when compared to the extraordinary enthusiasm of the early years. The vast majority, however, continued gladly to heed such missionary calls. Religious ideals clearly overruled economic considerations: "A brother, who has a vocation and ability to serve the Saviour, cannot be retained simply because he is invaluable in his particular profession."[37] At the same time some attempt was made to reduce the economic costs of this system of missionary selection to the choirs. After 1775 the Single Brethren were called upon to serve abroad less frequently but for longer periods of time. The gradual elimination of short-term missionary appointments thus contributed to a reduction of labor turnover and in so doing helped to improve the economic position of the choirs.[38]

The perpetuation of missionary work among the members of the Single Brethren's choir did not, on the other hand, preclude a decline in religious interest among certain members of the choir. The material success of the Single Brethren's choir posed a threat to the spiritual growth of its members. As one member of the Married People's choir observed:

We are not, however, without worry that, by and by, and here and there, something artificial and alien may creep in. To this we attribute for instance the fact that the master craftsmen among our Single Brethren are filled with a sense of professional achievement. Because they are now masters, and outwardly, as the saying in the world goes, have made their mark and are getting a good income, they are prone to forget their missionary ethic.[39]

The history of the Single Sisters' choir, seen from an economic standpoint, is a tale of perpetual woe. The Sisters were unable to find enough remunerative work to support their members. Opportunities for domestic employment had been severely curtailed after the Single Sisters had been forbidden to work in a house where male persons resided. The majority of Sisters had, therefore, to earn their livelihood by working in the choir kitchen or by helping to till the vegetable garden belonging to the choir. Various attempts to increase sources of employment within the Single Sisters' choir by introducing opportunities for weaving, dressmaking, and knitting failed. In the latter part of the seventeen-fifties some of this distress was temporarily relieved when a limited number of opportunities for work in the spinning of yarn were opened up to the Sisters.[40]

The economic situation of this choir was further aggravated by the fact that during the seventeen-forties and fifties on "two hundred days out of three hundred and sixty-five, because of Sundays, religious feasts and duties to the choir," [41] the Sisters were unable to pursue even what little employment they had. The other choirs sacrificed similar margins of their potential income to the religious life of the choir, but they, at least, had more remunerative employment to tide them over these periods of inactivity. Many of these economic hardships were not new to the Sifting Period, having been present throughout the early years of the development of the community of Herrnhut. But by the seventeen-fifties the initial religious enthusiasm and devotion of many of the Sisters had waned, and the infiltration of the aristocracy in the choirs had raised the Sisters' expectations as to what constituted an appropriate standard of living.

The members of the Married People's choir found themselves in an increasingly perplexing situation. The rigid enforcement of the principle of choir segregation had indirectly barred their access to the traditional source of supply of apprentices since the majority of apprentices were single and working and living in the Single Brethren's choir. The Children's choir in turn deprived the married people of the economic contributions of their offspring, an important source of revenue for the typical working-class family of the eighteenth century whose economy was based exclusively on the home. The fact that parents were supposed, whenever possible, to pay for the education and upkeep of their children, merely aggravated the family's economic plight. Although the choir of the Married People continued to grow during Zinzendorf's lifetime, its numbers changed little during the remainder of the century.[42]

The Children's choirs had, notwithstanding a certain amount of parental objection in the early years, increased their numbers considerably.[43] The economic stability of these choirs was jeopardized, however, by the fact that many of the parents could not afford to pay the costs of such an education for their children. The already precarious financial situation of the Unity was thus further burdened by the choirs' having to borrow in the seventeen-fifties and sixties about 600 talers annually to help defray the expenses for teachers' salaries.[44] The economic situation of the older Children's choirs, especially that of the Big Boys, generally aged twelve to seventeen, was worsened because the Single Brethren were loathe to apprentice more than a few of the Big Boys for fear of reducing their own economic output through lowering the level of skill among their choir members. Yet the Married Persons' choir, whose members were in desperate need of apprentices, was prohibited by the choir itself from employing any single, married, or widowed person. The Big Girls similarly were welcomed only in small numbers by the Single Sisters' choir, for whom they represented not an asset but a drain on their already strained economic resources.

Unfortunately the records dealing with the history of the Widows' and Widowers' choirs are very sketchy. Yet even these scanty documents show that their economic plight, too, was often aggravated by insistence upon choir segregation. The widowers especially found that not only were they deprived of the economic and social support of a daughter or granddaughter, but they were called upon to contribute their share to that same girl's upkeep in a separate choir institution. In addition, widowers were often deprived of their traditional occupation when the death of a spouse forced them to leave the Married People's choir. Many appear to have been unable to re-establish themselves occupationally in the Widowers' choir.[45] The widows would have been quite unable to earn even a pittance without drawing upon personal savings and community assistance. For some widows, however, the prohibition upon Single Sisters' serving as domestic servants or nurses in family households opened up opportunities that might otherwise have been closed to them. The majority, on the other hand, appear to have preferred to spend this time contemplating their ideal status as Christ's chosen brides. This preoccupation with their salvation often led them to ignore economic opportunities even when they did exist.[46]

The economic situation of the choirs of Herrnhut was thus throughout this period precarious. What saved them from bankruptcy and ultimately helped to guarantee their economic self-sufficiency was the fact that unlike the Bethlehem choirs they were able to draw upon bequests and donations from wealthy members and friends. Thus although the infiltration of the aristocracy may have encouraged many of the religious excesses of the Sifting Period, it also proved to be a vital source of revenue for the choirs at times when they would otherwise have been faced with virtual bankruptcy.[47]

In addition to these economic difficulties, the choirs of Herrnhut were also confronted with a number of social problems. By 1750 a second generation whose members had all been born into the community was growing up few of whom had experienced the kinds of personal conversions so instrumental in their parents' affiliation with Herrnhut. This was the generation that had been raised under the auspices of the choir and whose parents had had little to do with them once they passed out of the infant stage.

Although there must undoubtedly have been some young people whose behavior left little to be criticized, the records tell us almost nothing about them. They are preoccupied with the many persons whose socialization under the choir regime apparently failed to yield the religious and social graces which Zinzendorf had hoped for. The complaints are numerous, but invariably they center on the same points—namely, that the young men and women had become too worldly and lacked the spirit of religious devotion and enthusiasm which had been the hallmark of their parents' conduct.[48] Zinzendorf himself focused on another shortcoming of the educational system. He complained that the choirs had produced "good souls, but no particular heroes . . . good and faithful hearts, none [of whom] are particularly useful . . . they have become passive servants of the Lord rather than active Christians." [49] The problem thus was twofold. On the one hand many of the young people had apparently become worldly and had failed to develop a personal sense of religious commitment to the goals of the community. On the other, many of those who had remained immune to the pull of secular forces still lacked the active and militant *Streitergeist* of their parents.

Various attempts to limit the impact of secular influences by severely punishing culprits, and in a number of cases even by expelling the ringleaders from the community, served to curb but not to eradicate these outbursts of rebellion. Between 1740 and 1780 the number of members expelled from the community declined both proportionately to the total population and absolutely.[50] This trend reflects not a decline in deviant actions as such, but rather a change in the power structure in the community. The days of rigid authoritarianism were rapidly disappearing. As early as 1757 one hears of a Brother, expelled for bad behavior, who refused to leave and who finally had to be evicted by the civil authorities.[51] Such a step would have been unheard of ten years earlier. An attempt to evict one of the younger men for "stubborn and unbecoming conduct" was halted by the boy's father, who insisted that since the community had taken over the responsibility for his boy when he was but two years old, it could not suddenly turn him loose in the world, but must continue to shoulder its responsibility with regard to him.[52] By 1769 matters had progressed so far that the General Synod of the Moravian Church was forced to recognize that the civil authorities of the State could not be called upon to evict individuals from the community unless the deviant act committed constituted a criminal offense under Saxon law and not merely under the law of the Moravians.[53] After this the use of formal orders of eviction was discontinued. The Elders tried instead to put informal pressures upon "unsuitable persons" to seek residence elsewhere.

While the zealous old-timers of the community were lamenting the excessive worldliness of the younger generation, other more immediate problems needed to be solved. For one, the nature of the education given by the choirs often turned out to be impractical. The adult choirs had been very much interested in training their members in work for which there was a demand within the choir. In the Single Sisters' choir this might run to instruction in spinning, sewing, or washing. But a problem arose when Sisters left the choir, for instance to marry, and found that the same occupation could rarely be practiced elsewhere.[54] A similar problem existed among the boys and the young men, whose career choices were supposedly determined by the community but in practice were dictated by the specific needs of the choirs to which the young men belonged. Many of these boys, who had received a broad education in the Children's choir, could not find suitable jobs in the adult choirs and had therefore, to change their vocations. The enlightened educational policies of Zinzendorf were producing too many highly qualified persons for too few jobs. The limited economic expansion of the community precluded the employment of a large proportion of professional and highly trained persons. As a result these young people had, if they were to remain in the community, to be apprenticed into positions for which they had no previous training, little skill, and even less inclination. In spite of this, emigration remained relatively low.[55]

The choir system as an educational institution thus failed to produce the ideal second generation Zinzendorf had hoped for. Although the Count began toward the end of his lifetime to have some serious reservations about the advantages of the choir as a family surrogate, he never doubted its utility as an educational institution. He continued to insist that "we must hold to the underlying principles [of the choir system], unless the Saviour changes them through the lot." [56]

Four years after the Count's death a number of Moravians in Herrnhut were openly clamoring for a return to the traditional family. They demanded that the care and education of children become once more the sole prerogative of the family and specifically requested that the rights of the parents to bring up their own children as they pleased be recognized. But the actual modifications endorsed by the General Synod of 1764 were slight. Others were quick to point out that during the period in which the rights of parents in their children's upbringing had been curtailed parents had not only abrogated but often lost a "proper sense of responsibility," and the children in turn had often become alienated from their parents.[57] Thus the Synod of 1764, though recognizing that the responsibility for the rearing of children belonged properly to the family, was forced to admit that "no feasible possibility for change has yet been found."[58] A revised version of the choir statutes in 1767 continued to uphold the old order.

But by 1769 the newly emerging bourgeoisie refused to be silenced. This time their arguments were based primarily on economic grounds. Their claim that choir education imposed a very considerable financial burden upon the community was strengthened by a widespread recognition of the serious financial predicament of the Unity as a whole. Many of the parents deplored the fact that children were still going for walks in the country at an age when they could profitably help to earn their livings. Others decried the insubordination of their children and their lack of respect for authority. The Elders of the community, although more tempered in their criticism, supported these arguments.[59]

As a result it was decided to abandon choir education for the young. The only children for whom such education was still considered mandatory were the offspring of missionaries and young people who had shown "exceptional signs of grace."[60] The family was once more to shoulder the responsibility of rearing small children and ordinary local schools were to teach the children the rudiments of the three R's.

The Synod of 1769 not only stripped the choirs of their social responsibilities for the welfare of the younger members of the community, but advocated an overall decrease in choir membership. In an attempt to recapture the old "choir schools of the Holy Ghost" it was agreed that the choir members should ideally constitute only fifteen per cent of the total population of any given community, which in the case of Herrnhut involved reducing the total number of choir members to about 120 persons.[61] This was a radical departure from Zinzendorf's insistence on extending the choir rule to all members of the community; yet it is indicative of the genuine attempt made by the Synod of 1769 to modify existing choir institutions in an endeavor to bring them into line with changing conditions.[62]

During the next decade the effects of these far-reaching decisions continued to manifest themselves in the changing choir organization of Herrnhut. The principle of segregation of the sexes was no longer rigidly enforced. Parents were allowed to raise their boys and girls under the same roof, and men and women not related to one another by blood or marriage were able to work in the same house or workshop.[63] Widowers and widows were permitted once again to be cared for in the homes of their own sons and daughters, and as a result the Widows' and Widowers' choirs lost many of their members. But for those who had no close kin able or willing to look after them the choir houses continued to provide a home. Even inside the choir houses changes were made to soften the rigors of institutional living. It was admitted, for instance, that large rooms and mass sleeping quarters were not suited to the way of life of elderly people, and in the future the widows and widowers alike were to be given smaller rooms of their own and a greater degree of privacy.[64]

At the Synod of 1775 it was found that these modifications of the choir system had not met with universal approval. Many of the parents who six years earlier had clamored for the right to bring up their own children now wanted to return them to the choirs. These parents argued that they could not give their children "proper and appropriate supervision." [65]

The Single Sisters complained that the young girls entrusted to their care, after having first been brought up in their family homes, lacked the religious devotion, deference, and willingness to serve that had characterized earlier generations.[66] Thus the Sisters, for reasons of their own, supported the parents' demand for a return to choir education of the young. The Synod refused, however, to yield to these pressures, and insisted that too many of the parents were loathe to carry their own share of responsibility. It did acknowledge the Sisters' complaints but asserted that the parents had a right to bring up their children as they wished. The choirs should not interfere with parental education and upbringing, unless it could be proved that such education was injuring the "welfare of the soul" of the offspring concerned.[67] All members were urged to be patient with the young people and not to expect miracles of conversion.

From this point on, the choir principles of segregation were limited to a minority who entered voluntarily into this arrangement. The Children's and Married Persons' choirs disappeared completely. But the Widowers', Widows', and especially the Single Persons' choirs continued to operate well into the nineteenth century, sometimes even into the twentieth century. Thus in Herrnhut the choirs, although modified and limited, were able to survive long after their American counterparts had vanished. The responsibilities of the choirs in the nineteenth century differed from those they had assumed a hundred years earlier, and as time went by these choirs approximated more and more closely the pattern of a typical Protestant order, providing for a small minority a way of life in which they could continue to dedicate themselves exclusively to the work of the Lord. The employment of the choir principle as an inclusive mode of stratification for the total community and for purposes of regulating social interaction in matters of worship, work, and social intercourse had, however, vanished as the secularizing influences of the nineteenth century made themselves felt even in the rural backwaters of the Oberlausitz.

VI. MARITAL NORMS AND
BEHAVIOR

THE DEVELOPMENT of the choir system as a family surrogate had some serious repercussions for the maintenance of monogamy in Herrnhut and Bethlehem. The Moravians could not successfully reduce the saliency of an individual's family role as a spouse, parent, or child without attempting to control the very act which symbolized the taking on of new statuses within the family system— marriage. Zinzendorf's redefinition of the values underlying the marital bond and his specification of conditions governing mate selection provide a further illustration of the Moravians' attempt to subordinate family interests to the religious goals of the community.

The Count invariably stressed the religious goals of matrimony:

We regard the status of marriage as a holy ordinance of God, and as a counterpart of Christ and congregation. We regard the single status as proper and beneficial for many. It is to be commended to persons whose emotions or other circumstances might make marriage a dangerous proposition, and who therefore, for the sake of their salvation, should abstain from such a step. And we believe this all the more in as much as carnal desires [even within marriage] are detrimental to the welfare of the soul. But given certain natural temperaments there are situations where marriage is to be encouraged even under such circumstances. Thus we regard the prohibition to marry as a demonic teaching, and the total abolition of the status of marriage as a sin.[1]

The insistence upon total subordination of "natural inclinations" to religious goals, the explicit denial of the salutary effects of celibacy, and the corresponding emphasis upon marriage as a holy sacrament are basic to the Moravian conception of wedlock. Matrimony was viewed as a religious matter in which the interests of community and God overshadowed any personal inclinations or desires an individual candidate for marriage might have.

Marriage was regarded as instrumental for the achievement of religious goals because it permitted individuals "to minister unto the religious needs of members of the opposite sex." [2] It thus enlarged the field of service within which the Moravian could legitimately follow his missionary pursuits. The instrumental character of marriage is similarly reflected in the Moravian concept of the *Streiter Ehe* (the militant marriage), according to which marriage provided a unique opportunity for service, husband and wife participating equally in their work. The woman was regarded as the "helpmeet" of her husband, sharing whatever positions her husband occupied. If he was a member of the Elders Conference, she was included on the committee; if he was appointed to a missionary outpost, she was expected to assume that position also. [3]

Communal controls of matrimony were incorporated into the earliest statutes of Herrnhut: "No marriage may be contracted without prior knowledge of the Elders. Nor may an engagement be considered valid without the presence or prior consent of the Elders." [4] A similar regulation was enacted in Bethlehem.

It was assumed that every single Brother or Sister of marriageable age was automatically a candidate for marriage and admission to the Married People's choirs. [5] If an individual wished nevertheless to remain single, he or she had first to convince the Elders of the merits of such a step. The general procedure was for the supervisors of the Single choirs to nominate prospective candidates for admission to the Married choirs. These nominations were then discussed by the Elders Conference of the community, and character references of the individuals were examined. When these were deemed satisfactory, suggestions were made as to who should be married to whom. [6] Zinzendorf had prohibited any intermarriage between the Moravians in Bethlehem and other immigrants to or natives of Pennsylvania: "In particular I positively forbid the intermarriage of members of our Single Sisters' choir with natives of

Pennsylvania. Any Sister who takes such a step must be left to her own devices. These are two different kinds of people, that is for certain." [7]

The names and references of potential candidates were, during the early years of Bethlehem, frequently forwarded to Herrnhut in order that partners might be found for them from overseas. Correspondence between the two settlements turned frequently to the subject of marriage; a note from Zinzendorf reads as follows: "Gottlieb Bezold shall marry. We are thinking of sending him the Sperbach woman." [8] As far as the community was concerned, its criteria for selection of spouses were based on evaluations of the abilities of individuals to carry out specified religious assignments. It was taken for granted that there would be no serious incompatibilities of personality.

The authority of the community in matters of marital selection was not unlimited. The Elders, including Count Zinzendorf himself, were authorized only to make suggestions, not to issue orders. But the right of acceptance or refusal of such suggestions did not rest solely with the candidates concerned. The recommendations of the community had, by means of the lot, to be ratified by God himself. Recourse to the lot in questions of marital selection thus absolved the community Elders of ultimate responsibility for their suggestions. And the fact that God had indicated his approval of a particular union was far more likely to silence the personal doubts of such candidates than would have been the case had the community Elders themselves made such a recommendation.

The religious importance of marriage cannot be understood solely in terms of the instrumental advantages adhering to this status. The very act of marriage also signified the achievement of a new relationship to God. Not only did wedlock join two human beings but it also united each human being with Christ. When the individual entered the Married People's choir his relationship to his Creator underwent a subtle change. No longer was Christ portrayed as the chaste bachelor whose "holy celibacy till death transformed his choir

companions into virgins." [9] Now He became husband to the souls
of the married Brother and Sister:

> Jesus' Sire consented,
> That to him cemented
> Thou should'st ever be;
> Jesus did it merit
> And the holy spirit
> Beautifieth thee.
> Through Christ's blood,
> The Three-One God
> Owns thee as his near relation,
> O Lamb's congregation.[10]

. . .

> The Married choir the conduct fair
> Of the blest Trinity do share,
> And every daughter-in-law of God
> Unhurt goes on her road.[11]

During the time of the Sifting, in which preoccupations with the
mystical ties of marriage were at their height, the earthly marriage
was assigned second place. It is referred to as an "interim wedding,"
a "proxy marriage," until such a time as the soul may be forever
united with Christ.[12] The Moravian view of marriage thus emphasized both the instrumental values of matrimony for the pursuit of
missionary goals and the emotional gratifications inherent in man's
union with God.

Problems in Controlling Marriages

A mere delineation of marital norms could not guarantee their
acceptance by the members of Moravian settlements. In their attempts to implement these regulations, the leaders in Herrnhut and
Bethlehem were thus beset with a series of administrative problems.
A number of them related specifically to matters of social and
demographic planning. What, for instance, constituted the ideal
proportion of single, married, and widowed members in a given
community? How could such statistics be translated into reality?

How, in other words, did one go about the matter of getting the proper ratio of nubile men and women in the right places at the right time? Other problems were associated with the need to motivate the individual Moravian to abide by the newly defined marital regulations. How could a Sister or Brother be induced to accept the choice of a spouse recommended by the community? How could she or he best be persuaded to exchange the status of the single for that of the married? Could effective socialization procedures predispose the individual toward concurrence with the official viewpoint? How could the community best come to terms with recalcitrant members who were either hesitant or unwilling to accept the official ruling? How, in short, was the Moravian leadership to maximize its control over the individual without at the same time minimizing the individual's motivations for compliance?

Once the community had clearly defined the conditions under which the marital state was to be preferred to that of the single person, the leaders were confronted with an obligation to ensure, to the best of their ability, that adequate opportunities for marriage did exist. Since married persons were preferred for all the major occupational categories, especially those in the missionary field, this meant that the citizen of Herrnhut or Bethlehem had to be given the opportunity to secure himself such a helpmeet. A reasonably balanced sex ratio and an age distribution of the total population favorable to marriage thus became a basic requirement for every self-contained Moravian community. Yet Bethlehem was continuously plagued by a serious shortage of nubile women. In 1754, at the height of activity during the General Economy, there was only one Single Sister for every seven Single Brethren.[13] In Herrnhut, on the other hand, the situation was reversed. In most years there was a considerable excess of nubile Sisters over eligible bachelors, frequently as many as 150 Single Sisters to every 100 Single Brethren.[14] Thus even if every Moravian had been highly motivated to marry whomsoever the community proposed, the demographic characteristics of the situation effectively precluded the objective realization of such goals by a sizable proportion of potential aspirants to the marital state.

The question then arises as to what extent, if at all, the leaders of Bethlehem and Herrnhut attempted to correct these discrepancies in the sex ratios. A number of Spangenberg's letters to Zinzendorf written during the seventeen-forties and fifties contain specific requests for more single Sisters to be sent from Herrnhut to Bethlehem: "We are all agreed that our greatest need is for a shipload of Sisters. A group of about 60 young women, especially of the type who settle here most readily, would be neither too small nor too great a number." [15] A number of direct requests for spouses for certain Brethren were also made: "Send Sisters to be married to the following Brethren. . . ." And a long list follows of eligible bachelors from the Single Brethren's choir in Bethlehem.[16] Many of these requests were ultimately granted, but no definitive migration policy was ever put into practice.[17]

The rigid rules requiring segregation of the sexes created additional problems for the transport of the Single Sisters. We find, for example, that the Moravian congregation in Wachovia, North Carolina, asked Bethlehem to spare them two to three Sisters for their men. Bethlehem granted the request, but its fulfillment was no easy matter. Since the Single Sisters could not possibly be entrusted to a strange wagoner, or even a Single Brother from the South, it was finally suggested that one of the Single Brethren from South Carolina should come and be married in Bethlehem in order that, as a married man, he might then in all propriety be able to shepherd the several Sisters back with him to the waiting widowers.[18] The problem of ensuring the safe conduct of Single Sisters across the Atlantic was no less a problem for the authorities in Herrnhut.

The Count himself appears to have been unperturbed by these problems. His original plan to solve the marital difficulties of Herrnhut by providing extensive colonization projects in the New World to which the surplus of nubile men and women could be

sent remained a grandiose scheme on paper. In reality it ran into
financial difficulties from the very start, and even Bethlehem, instead
of alleviating the marital problems of the German Moravians,
merely served to aggravate them.[19] What Zinzendorf failed to perceive was that his haphazard emigration policy and his refusal to
become involved in mundane details of demographic planning ultimately impaired the success of the missionary efforts he was so keen
to foster.

Only after Zinzendorf's death do we find the first real attempts
made to grapple with the problem of determining ideal ratios of the
single to the married. At the Synod of 1769 Spangenberg made the
following observations:

> We have many people in the choir houses whom we are not in a posi-
> tion to marry and to provide with a living. We have taken upon our-
> selves an obligation which we cannot fulfill. . . . Ideally there should be
> a fixed ratio between the choirs in a community, so that when the com-
> munity numbers 800 the Single Brethren's and Single Sisters' choirs ac-
> count for about 120 members each.[20]

The elaboration of such ideal standards provided for the first time a
yardstick for the formulation of a coherent population policy. But
the proposals came too late, the great waves of emigration from
Herrnhut to Bethlehem having occurred in the seventeen-forties and
fifties. By 1769 the failure to control the discrepancies in the sex ratios of the two communities had already helped to nurture personal
discontents which in Bethlehem had contributed to the decline of
the Pennsylvania choir system. In Herrnhut the consequences of
such discontent for the maintenance of the choir system were less
severe.

The Moravian leaders' attempts to induce members of the Single
choirs to accept the choice of the spouse recommended to them met
with varying degrees of success. For the vast majority of Herrnhuters the saliency of the religious ideals underlying the marriage contract was indisputable, and no economic, social, or even purely
personal considerations could alter this. We hear of a Single Sister

who "according to the will of the Saviour and for the sake of service in the community, accepts the hand of an important Brother, even though on her part the step is undertaken in pain and has cost her many a death." [21] In the early years of Herrnhut such a subordination of personal inclinations to religious ideals was the rule. Although there arc a few references in the seventeen-forties and fifties to an "unbecoming" attitude on the part of a Sister or Brother, such rebelliousness was rare. During these years Herrnhut was, moreover, able to impose rigid controls upon the individual's choices and chances of marriage. The commandment that individuals should, in matters of marriage, be guided only by a concern for the Saviour, the community, and the welfare of their own souls was taken literally and enforced indiscriminately. A Sister who received a letter from her former sweetheart was placed in solitary confinement until such time as she had completely severed the "emotional remnants of this old bond of friendship." [22] Those who retained secret hopes of attaining purely personal happiness and who continued to indulge in fantasies that they could be guided primarily by personal desires in matters of marriage were excluded from the choir. We hear that "with tears and heavy hearts the Sisters agreed to this viewpoint." [23] When subordination of personal desires to religious ideals was not achieved, excommunication could be, and at times was, used as a last resort.[24]

After Zinzendorf's death the Moravians' acceptance of communal controls over marriage declined gradually. The nature of the explanations tendered by the Single Brethren and Sisters who refused offers of marriage indicates that personal considerations of economic advantage were gaining primacy over purely religious motivations. The minutes of the Elders Conference of Herrnhut contain numerous references to members of the Single Brethren's choir who showed no particular desire to sever their present choir affiliation. To mention but a few, we find a bookbinder who vehemently declines an offer of marriage and economic independence in favor of continued residence in the Single Brethren's choir.[25] A young carpenter is willing to ply his own trade but prefers "not to marry for the time being."[26] Similarly, a glazier confesses that he has no inclinations toward marriage and would much rather remain in the Single Brethren's choir.[27] Similar comments by members of this choir are to be found throughout the latter part of the eighteenth century. Underlying the refusal of most Single Brethren to take a wife was a genuine fear of poverty, if not destitution. Marriage meant that the Brother would have to abandon the relative economic security of his trade within the Single choir and venture forth as an independent craftsman. It was this uncertainty of economic prospects rather than any misgivings about the personal qualities of his prospective wife which led many a Single Brother to cling to his livelihood within the Single choir.

The Single Sisters of Herrnhut were more likely to agree to marriage, as well as to whomsoever the community proposed, than were the Single Brethren. In part this was due to the fact that marriage rarely affected the economic standing of a Sister adversely, the economic support given by the Single Sisters' choir having always been minimal. In addition, the very fact that objectively, by virtue of the imbalances inherent in the sex ratio, the Single Sister had a smaller probability of marrying than the Single Brother may well have enhanced the marital status with a certain scarcity value.

In Bethlehem Spangenberg had his own troubles. In a letter to Zinzendorf in 1755 he noted that the suggestions and offers of marriage did not always meet with success. The Count himself appears to have had little patience with such dillydallying and continued to issue recommendations as to who should be married to whom. But Spangenberg did not find it easy to follow through upon these recommendations, as the following letter to Zinzendorf demonstrates:

Now when I left you, you entrusted me with the following mission: Once a year we were to go over all our Single Brethren and Sisters and ask ourselves whether any of them should be recommended for marriage. Well, that was an assignment which could not have been made more difficult for me had you ordered me to move mountains. I have great difficulty with Brother Gottlieb, who otherwise is such a good soul. With Annie Rosel, who normally is our pride and joy, it goes no more readily. . . . But dear me, what does one do when the marriage offer miscarries, *ergo* when a Brother or Sister just won't, or at least not willingly? I have been thinking that if Joanna [the supervisor of the Single Sister's choir] could be empowered to act on their behalf, we could select spouses according to individual circumstances. If we do not do this, we are likely to be faced with failure before we have even begun to negotiate. This is what happened in the case of . . . [there follow several names] where the Brother or Sister did not want the other person.[28]

The length to which Spangenberg would go in trying to persuade an individual to marry is brought out in the following cryptic notification of a marriage: "Now we have married off Brother Sensemann, otherwise the Pachgatgoch Mission could not have been manned. For six years we have been negotiating to and fro and yet every time when it came to a decision, the marriage proposals turned to water." [29]

Yet the situation in Bethlehem differed from that in Herrnhut in at least two important respects. In the first place dissatisfaction with existing marriage arrangements occurred earlier and appears to have had more serious repercussions for the perpetuation of the choir system than was the case in Germany. In 1752, only ten years after the founding of the community, a number of Moravians were already rebelling against communal controls of marriage. Spangenberg reported that:

There are several among them who are no longer reconciled with living in the [Single Brethren's] choir. They left Europe with the assurance that they would be taken care of and be married as soon as they had spent a few years here. But so far nothing much has happened. Should we simply permit these young people to leave the community and marry according to their own inclinations? I think not. For these are people who in their own way could contribute much, and with whom the Saviour is certain to attain a given end, even though He may not be able to achieve everything with them.[30]

Zizendorf remained adamant in his refusal to permit any member of the Bethlehem congregation to marry an outsider, notwithstanding the shortage of nubile Sisters within the settlement. Although such separation from the influences of the outside world was essential to Zinzendorf's ideal of a "closed" community, the young people appear to have been less and less willing to permit the church to dictate their marriage chances and choices. After 1770 the number of non-Moravians brought into the community through marriage increased rapidly, and their presence accelerated the demise of religious exclusivism.[31]

Communal authority over marital affairs was declining rapidly. Ettwein, the leader of Bethlehem during the American Revolution, openly admitted that the authorities were so hard pressed by the insistent demands of a few Single Brethren for marriage that they were forced to meet these requests even though this meant deferring the chances for marriage of many a Single Sister whose personal fitness for marriage was much greater.[32] Some of the most obstreperous candidates for marriage were to be found in the ranks of the widows and widowers, many of whom were loathe to remarry for the sake of the church. A widow Bennet in Barbados, for example, adamantly refused to accept the recommendation of the Bethlehem Board that in order to continue to stay in missionary service in Barbados she marry her deceased husband's successor. The Bethlehem administration had apparently planned to send a Brother out to Barbados to woo her. In the end they gave up this plan because "It was to be feared that the widow Bennet might abide by her decision." [33]

The greater degree of impatience with existing marital conditions found among the single persons residing in Bethlehem can be explained, in part, by differences in the expectations of marriage held by the Moravians of Herrnhut and Bethlehem. Whereas the Herrnhuters could not hope to alter their chances of marriage in any radical way in the near future, the members of the Bethlehem community had, prior to their emigration, been assured that they would be able to marry in the very near future.[34] But the situation in Bethlehem differed from that of Herrnhut in yet another respect. Whereas in Herrnhut the economic prosperity of the choirs had led many Moravians to refuse marriage because it meant giving up a reasonably assured source of income, in Bethlehem the economic growth of the choirs merely strengthened the Moravians' desires to achieve their own economic ends and thus intensified their antagonism towards communal control over their personal affairs. In both communities these developments ultimately jeopardized the legitimacy of the official Moravian marital regulations.

Moravian Marriage Trends: 1727–1850

In order to be able to evaluate more fully the consequences of Moravian marital norms for actual behavior, data on the marriage rates of Herrnhut and Bethlehem need to be examined with some care.[35] In both communities there were considerable fluctuations in the number of marriages contracted annually. In Bethlehem the greatest number of marriages within any given year occurred in 1749, when seventy-four individuals were bound to one another in wedlock, fifty-six of whom were wed on the same day in what has come to be referred to as "the Great Wedding."[36] An unusually large number of marriages were also contracted in 1751, when there were twenty-one such events and in 1755 when there were sixteen.[37] These times of sudden prosperity in the marriage market were offset by long periods in which no marriages took place at all, as for example in the years 1751, 1760, 1765, and 1776–1777.[38] The fact that no marriages took place in Bethlehem from December, 1775, to August, 1778, suggests that the uncertainties stemming from the Revolutionary War may well have prompted the Moravians to delay so important a step as marriage until life became more predictable.

A clearer picture of the changes which took place in eighteenth-century Bethlehem may be obtained from an analysis of the average annual number of marriages contracted within a given decade. The mean annual number of marriages declined steadily from a high of thirteen in the seventeen-forties to a low of four in the last decade of the eighteenth century.[39] The crude marriage rate declined even more sharply (from twenty-nine per 1000 population in the seventeen-forties to seven in the seventeen-nineties), indicating that the overall decrease in marriages was occurring at a time when the population of Bethlehem was still expanding.[40] The social implications of the declining marriage rate become even more serious when one bears in mind that the tradition of marrying prospective immigrants immediately prior to their departure for America was widely practiced in the early years of the community but was abandoned after mid-century, when the immigrants were almost all single men and women.[41] This would suggest that after 1750 the actual percentage of the total population which was single rose very considerably, while the proportion of Bethlehem's married couples declined consistently.

The statistics should be interpreted with caution. It must be remembered that we are dealing with an immigrant population with a characteristically very high proportion of the total population in the younger adult groups and a correspondingly small percentage represented by the very young or the old. This means that the percentage of the total population within the marriageable age group of fifteen to fifty is very high. It is, therefore, not surprising to find that the Moravian crude marriage rates seem to be high rather than low when compared to the crude marriage rates of other societies. Only after taking into account the peculiarities of the age structure of an immigrant population can one get a proper indication of the sizable proportion of Moravians who continued to remain in the choirs of the Single Brethren and Sisters.[42]

But the structure of Bethlehem's population was unusual in another respect. It was characterized by a very skewed sex ratio, which was most marked among the single. Thus we find that in the year of the founding of Bethlehem there were sixteen Single Brethren and only seven Single Sisters, yielding a ratio of approximately two to one. By 1751 the ratio stood at three to one, and two years later it had risen to seven to one.[43] This enormous discrepancy in the objective chances for marriage of men and women unquestionably contributed to the decline in the marriage rate of Bethlehem.

Finally, a word needs to be said about remarriages. Since the marital status was considered to be a precondition for the fulfillment of many occupational duties, especially those of missionaries, the community frequently insisted upon early remarriage where a member lost his or her spouse.[44] The Moravian was under strong pressure to remarry if he was to continue to carry out his religious activities to the best of his ability. An interesting sidelight is thrown on the matter of remarriage in a letter of John Ettwein, a prominent leader and bishop of the American Moravians, who having lost his wife at the age of sixty-one was determined not to remarry. He justified his decision by noting:

I have no special office in the congregation which would involve much intercourse with the Sisters. And even should I conduct a liturgy for the Single Sisters' or for the Widows' choir in some emergency, or preach to them, it could be done without scandal here.[45]

Even the venerable head of the American Moravians could be excused from the obligation to remarry only because he was able to prove that the fulfillment of his religious duties would not be thereby impaired.

Moravian marriage statistics thus include a high proportion of remarriages. In Bethlehem during the years 1742–1800 approximately one marriage out of every seven constituted a second marriage for one or the other or both partners. These include 101 second marriages and eight instances of third or even fourth marriages.[46] In contrast an examination of remarriages for the period 1841–1850 shows that the ratio of remarriages to first marriages stood at one to twenty-five, and there are no records of third or fourth marriages.[47] The decline in the proportion of remarriages may be attributed in part to the greater longevity of the population; fewer died young and the total number of young widows or widowers was, thus, correspondingly smaller. In part it reflects also a lessening acceptance of the official Moravian regulations governing remarriage.

The situation in Herrnhut was not markedly different from that in Bethlehem. The crude marriage rate declined from thirty-three per 1000 population in the seventeen-forties to four per 1000 at the end of the eighteenth century.[48] Herrnhut similarly had a skewed sex ratio, only in this case the women outnumbered the men. In 1754, for example, there were only seventy-one Single Brethren for every 100 Single Sisters. By 1765 the sex ratio had risen to eighty-two, but in the following decade it declined to sixty-two, and remained in the sixties for several decades.[49] When the members of the Single choirs in Herrnhut did finally get married, the men were in their forties and the women in their thirties. By the beginning of the nineteenth century the married accounted for only ten per cent of the total adult population of Herrnhut.[50]

The seriousness of this situation, never recognized by Zinzendorf, was clearly grasped by his lieutenant, de Watteville, one of the few who dared to be critical of Zinzendorf's work during the Count's lifetime:

When I have the two Single choirs in front of my eyes and become aware of the fact that half of their members are already well beyond the normal age of marriage, I cannot refrain from blushing with shame. . . . These people have pledged themselves with body and soul to the work of the community, and expect in turn that their material and spiritual welfare and destination will be taken care of by us. I see among them many whose personal qualities would make them most admirable husbands and wives. They would, beyond any thread of doubt, like to get married, and the Saviour may even have called them to such a status. Yet all these people have already turned into elderly bachelors and spinsters. And the cause of all this rests alone in the fact that their expectations of receiving a proposal of marriage were never fulfilled. . . . It is only to be regretted that we do not have every year at least 15 marriages in a place such as Herrnhut.[51]

But de Watteville's misgivings were not shared by his contemporaries. As a result, no serious attempt to remedy the situation was made until after the Count's death, by which time most of the recommendations came too late to be of value to the community.

The central clue to the low rates of marriage in both communities is to be found not in the religious norms of the Moravians, which consistently and unambiguously defined the status of marriage as preferable to that of the single, but in the economic and social conditions which mediated the actual marriage chances of a given individual. The economic conditions prevailing in Herrnhut in the eighteenth century were not conducive to a high rate of marriage. The fact that "only those who are in a position to feed and care for a mate and children and raise and educate them properly, are to be permitted to marry" [52] meant that many a Single Brother simply could not afford to take such a step. The Synod of 1775 was forced to admit openly that Herrnhut had reached a point where many had to remain single because their financial means did not permit them to establish their economic independence from the Single choirs.[53] As a result, individuals whose earnings were relatively low, such as servants, unskilled laborers, and apprentices, were rarely permitted to marry.

This insistence upon proof of the ability of the husband to support a family meant that those on the lower rungs of the socioeconomic ladder were effectively excluded from the ranks of the married, while members of the professions were over-represented in the married choirs. This was not only because they were more likely to be able to provide adequate economic support for a family, but also because the Moravians rarely permitted important professional activities to be carried out by a man unless he had a "helpmeet" by his side. The absence of any real poverty in Herrnhut must be attributed in part to this rigidly enforced prohibition on the marriage of the lower socioeconomic stratum.[54]

Another economic factor which tended to lower the rate of marriage is to be found in the differential wage scales for the single and the married. Since the single person invariably received lower wages, it was to the advantage of the community that its economic enterprises should be staffed by single persons rather than by the married.[55]

The bachelor contemplating marriage thus had either to leave the security of the Single Brethren's choir for the uncertainties of self-employment or else try to secure employment in one of the communal enterprises, where he was forced to compete against single men who could command lower wages for the same work. His situation was aggravated by the fact that his very involvement in the enterprises of the Single Brethren's choir not only had trained him in occupations which were frequently the sole prerogative of this choir, but at the same time had effectively prevented him from setting up his own business prior to marriage. Had he at least been able to do the latter the initial fluctuations of such an enterprise could have been weathered without having to shoulder the additional worries of supporting wife and child.

During the latter part of the eighteenth century the leaders frequently complained that far too many of the young people expected the community to take care of them. "We hear from many a married Brother the opinion voiced: They gave me a wife and now they must also provide for my economic support." [56] What the administration ignored was that these same individuals who were insisting that the community continue to take care of them had been raised in choir institutions as infants, children, and young men and women, in which all major decisions for their welfare were invariably made by the choir supervisors and not by the individuals themselves. The young men's reluctance to shoulder suddenly the economic and the social responsibilities of marriage must, therefore, be understood in the context of their choir upbringing.

In Bethlehem the social and economic conditions which contributed to a low marriage rate appear to have been very similar to those operating in Herrnhut, where one married whenever there was a need for workers. The fact that the marriage rate of Bethlehem, although low, was consistently higher than that of Herrnhut must be attributed primarily to the ability of the Bethlehem community to expand its economy more rapidly than was possible in Herrnhut.

This preoccupation with the economic and social hazards of matrimony contrasts strongly with the spirit which animated the early years of both settlements. The pioneers of Herrnhut and Bethlehem, even though objectively faced with economic and social problems far greater than those encountered by their descendants, were sustained by a faith and a devotion to service which enabled them to overcome all these difficulties. The fact that preoccupation with material welfare manifested itself in Bethlehem several decades before it took root in Herrnhut suggests that the salience of religious values for marriage began to decline in America somewhat earlier than in the German community.

PART FOUR. THE ECONOMY

*Our economic systems cannot
maintain the same course
for more than a generation.
They may well conserve themselves,
so as not to perish. But they
must be capable of being poured
into as many different moulds
as it pleases the Saviour
for eons on end.*

—JÜNGERHAUS DIARIUM
June 13, 1751

VII. THE REGULATION OF PROPERTY

THE HISTORY of the economic institutions of Herrnhut and Bethlehem in the eighteenth century furnishes a detailed picture of the
extent to which even the material interests of the Moravians were
guided by religious values. The historical records serve to highlight,
moreover, the problems confronting the Moravians in their attempts
to subordinate all economic interests to religious goals. The professed norms and practices of the Brethren, with their uneasy
vacillation between private and communal ownership, may be taken
as a point of departure for an examination of these problems. Max
Weber, in his analysis of the property norms of religious groups,
commented on the strong proclivities that exist within the more
emotional Pietistic sects toward communal ownership of goods.[1]
Herrnhut and Bethlehem provide two interesting case studies of the
consequences of a Pietistic value system for the retention, modification, or abolition of private property.

Property Ownership in Herrnhut

The earliest regulations concerning property held by the Herrnhuters were incorporated into the Communal Statutes of 1727,
which dealt with the levying of work and property taxes by the
community.[2] As regards the payment of taxes levied, not by the
community of Herrnhut but by the provincial administration of the
Oberlausitz, the Moravians were instructed to render unto Caesar
what was Caesar's. Only payment of taxes earmarked for expenditures on activities in which Moravians clearly took no part, such as
military or State church taxes, could be waived. The limits of com-

munal responsibility for the welfare of its members were clearly delineated: "Every resident of Herrnhut shall work, and eat his own bread. But when he is old, sick or destitute, the community shall take care of him."[3] This suggests that, although Herrnhut was ready to practice Christian charity, its concern for the economic welfare of its Brethren and Sisters in no ways approximated the sharing of worldly possessions characteristic of many of the early Christian communities.

The Statutes decreed further that all ground for building purposes was to be allocated by the community Elders. Furthermore, construction of a house could not commence until after the architectural plans had been approved by the community. The Judiciary Council retained the right to buy back the property should the present owner choose or be forced to leave the community. The Judiciary Council also supervised all rental arrangements and leases of property in Herrnhut.[4] With the gradual emergence of the choirs, the importance of these regulations declined; more and more members of the community sought bed and board in the choir houses.

During the next two decades property regulations changed little. An occasional attempt was made to introduce common ownership of goods, as when the Single Sisters' choir agreed to share their worldly possessions. Such developments were sporadic and short-lived, and moreover they failed to alter the fundamental attitudes of the community regarding private property. Although the choir system did exert some pressure toward greater communal ownership of goods, this was more than offset by the fact that the real power-holders in Herrnhut at that time were for the most part members of the aristocracy.[5] Even Zinzendorf, for all his spirit of religious devotion, had no intention of sharing his material possessions with a band of refugees from Moravia. His belief in the equality of man before God never really interfered with his fundamental belief in the validity of the social distinctions of this world.[6] For this reason the economic ethics of Herrnhut during these early years bore the imprint of the property attitudes of the privileged landed aristocracy of eighteenth-century Germany.

A considerable amount of responsibility for communal welfare was accepted by Zinzendorf and other members of the aristocracy. They owned three of Herrnhut's major social amenities: the inn, the orphanage, and the drugstore.[7] The history of the inn is particularly interesting since it presents in a nutshell the clashes between religious and economic interests which occurred in Herrnhut during the first half of the eighteenth century.[8] Most of the early attempts to operate such an establishment failed because of the difficulties encountered by the innkeepers in abiding by the Count's regulations governing "a pious innkeeper of a Christian tavern."[9] For example, in 1727 Zinzendorf leased a building to one of the Moravian immigrants, Gottlieb Lehmann, under the following conditions:

The innkeeper shall be responsible for the welfare and upkeep of the aforesaid premises. He is to counteract all worldliness and blasphemy and defend our cause to the guests to the best of his ability. He is to provide no one with more drink than necessary; the moment he notices any excesses, he is to refuse to serve the guests any more, and if such guests become troublesome, he is to seek the aid of nearby residents. He is never to disparage our community, and for the sake of God's greater glory he is to try to help the guests mend their ways. . . . The inn is to be under the supervision of the Elders, and no one may be permitted to stay overnight unless prior permission has been obtained from the Elders. Closing time shall be at nine in the summer, and at eight in the winter, after closing time only carters and foreign travelers may sit more than two at a table.[10]

It is not surprising to discover that Lehmann found it difficult to make the inn a paying proposition, for not only did this contract deprive him of most of the local clientele during the evening hours but it also imposed conditions which non-Moravian guests were unlikely to cherish. When in 1731 the Single Brethren's choir moved into the inn and agreed to supervise the tavern, Zinzendorf's insistence upon the need for segregation of the sexes posed additional dilemmas: "The beloved married Sisters agreed to do the work which cannot be undertaken by the Brethren themselves. Brother Kremser is learning a little about cooking." [11] Since even married Sisters were not permitted to stay at the inn overnight, a serious problem arose every time a female visitor, irrespective of whether she was accompanied by her husband or not, sought lodgings at the inn. The Brethren were under strict instructions not to take in any womenfolk unless it was impossible for the women to travel on to Strahwalde or Eulkretscham the same night.[12] Such regulations failed to promote the inn's reputation for hospitality and conviviality.

Under these circumstances one is not surprised to learn that the inn continually changed hands. Most of the innkeepers ran into trouble either because they followed Zinzendorf's instructions to the letter, as a result offending guests and failing to make an adequate living, or because in striving to make a living they permitted behavior that the Count in turn was unwilling to tolerate. In the seventeen-forties the increased emphasis on conformity and social control further reduced the number of Brethren and Sisters frequenting the inn, and since too few foreign travelers passed by, it had to be abandoned.[13]

With the community drugstore Zinzendorf was more successful. The store stocked not only drugs and medical supplies but also "sugar, coffee, tea, dried currants, almonds, tobacco, snuff, starch, powder, lime, ammunition, down, chalk, corks, plain and colored paper, and kindling." [14] Its capital assets rose from 317 talers in 1733 to 4,010 talers in 1744, all of which was owned and controlled by Zinzendorf and his wife.[15] Not all the Moravians were pleased by these arrangements. The fact that most supplies were in the hands of the aristocracy and could not be purchased elsewhere, since permission to set up other stores was withheld, led to some discontent in the community. Zinzendorf's order that all salt had to be bought at his inn provoked a storm of protest, which was intensified when it was discovered that the measure used was short weight.[16] Zinzendorf's rejoinder to these complaints brings out clearly how far removed his economic ethics were from those which inspired the early Christians to share their worldly goods. The Count vehemently denied that the aristocracy was trying to make a profit and pointed out that if the Moravians were living on some other nobleman's estate they would begin to see how well off they really were with him. He closed with this admonition: "Christ's position on this issue is clear, one should be silent and a little more willing to suffer injustices." [17]

It is precisely because Zinzendorf saw himself as a pious Christian lord of the old feudal regime and not as a member of the emergent class of capitalists that the profit motive cannot be used satisfactorily to explain his actions. This becomes even clearer if we look at a third major communal enterprise in which he had a stake, the orphanage and educational institutions of Herrnhut, for here the Count lost money almost from the beginning. Guided by an overriding desire to provide a Christian upbringing for waifs and strays as well as for the children of the aristocracy and of the Moravian immigrants to Herrnhut, he never paid much attention to the question of whether or not the parents or guardians of these children could help defray the costs of their education.[18] For Herrnhut, however, the provision of these facilities was crucial. Had it not been that Zinzendorf was willing to bear the costs of this educational institution, the majority of Moravian children would have had to do without a formal education during the pioneering years of the community. This same institution, subsequently converted into the Children's choir, helped to free parents of the traditional responsibilities for the upbringing of their offspring and thus gave them greater opportunities to devote themselves to the service of God.

Zinzendorf's exile from Herrnhut in 1736, by order of Frederick Augustus the Third, Elector of Saxony, created a serious financial crisis precisely because so many of the community's enterprises were intimately linked with the economic fortunes of the Count. Two years after the Count's banishment the orphanage was indebted for over 2,000 talers, a not inconsiderable sum of money for the Herrn-huters in those years. Zinzendorf tried to hand over the financial responsibility for the orphanage to the community of Herrnhut, but the Moravians were quick to point out that since they were themselves very poor and constantly fighting to keep out of debt they could not possibly take on such a financial liability. At this critical juncture Herrnhut was once again saved from bankruptcy by the intervention of an aristocrat, Count Promnitz, who agreed to shoulder most of the debts incurred by the orphanage.[19] Clearly, Herrnhut in its early years could not have survived financially had it not been for the continuous assistance of Zinzendorf and his well-to-do friends.

The first real attempt by the community of Herrnhut to take over certain financial responsibilities began as early as 1728 when a communal poor-relief fund was inaugurated. Although the fund, raised through personal and property taxes, was small, it nevertheless assured for the Moravians a modicum of self-sufficiency and independence which effectively counteracted the emergence of a typical feudal type of relationship between lord of the manor and vassal.

In the latter part of the seventeen-forties the religious enthusiasm of the Sifting Period began to have some serious repercussions on the economy of Herrnhut and for a time altered the property norms of the community. In the first place, the Moravians, inspired by a simplistic belief in God's providence, began to borrow considerable sums of money for the expansion of their communities. In Herrnhut a number of well-to-do aristocrats declared themselves willing to extend credit up to 21,000 talers to the community at an annual interest rate of one per cent.[20] With this money the community managed in the following years to buy from Zinzendorf many of the enterprises initially developed by him. In 1747 the community thus acquired Zinzendorf's general store and the drugstore for a sum of 3,133 talers.[21] But the social and religious excesses of the Sifting Period continued seriously to deplete the funds of the community. Having been able to make a small profit from the operation of the community store and the sale of drugs, the chairman of the committee on communal credit, von Damnitz, urged an expansion of the socialization of property within Herrnhut. He suggested, for example, that it was unfair for the bakers and butchers of Herrnhut to thrive while other Moravians had to be supported from the poor relief fund, and that this situation might best be remedied by turning over all bakeries and butcher's shops to the community.[22] During the seventeen-forties the community did in fact acquire property rights to many of these enterprises, and for a time the profits of such stores helped to defray some of the community's mounting expenditures in the missionary field. But the general financial situation remained precarious, for Herrnhut was never in a position to pay back any of the capital it had borrowed in order to acquire these properties for the community.

This socialization of some of the basic commercial enterprises of Herrnhut did not spring from any desire to emulate "the communism of love" of the earliest Christian communities. It was motivated rather by practical financial considerations as to how the community might best support its costly religious culture and its missionary ventures. The impetus for this socialism came not from Zinzendorf but from men like von Damnitz, by whose efforts Herrnhut was saved from the worst economic repercussions of the excesses of the Sifting Period. Had matters been left in the Count's hands it is doubtful whether Herrnhut would ever have been able to weather the economic crises of the seventeen-forties and fifties, for Zinzendorf continued to consider any rational evaluation of economic affairs below the dignity of the devout Pietist. His criticism of the early attempts at socialization of communal enterprises was outspoken:

Trade and commerce, shops and stores, are not befitting to our communities, they should be left to private individuals and partnerships. All professions and commercial transactions from which a community profits give the semblance of a *Communionis bonorum* and are therefore an abomination in the eyes of the ecclesiastical Ordinary. Furthermore they

make it necessary for a community as community to borrow more and
more capital and to become enmeshed in monetary transactions and
market situations.[23]

The Count clearly regarded any attempts by the community to
take over property as a threat to the religious character of Herrnhut.
Yet his criticism all too often was not voiced until after the event
had taken place. Had he really felt these matters to be issues of principle he could undoubtedly have refused to sell the general store and
the drugstore to the community. His views on economic affairs both
retarded and at times impeded the economic development of Herrnhut as a self-sufficient community, but they did not fundamentally
alter the direction of development.

Viewed in the light of the history of the community as a whole,
even during the years of greatest religious enthusiasm and emotionalism, Herrnhut never departed radically from adherence to the
norms protecting private-property rights. It is true that from a
purely religious standpoint the Moravians regarded all economic
wealth as ultimately the property of God alone: ". . . we owe our
body and soul, our abilities and wealth to the Lord alone, and it is
He, not we, who has complete power of disposition over all that we
possess." [24] But this ethical maxim was never in fact translated into
a practical maxim governing economic action. Herrnhut's property
regulations, although they bore for a few years some limited traces
of socialism, remained for the most part tied to the traditional
feudal order. The sanctity of private property was never seriously
endangered by the religious enthusiasm of these people.

Property Ownership in Bethlehem

The economic organization of Bethlehem in its earliest years is
buried in obscurity. The documents and diaries pertaining to the
period 1742–1744 make no reference to the property arrangements
of the community, nor do they deal with any questions regarding
the types of industry or employment envisaged for the new settlement. Most of the account books going back to this time are simply

inventories of the amount of money brought over by various immigrants, shedding little light on the manner in which these people
were making a living on the forks of the Delaware. This total silence about economic matters suggests that the Moravians were in
those first years so completely taken up by their religious life and
the prospects of extensive missionary activities that little or no systematic thinking was brought to bear upon economic problems.
Certainly men and women alike pursued various occupations, and
the extensive building programs and the cultivation of the land attest to their activity. But what was apparently lacking was any concern for the way in which these day-to-day economic arrangements
might work out in the future.[25]

In 1744, upon Spangenberg's return from Europe, the first formal
provisions for the development of a self-sufficient economic system
were made. But the General Plan of Bethlehem spelled out the economic goals of the new settlement in very broad terms. According
to this plan every member was to devote all his time and labor to
the community, in return for which he would receive free bed,
board, and clothing.[26] No one signed any formal contract; the
whole system rested upon a voluntary verbal agreement and shared
trust. In these early years the mutual devotion to the ideal of service
in the name of the Lord was apparently sufficient to guarantee the
feasibility of such an informal arrangement.

To get a more detailed view of the property norms incorporated
into this system we need to turn to the Brotherly Agreement of 1754,
which for the first time laid down in some details the rules and regulations that had been implicit in the system since 1744, and which
sheds some light on the ownership of property in Bethlehem. Most
Moravians have insisted that there was never any real community of
goods in Bethlehem, even during the years of the General Economy
(1744–1761). For example, Ettwein, in a letter to George Washington in 1778, insisted that the Moravians'

. . . poverty and the wild State of these Parts, made them deny many
conveniences of this life & they lived in Simplicity & Brotherly Love as

one family, worked all for the Benefit of the Whole & desired Nothing but Food & Raiment; If one or the other had some private Property, he deposited it or disposed of it, as he pleased, for his own Interest, for there was no Communion of Goods, tho' it appeared so. . . .[27]

That the sharing or relinquishing of one's worldly goods was not a matter of principle seems evident. But at the same time one should beware of automatically assuming that this principle of complete retention of private property was put into practice. The second paragraph of the above-mentioned Brotherly Agreement suggests that the property arrangements were in fact a good deal more complex:

We all belong to the Saviour, as He is our Lord, and what we have, that all belongs to Him, and He shall dispose of it as pleases Him. Our worthy Brother David Nitschmann, whom we love and honor as a father among us, is, indeed, in the eyes of the world for the sake of good order recognized as the Proprietor of Bethlehem and its appurtenances and the possession goes under his name and the names of his heirs, and shall be administered by his executors, after his death for the same objects as hitherto. Yet he is, in truth, as are his heirs, the one who possesses it in fee for the Saviour. We, however, will at the same time, regard him, his heirs, assigns, executors and administrators as tutors given us by the Saviour and carefully avoid all appearance of arbitrary appropriation.[28]

According to this statement the Moravians did not necessarily adhere to the traditional norms sanctifying private property. Fundamentally they believed that all worldly goods belonged not to man but to the choirs and the community, which acted merely as administrators of God's wealth. They were, however, aware that such a belief could not readily be incorporated into their regular economic dealings with non-Moravians. To avoid unnecessary ostracism and antagonism, they hit upon the convenient formula of holding most of their property under a system of proprietorships. Most of the land upon which Bethlehem was built had originally been acquired by Zinzendorf's wife, the Count having transferred all his worldly possessions to his wife prior to being exiled in order to avoid the danger of their confiscation by the authorities in Saxony. Since under the British colonial law no property could be owned by aliens residing outside Pennsylvania, the land was held in the names of three trustees of the Unity, David Nitschmann, Henry Antes, and August Spangenberg.[29] In 1751 the ownership was transferred to Nitschmann alone, and upon his death to Nathaniel Seidel. This principle of proprietorship was maintained until the middle of the nineteenth century, and thus survived long after the General Economy as such had been abrogated.

Thus, although in theory the norms of private property were held inviolate, in practice the Unity of the Brethren had sole control, if not ownership (the latter being technically reserved for the Saviour) of land and property in Bethlehem. In practice, therefore, the individual immigrant to Bethlehem in the seventeen-forties and fifties had no opportunity to buy land or to start up his own business, since all land and property belonged by definition to the community as a whole.

The arrangements made for the disposal of personal incomes required all members to hand over their personal savings to the community account. The transaction was carefully entered into an account book, and although the immigrants received no security or interest for this sum, "the capital remained theirs, and they can claim at any time whatever increment they find they need."[30] The fact that in 1748 only thirteen out of 400 members had any private property suggests that the total amount of these contributions was very small.[31] Although the members were technically free to use this money as they pleased, the very fact that the community took care of most of their physical and social needs and that there was no opportunity in Bethlehem to invest such savings in a personal business meant that most of this money remained in the communal fund. In many cases these sums were ultimately bequeathed to the community upon the death of their owners.[32] By 1761, when the General Economy collapsed, the total amount of private capital to be returned to individuals amounted to £3690/18/6½ sterling, but with a total of over 1,300 members this amounted to an average of less than two pounds per capita.[33] Had the private incomes of individual members been greater it is unlikely that this arrangement could have worked out as well. Not only would the individual depositors have had a greater interest in securing some interest on their money, but the community itself would have been less likely to permit such capital to lie fallow.

Another aspect of these property arrangements has to do with the nature of the labor contract that was developed in the Brotherly Agreement of 1754:

> We do not accordingly, regard ourselves as men-servants or maid-servants, who serve some men for the sake of a wage, . . . but we are here as Brethren and Sisters, who owe themselves to the Saviour, and for whom it is, indeed, a token of grace that they may do all for His sake. . . . We declare therefore, . . . that we do not for this time nor for the future pretend to any wage or have reason to pretend to any.[34]

The contract signed by all members in 1754 is even more explicit on this point: ". . . we will not on any Occasion whatsoever have demand or sue for any Wages or Hire for our Labour or Services which we shall do in or for the aforesaid Family or Congregation, promising therefore to be content with our Food, Clothing and such other Accommodations as aforesaid." [35]

Every member of the Bethlehem General Economy was expected to give his labor to the community in return for food, clothing, shelter, and education for his children. During these years the community also had the right to assign a man or woman to whatever task it desired. Occupational assignments were controlled by the various economic and trade supervisors and not by the individuals themselves.[36] Finally, individuals were not permitted to borrow any funds without the consent of the community as a whole, for "As we all stand for one, so shall and will no one among us borrow anything or take up money whether for his own person or on account of the Economy, . . ."[37]

In contrast to Herrnhut, Bethlehem during the years of the General Economy had an economic system which, although in theory not opposed to the sanctity of private property, in practice incorporated a communism of property, production, labor, and consumption. Technically the community never appropriated the worldly goods of its members, but it effectively prevented them from making any use whatever of possessions they had brought with them. And by insisting upon a communal sharing of land, trades, and commerce, of individual labor as well as of the consumption of the fruits of this labor in the form of food, drink, and shelter, the community in fact destroyed the very foundations for a system of private property.

The Generation of a Religious Work Ethic

The religious convictions of the Moravians not only manifested themselves in their property regulations but also found striking expression in their attitudes towards work. The virtues of diligence, simplicity, frugality, punctuality, conscientiousness, and continence came to be considered not only as highly desirable attributes in and of themselves but also as essential qualities of a truly Christian way of life. In Zinzendorf's eyes work came to be considered ultimately a goal in life: "One does not only work in order to live, but one lives for the sake of one's work, and if there is no more work to do one suffers or goes to sleep. . . ."[38] The Count was constantly reminding the Brethren and Sisters to bear in mind how essential hard work was to a devout Christian. The old German proverb "Ohne Fleiss kein Preis" (No reward without hard work) thus took on a very special meaning for the Moravians, whose reward was ultimately to be measured in religious rather than economic terms.

Max Weber has pointed out that with the emergence of a Protestant ethic hard work became "not the cause of salvation, but the sole means of recognizing it."[39] Certainly the religious ethic of the early Moravians in Herrnhut and Bethlehem, by redefining the relationship between work and salvation, gave a very powerful impetus to the enhancement of economic output. Zinzendorf optimistically calculated that in Herrnhut the twenty-four hours of the day could readily be divided as follows: five hours for sleep and rest, three hours for the "nourishment of body and soul," leaving a total of sixteen hours for physical labor.[40] In actual fact, however, this division of the day was rarely maintained; religious love feasts and the thousand and one demands of choir life more often resulted in the bulk of a day being given over to the nourishment of the soul rather than to the production of material goods.

In Bethlehem a similar redefinition of the place of work in man's life had taken place. As a result it becomes very difficult to draw a hard and fast distinction between sacred and secular activities, between religious work and economic work, for to the Moravians of that day all work was religious work in the sense that all work was intimately linked to man's salvation. Spangenberg, speaking of the General Economy, noted: "In our Economy the spiritual and the physical are as closely united as a man's body and soul, and each has a strong influence upon the other. As soon as all is not well in a Brother's heart, so soon we notice it in his work." [41]

The various hymns composed by the Moravians to bring out the religious and spiritual significance of man's toil and labor as shepherd, ploughman, thrasher, reaper, spinner, knitter, tailor, or washerwoman, convey to this day a sense of the extent to which all work was regarded as God's work and thus required man's utmost diligence and industry. The hymn composed by Spangenberg for the spinners may be taken as an illustration:

> Know, ye sisters, in this way
> Is your work a blessing,
> If for Jesus' sake you spin,
> Toiling without ceasing.
> Spin and weave; compelled by love;
> Sew and wash with fervour,
> And the Saviour's grace and love
> Make you glad forever.[42]

All secular work became in fact a legitimate domain of the sacred. Thus in 1746 Spangenberg was able to report on the state of the

Bethlehem economy in the following words: "They mix the Saviour and His blood into their harrowing, mowing, washing, spinning, in short into everything. The cattle yard becomes a temple of grace in which priestly manners are maintained." [43] Not even the cattle were immune from this religious ethic. A directive to the cattle tenders pointed out: "One must take care of the cattle in such a way, that they may always be happy, and in their own way thank God for having placed them under such good care." [44]

The importance of the religious significance of work, no matter how menial the task might appear to the world outside, was constantly reiterated in the so-called Moravian love feasts. Such love feasts centered on the partaking of a common meal in celebration of some event. Love feasts were held on numerous occasions, such as the completion of the haying of the fields, the spinning of a shipment of wool, the completion of a building, or laying the cornerstone of an oil mill.[45] In such an atmosphere it was impossible for a person to remain unaware of the religious implications of his economic labor, whatever his occupation.

The identification of man's religious calling with his economic calling thus provided a powerful stimulus to the economy. Not only did it make him more willing to defer the gratification of personal wants and thus free additional resources sorely needed for economic expansion, but by making work a virtue it also raised the level of industriousness in the communities concerned. This same preoccupation with religious goals served at times, however, to impede the development of a self-sufficient economy, particularly in the sphere of business and industry. Instances of such obstruction will be given in the course of analysis of the diversification of the Moravians' economic institutions.

One problem which derives from certain incompatibilities between the religious and economic norms of the Moravians deserves brief mention at this point. The Brethren had, as we have seen, incorporated into their religious value systems the norms of brotherhood and equality. The maintenance of these values posed some serious difficulties for the operation of their economic institutions. A community which lays considerable stress upon the values of fraternity and equality, and furthermore is oriented towards essentially noneconomic goals, is usually confronted by the problem that its economic system tends to require an occupational specialization in direct opposition to the egalitarian norms of the group.[46] In such a community it becomes almost impossible for the group's solidarity to be conserved or enhanced by the division of labor, since such a differentiation of roles, while favorable for economic productivity, is decidedly unfavorable for social integration.[47] The Moravians were confronted with the problem of maintaining the core values of equality and fraternity while at the same time instituting a system of rewards which would not be in conflict with the evolving occupational specialization within the economy.[48]

The histories of Herrnhut and Bethlehem suggest that in practice, though not in theory, neither community adhered to an absolute commitment to the value of equality. In Herrnhut, for example, although the complete equality of man before his Maker remained undisputed, the question of equality among men was interpreted relative to the social conditions of the day. Zinzendorf himself regarded the social and economic stratification of society as ordained by God and considered it not only foolish but impossible to try to interfere with the natural order. Although the Count was the last person to deny the ultimate equality of man before God, he at no time advocated the application of this egalitarian principle to the social order of his own community. He believed that in their social and economic relationships the Brethren should support the status quo, and he urged them to be "good lords of the manor, good vassals." At no time did he consider the possibility of abolishing such social distinctions.[49] For him the anomaly of religious equality and social inequality simply did not exist. The leadership of Herrnhut continued to support this view in the years after Zinzendorf's death. Their viewpoint is clearly expressed in the "Brotherly Agreement" of 1770:

Just as the abrogation or even intermingling of social classes is contrary to the arrangement of human society established by God, so in our own community of faith and equality of the inner calling, the divine regulation of the social differentiation of classes shall not be lost sight of, even in our own congregation.[50]

It thus becomes clear that in Herrnhut the problem of maintaining the norm of equality in face of the need for role differentiation in the economy was in practice resolved by relegating egalitarian values to the religious sphere alone. In this way the ultimate equality of men could be supported without threatening the class structure, since both were considered to be divinely ordained. The values of the old feudal order were so strongly entrenched in Herrnhut that, with the possible exception of the Sifting Period, the egalitarian norms were never extended to the social and economic spheres. This was not the case in Bethlehem where, as we have seen, the values of egalitarianism manifested themselves not only in the Moravians' religious ethics but in their communal organization of consumption and production as well. The Moravians in Bethlehem were careful to avoid an absolutist position on the matter of economic equality: "To insist upon universal equality with regard to board, clothing, work, etc. would go against common sense, love, and Christ's intention, for the circumstances of the people are so very different. But whenever the circumstances are the same equal treatment of all is essential." [51]

This refusal to adopt an absolutist position with regard to the value of equality thus left the way open for the retention of at least a modicum of role specialization and differentiation of rewards within the economy. The egalitarian norms of the Moravians were thus never extended systematically to economic activities. The Brethren's failure to adopt an absolutist and consistent stand on the matter of human equality indirectly served to reduce the amount of potential conflict between religious norms and economic conduct.

VIII. THE DIVISION OF LABOR

FROM THEIR INCEPTION Herrnhut and Bethlehem were expected to strive for communal self-sufficiency. The Zinzendorfian model of an exclusive settlement was inspired not by a desire to flee from the snares of the sinful world, as was the case with the Amish or the Hutterites, but by a determination to establish a degree of independence from the outside world which would permit the Moravians to pursue their religious goals unhampered by the limitations imposed by a dependence upon non-Moravian resources.[1] In both Herrnhut and Bethlehem it became mandatory to establish an economy which could effectively support a resident population and also a large number of itinerant missionaries for whom such settlements provided a stopover on their journeys to more distant lands. In Herrnhut the basic economic unit was coextensive with the political boundary lines of the community. In Bethlehem, however, during the first two decades of settlement the economy included a number of neighboring agricultural settlements, notably Nazareth, Gnadenthal, Christiansbrunn, and Friedensthal, all of which constituted what came to be referred to as the General Economy of Bethlehem.[2] In order to understand more clearly the problems encountered by the Moravians in their attempts to establish economically independent communities, we must examine the patterns of occupational specialization prevalent in eighteenth-century Herrnhut and Bethlehem.

The Occupational Structure of Herrnhut

In 1727, five years after the founding of the community by a band of immigrants on a deserted piece of swampland, Herrnhut had already begun to lay the foundations for a self-sufficient economic enterprise. The range of occupations pursued covered at least twenty-four different economic activities.[3] Most of these occupations were concentrated within various trades which supplied the community with the basic necessities of food, clothing, and housing. Other occupations, such as organmaking, were beginning to provide for some of the higher enjoyments of life.

By far the most important activity was the building of houses and roads for the rapidly expanding community. More than one quarter of adult males employed in 1727 were engaged in the building trades; they included carpenters and masons, as well as construction laborers.[4] The textile and garment industry, which included linen weavers, wool cloth weavers, spinners, and tailors, accounted for almost one fifth of the employed population. Here were laid the foundations of the only industry which was to achieve a reputation outside the walls of Herrnhut itself. Cutlers, potters, leather craftsmen, and wood craftsmen also played an important role in the community. Together, these skilled tradesmen accounted for more than one half of the economically active population.

Close to one sixth of the working population were listed as landlords. Unfortunately no detailed information on the nature of their business is available.[5] Unskilled workers accounted for a little over one tenth of the economically active population, and undoubtedly included a good many of the peasants who, having had to leave their land and lacking any trade skills, had to take whatever work came their way. Those engaged in agriculture accounted for only two per cent of the male working force, an unusually low percentage considering that about one half of the Moravian immigrants were farmers.[6] It should be remembered, however, that Herrnhut was being built at the foot of the Hutberg on land that was swampy and clearly unsuitable for cultivation. Had the land been easier to till, Zinzendorf would most likely have done so before the Moravians ever set foot on his estate. The land which was already under cultivation was in the hands of the villagers of Berthelsdorf, the original residents of the Count's estate. Under these circumstances the development of any extensive agricultural activity among the Herrnhuters was not possible; at best they could hope to supply at least part of their own needs for produce. Herrnhut had at this time two bakers, but no millers or butchers.

In these early years those engaged in full-time missionary pursuits accounted for less than one tenth of the economically active population. Furthermore, no one was at this time engaged in any commercial activities on a full-time basis. Whatever economic transactions had to be carried on with the outside world were handled either by the leaders of the community or by the tradesmen themselves. This was, in brief, the division of labor in Herrnhut in 1727. Although the community was not as yet entirely self-sufficient, it had already begun to lay the foundations for a diversified economy in which skilled trades were to play a major role.

Two decades later the population of Herrnhut had risen from 300 to more than 800. The number of different occupations had jumped from twenty-four to seventy-three.[7] The textile and garment-making trades now constituted the single most important group, accounting for over one fifth of the total work force. They included at least fourteen different occupations. The metal, wood, leather, pottery, and stone trades showed a similar increase in the variety of occupations pursued, even though individually their respective share of the labor force was considerably smaller than that of the textile group. At times the uneven growth rates of specific occupations were economically disadvantageous. The shoemakers and menders, for example, continued to increase far too rapidly; by 1747 there were twenty-four of them, which meant that there was one shoemaker for every thirty-five persons in the community. Trades concerned with food production and the making of household requisites had also become more diversified. By 1747 they included bakers, butchers, millers, soap and starch makers, and even a brewer, accounting for just over five per cent of the working force.

In contrast, the proportion of the population engaged in building and construction had declined sharply; it now accounted for less than five per cent of the economically active labor force. The initial building boom had lost its momentum, and the introduction of choir living arrangments further reduced the demand for individual family housing. The percentage of the adult male population engaged in agriculture had risen from two to six per cent. The striking decline in the percentage of the unskilled, who by the mid-forties represented only two per cent of the male working force, speaks well for the economic growth of the community as a whole.

Occupations in the professions, which included physicians, surgeons, theologians, laboratory assistants, apothecaries, lawyers, and schoolteachers, all notably absent in 1727, represented another five per cent of the work force. The ranks of the aristocrats, a term first used as an occupational designation in 1736, had increased to almost ten per cent and appear to have been accompanied by a similar rise in the number of domestic workers, most of whom were employed as servants to the aristocracy. Full-time missionaries now accounted for more than ten per cent of the male working force of Herrnhut, though it is likely that this figure under-represents the actual number of missionaries from Herrnhut active in the field.[8] Administrative personnel, which included mostly full-time choir supervisors and assistants, accounted for eight per cent of the male labor force. Herrnhut was clearly establishing itself as a center of skilled trades in which agriculture played an insignificant role.

By the middle-sixties more than eighty different occupations were being practiced in Herrnhut.[9] If one includes the array of women's occupations the figure is even higher. Although new occupations were still being added, the rate of occupational diversification had apparently slowed down after mid-century. Textiles continued to dominate the occupational structure of the community, accounting for about one fifth of the total working force. The position of the leather trades was still prominent, accounting for more than ten per cent of the employed men. The share of the male population employed in the wood and paper, iron and metal, building, and pottery trades fluctuated little throughout this period. Skilled craftsmen thus continued to provide the backbone of the Moravian economy in Herrnhut.

The major change in the occupational distribution of Herrnhut in the seventeen-sixties is to be found in the field of commerce. An entirely new form of business enterprise had been opened to the Moravians. Approximately ten per cent of the men in Herrnhut were engaged in packing, merchandising, selling, transporting, and balancing accounts for goods that included tin plate, sheet iron, leather, yarn, pharmaceutical products, textiles, toys, and trinkets.[10] The only other major occupational grouping new to Herrnhut in the fifties and sixties was that of the semiskilled, who were increasingly finding employment in the textile, printing, and tobacco works of the community, and who by 1764 were accounting for about eight per cent of the male labor force.[11]

The production of food, including milling, baking, butchering, and cooking, provided jobs for a higher proportion of the labor force in 1764, which may be attributed in part to a general rise in the standard of living. The influx of the aristocracy played an important role in this by elevating the gastronomic tastes of the population. Yet in spite of this increase in the overall standard of living, the percentage of the adult male population employed as day laborers in essentially unskilled work had increased during the seventeen-fifties to almost ten per cent, a figure which had not been equaled since 1730.[12] Most of these day laborers came from the ranks of the Married and the Widowers' choirs. This differential was attributable not to the fact that the Single Brethren's choir attracted a lower proportion of unskilled persons, but that it alone provided any organized occupational training for new members.

Persons engaged in administering the affairs of the choirs, the community, and the Unity as a whole accounted in the seventeen-sixties for a smaller share of Herrnhut's working men than had been the case in the first half of the eighteenth century, although the absolute number of persons pursuing such occupations had increased. The need for administrative personnel did not rise in direct proportion to the increase in the population of the community. In like manner the professions showed a similar percentage decline during the fifties and sixties.

Regrettably we do not have any reliable information on the number of Herrnhuters engaged in missionary activities during this later period. The fact that missionaries were forced to leave Herrnhut in order to minister to the unconverted meant that de facto they were no longer part of Herrnhut's population. As a result, the failure to enumerate missionaries in the occupational statistics of Herrnhut was based on an arbitrary and changeable decision of the record keepers from one period to the next. All that can be established with any degree of certainty is that the duration of missionary assignments increased and the number of persons temporarily absent from Herrnhut was severely curtailed.[13]

Finally, a few comments may be made about the occupational pursuits of the women of Herrnhut. In contrast to the men, the women showed only a limited degree of occupational specialization, being almost invariably employed in positions requiring far less skill. During this period over three quarters of all working women were employed either in domestic service or as cleaning women. The only major skilled occupations to which women were admitted in any number were in textiles, where they found work as spinners and wool cloth weavers. During this same period textiles absorbed sixteen to eighteen per cent of the female labor force. Some of the better-educated women were able to secure employment either as teachers or as administrators in the choirs. By 1764 twenty-eight women were listed as aristocrats.[14]

Ironically, despite the fact that the system of choir segregation had freed the women of their traditional burdens of child-raising and housekeeping, the Moravians failed to capitalize upon this situation from an economic standpoint. They failed to train and educate women for occupations that might well have contributed to the enterprises of the community and would have enabled the women to earn their own livelihoods. As it was, many women having no specific skills were unable to find employment, and the Single Sisters' choir and the Widows' choir were almost constantly in financial straits. It is doubtful whether these choirs could have continued to exist at all had it not been for the economic support they received from their wealthier aristocratic Sisters, who provided both direct financial subsidies and occupational opportunities for other Sisters to serve as their personal maids.[15]

The economic welfare of the community rested disproportionately in the hands of men and especially in the hands of the members of the Single Brethren's choir. Although this choir provided within its own house more occupational opportunities than any of the other choirs, it was nevertheless forced to send many of its members to work elsewhere.[16] The fact that single men were permitted to work not only for their parents but even for married persons to whom they were not related indicates that the economic necessity of earning a livelihood was seriously weakening the degree of choir segregation. By partially subordinating the choir principle to that of economic advancement, Herrnhut had in the second half of the eighteenth century become a reasonably self-sufficient economic unit in which a considerable variety of trades and commercial activities were being carried on.

Although no precise statistics on the extent of unemployment are available, there are indications that throughout the eighteenth century a significant number of individuals were unable to secure employment. For example, one finds mention of the fact that in 1732 Zinzendorf ordered that every Brother who could not find full employment be permitted to work in the Count's gardens, "in order that he [the Brother] may more readily make ends meet."[17]

An alternative solution recommended by the Count, especially with regard to the problem of seasonal unemployment, was for the unemployed to go out in pairs, spreading the word of God and earning their bread from place to place. Many did indeed resort to this step. During the winter months, for example, most of the persons engaged in the building trades would venture forth as missionaries. In 1736 one finds mention of Herrnhut missionaries in the following places: two in Lapland, four in Greenland, thirty-one in Georgia, two in St. Thomas, and seven in St. Croix, and two in Surinam.[18] Frequently, however, such missionary activities brought only a temporary surcease from economic problems. In the early years most of the missionaries were sent abroad only for limited periods of time, and upon their return had then to be reintegrated into the communal economy of Herrnhut. Thus, although permanent emigration of missionaries would have helped to reduce the rate of unemployment, this pattern of emigration was rare.

One solution to the unemployment problem was for those out of work to seek employment outside Herrnhut. Many did in fact resort to such employment in the early years of the community. The major disadvantage of this step was that it interfered considerably with Zinzendorf's plan for a closely knit and self-sufficient communal enterprise within Herrnhut. For this reason outside employment was actively discouraged by the Count, and by the seventeen-forties was forbidden. By ruling out the possibility of employment in the world outside, Zinzendorf had at times to resort to an alternative and even more drastic solution: the restriction of immigration to the community. The refusal to accept any unskilled persons after 1736 was dictated primarily by the necessity of curtailing the entry of persons who could not readily be absorbed into the economy. By the same token, we find that in 1740 two scribes from Norway were refused admission to the community because there was no opportunity in the near future for them to ply their own trades.[19]

Thus, although Herrnhut was able to achieve a considerable degree of economic specialization and lay the foundations for a self-sufficient economic system, it did not entirely resolve the problem of unemployment, a problem in large measure due to the absence of opportunities for the unskilled in agriculture. Unfortunately we do not have any detailed information about the productivity of the community during these early years.[20] But commentaries accompanying the various occupational inventories alluded to earlier suggest that Herrnhut's economic expansion barely managed to keep abreast of the population increase. Although the vast majority of the population were able to support themselves adequately, the unemployed and those too old or too young to earn their livings could not have survived in Herrnhut without the financial support of the aristocracy.

The Occupational Structure of Bethlehem

In 1747, only three years after the establishment of the General Economy, one finds in Bethlehem and its neighboring communities a considerable degree of economic diversification; approximately forty different occupations were being practiced.[21] Agricultural pursuits occupied a major proportion of the community members, in particular among those residing in Nazareth, a few miles north of Bethlehem. In their ranks were to be found caretakers of oxen, sheep, and cattle, threshers, wood choppers, and vegetable gardeners.[22] The farms, mills, gardens, and vineyards tended by the Moravians reduced the dependence of Bethlehem upon the outside world for the supply of many of the basic needs of its members and were a source of revenue as well. Bethlehem was thus able to support its own people to a degree never attained in Herrnhut. Although agricultural production did not keep abreast of the community's population growth, it nevertheless provided a very crucial source of economic support for the General Economy.

The General Economy was not, however, at any time a purely or even predominantly agricultural commune. Trades came to play an important role in Bethlehem not only in meeting the clothing, household, and building needs of the community, but also by providing a small surplus which could be used to purchase such items as sugar, glass, and iron. In 1747 the most lucrative business in Bethlehem appears to have been the tannery. In building and construction the demand for labor frequently outstripped the supply. Masons especially appear to have been in great demand. Owing to the small number of Moravians employed in the building trades, additional Brethren had at times to be recruited from the Single Brethren's choir to lend a hand in the construction of a choir house or farm building.[23] The woodworkers in 1747 included joiners, turners, coopers, saddlebow makers, box and spindle makers, cabinet makers, and wheelwrights. Most of the work in textiles was in linen weaving, much of which was carried out by the Sisters. Two blacksmiths and a locksmith provided some of the basic tools of the community but did not supply any implements to outsiders at this time.[24] Those engaged in the processing or manufacturing of foods and household goods included the proverbial butchers, bakers, and candlestick makers, as well as brewers, millers, and soapmakers.

Those in the professions, mostly schoolteachers and doctors, constituted a small but significant minority of the economically active population of Bethlehem. The number of persons supported by the Economy who were consequently able to devote themselves to missionary activities was truly astounding for a community that was only just emerging out of the wilderness. In 1747 approximately fifty out of a total population of over 400 were away on missionary duty.[25] The absence of any full-time administrative personnel suggests that in contrast to Herrnhut all such activities continued to be carried out on a part-time basis by persons already engaged in the economy. The absence of an aristocratic class also obviated the need for servants.

During the next decade the most striking increases in the proportion of the population engaged in specific occupational groups took place among the textile and garment workers, the metal workers, and the leather workers. In each of these groups the increase was due not to greater diversity of trades but to the augmenting of workers in an already existing trade: in garment manufacturing to a sudden influx in tailors; in the leather trades to an influx of shoemakers; and in the metal trades to a somewhat smaller influx of blacksmiths and locksmiths. Those employed in the building and construction trades also grew in numbers during these years.

Most of the other trades, the professions, and agriculture showed small increases in the absolute number employed, but these were more than offset by the increase in the total population of the General Economy. The total number of different occupations pursued in the General Economy had, by 1752, risen to over sixty.

The General Economy of Bethlehem, begun in 1744, was finally abrogated in 1761. In order to comprehend better the factors which precipitated its collapse we need to compare the division of labor of Bethlehem in the early years with occupational statistics for the period immediately preceding the breakup of the General Economy. By the end of the seventeen-fifties the total number of different occupations practiced in the community of Bethlehem, excluding Nazareth and the Upper Places, numbered sixty-three.[26] The major innovations occurred in the fields of administration, trade, and commerce. In its pioneering years Bethlehem had been unable to permit any of its members to pursue administrative tasks within the community on a full-time basis, but by 1759 the choirs at least were being staffed with full-time supervisors. The number of such administrative personnel both in absolute terms and on a per capita basis was, however, considerably below that of Herrnhut, in spite of the fact that, from a purely materialistic point of view, Bethlehem could afford such administrators more readily than Herrnhut.

Commerce, an area in which the early Moravian settlers in Pennsylvania had shown little interest or inclination, now accounted for a small but significant percentage of the male labor force. By 1759 bookkeepers, storekeepers, and secretaries were handling much of the paper work resulting from the growth of trade with the outside world. The emergence of full-time guides for strangers and Indians and the rise in the number of innkeepers in the community suggest that Bethlehem, in spite of its official doctrine of exclusivism, was both willing and able to cater to the needs of tourists and visiting fellow Moravians. Finally, one finds a greater diversification of labor in the area of food production. By 1759 cooks, brewers, beer carriers, and a keeper of the cellar had found employment in the community. One suspects that the general standard of living, as reflected in the consumption patterns of the Moravians, had risen.

Yet at a time when many occupations were being practiced in Bethlehem for the first time, a large number of trades pursued by Moravians in the pioneering years of the community had been abandoned. In the ranks of the professions no apothecary or surgeon could now be found. In the building trades brickmakers, tarmakers, and tilemakers had disappeared. Blacksmiths, goldsmiths, pewterers, clockmakers, and plumbers had vanished from the ranks of the iron and metal workers. Leather, hemp, and wood workers now operated without the skills of a ropemaker, tawer, harness maker, wheelwright, box and spindle maker, and cabinet maker. And the community was apparently unable to continue to support a wigmaker, a barber, or for that matter, rather understandably, a sailor. To a large extent the elimination of these occupations undoubtedly reflected the gradual absorption of the immigrants into the economy of Bethlehem, in the process of which many persons were forced to abandon their former occupations in favor of a skill more immediately required in the new community.

Certain shifts in the proportional significance of various occupational groups may also be detected. In 1759 the occupation of missionary constituted the single most important group within the community, accounting for approximately thirty-six per cent of the male labor force. In absolute numbers this group had more than doubled itself within the past decade. It included all persons who devoted themselves on a full-time basis to a religious calling, such as missionaries, preachers in the Diaspora, and teachers in Moravian educational institutions, as well as bishops, deacons, and ministers. The significance of this group's size for the economy of the community can only begin to be grasped when one realizes that all of these able-bodied men were working in professions for which there was no material recompense, and were thus dependent upon their fellow Moravians in the settlement to support them. Furthermore, since the Moravians required that all official positions should preferably be staffed by both a man and a woman, almost every male missionary had a female helpmeet at his side, thereby further depleting the wage-earning ranks of the community. The dependent children of such persons also were expected to receive their economic support not from their biological parents but from the skilled craftsmen and farmers of the community. From a purely materialistic standpoint, the economic survival and welfare of the community of Bethlehem were, therefore, dependent upon the labors of approximately one third of the total population.[27] When one realizes that the ratio of the economically active members to the dependent population of eighteenth-century Bethlehem finds a parallel only in modern industrialized American society, one begins to get an idea of the extraordinary handicaps under which Bethlehem was forced to operate during the Colonial Period in order to attain the religious goals of the community.[28]

By the end of the seventeen-fifties agriculture constituted the second most important occupational group. The original plan of creating in Bethlehem a place of skilled craftsmen while leaving agricultural pursuits to the Moravians in nearby Nazareth and the Upper Places had apparently failed, for the data for 1759 indicate clearly that in Bethlehem alone over ten per cent of the male population was engaged in farming of one kind or another. For the General Economy as a whole the percentage must have been considerably higher. The efforts of the Moravians to recruit Brothers to the land seemed to be at least partly successful.

In 1759 the professions, textile trades, and leather and hemp craftsmen each accounted for close to nine per cent of the male labor force. But whereas textiles and leather crafts had played a similarly important role in the occupational structure of Bethlehem in its early years, the professions had expanded only recently, due primarily to a very sharp rise in the number of full-time teachers employed in the community. In 1747 there were only two teachers for the whole of the General Economy. Only two decades later there were twenty-two in Bethlehem alone. Although the ranks of the potters, woodworkers, food preparers, and iron and metal workers showed slight gains in absolute numbers during the seventeen-fifties, their respective shares of the total male work force changed little.

The only occupational group to suffer a major setback during this period was that of building and construction. As late as 1752 there had been at least twenty-two building and construction workers in the community, yet by 1759 there were only two, and this at a time when Bethlehem was expanding both in population and housing. Unable to supply its own demand for such labor, Bethlehem was forced to rely upon outsiders for much of the work that went into the building of the community.[29]

Such then were the major characteristics of the division of labor in Bethlehem during the years of the General Economy. Although Bethlehem's occupational structure still bore some resemblance to that of Herrnhut, as evidenced in the role of skilled trades, especially textiles and leather, and the movement of both communities into the realm of commerce, there were some important differences. Bethlehem had virtually no aristocracy and as a result domestic service was not, as in Herrnhut, a major avenue of employment either for men or for women. Nor had Bethlehem, in spite of its economic growth, developed a group of full-time administrators and choir functionaries that could come anywhere near to matching the size of the one in Herrnhut, either absolutely or relative to the total economically active population. In Herrnhut during this same period the unskilled laborers represented as much as ten per cent of the male labor force and eighteen per cent of the total economically active population, whereas in Bethlehem unskilled Moravian workers were virtually unknown and the community had therefore to rely upon neighboring communities for an adequate supply of such labor.[30] The most striking difference between the two communities lay in the fact that Herrnhut had by the seventeen-sixties abandoned all attempts to develop an agriculture of its own. In Bethlehem, on the other hand, this branch of the General Economy, although unable to meet all demands of the growing community, was nevertheless able to supply a significant portion of Bethlehem's food.

Finally, our information about the occupational structure may, for Bethlehem, be supplemented with data on the production and consumption patterns of the Moravians during the years of the General Economy. These patterns may best be described with reference to the way in which three of man's most basic needs—for food, for clothing, and for shelter—were met. In these years all the food for the population had to be produced by the community, for there was no surplus capital which could be spent on the purchase of this basic commodity. By 1747 the Moravians had acquired considerable land. In and around Bethlehem there were 200 acres of arable land and an additional twenty acres of meadowland for sheep and cattle. Nazareth provided 250 acres of arable land and a further twenty acres of pasture. Gnadenthal and Christiansbrunn together accounted for 130 acres of arable land and four acres of meadowland.[31] Additional land which belonged to the Moravians had not yet been put under cultivation. All the agricultural produce of the Moravians came from these tracts of land, most of which had been transformed from forest to arable fields during the five years in which the Moravians had been resident in that area.

Although we do not have many details on the development of agriculture in the Bethlehem area during these years, a number of comments by Moravians as well as more independent-minded outsiders leave no doubt about the astounding progress that had been made. Even the level-headed Spangenberg was driven to remark in 1752 that "The fruit of our fields is beautiful to behold, it is well nigh impossible to find anything comparable between here and New York. It is a miracle to all men, for our soil has often been depleted through excessive usage."[32] Outsiders noted that Bethlehem's agricultural prowess set an example for the whole of the Lehigh Valley.[33] During these early years, in addition to an extensive cultivation of wheat, corn, and flax crops, the foundation of what was to become the single largest cattle-farming industry in Pennsylvania was being laid.

In 1747 Bethlehem's population of about 300, the vast majority of whom were people in their twenties and thirties, consumed the following quantities of food: 2,307 bushels of wheat, 12,832 eggs (an average per person of one egg about every ten days), and 15,586 pounds of meat (an average per person of about two servings of meat a week).[34] No details are given on the amounts or types of home-grown vegetables which supplemented this rather Spartan diet. Cammerhoff provides a graphic description of the eating habits of the Moravians in these early years:

Normally we eat meat twice a week. Our other staples consist of soups, farina puddings and side dishes of vegetables, depending on what the season has to offer. Occasionally there is added to this a little butter. Coffee is made from barley oats; tea and chocolate are prepared by the doctor from his collection of herbs. We brew very little beer, mostly only for sick or ailing persons. Nor are our children exposed to delicacies, although it is true that the food which they eat is a little easier to digest than that given to the Brethren and Sisters who of course work up a good appetite in their work.[35]

Although the fare was somewhat monotonous, everyone was fed adequately and there was little recorded illness among the Moravians in these early years.

The Moravians in Bethlehem relied from the very beginning either on clothes they had brought with them from Germany or on clothes made by one or other of the trades in their new community. Linen weaving, most of which was, as we have seen, carried on by the Single Sisters, provided cloth for shirts and dresses as well as sheets for the choir houses and the nursery. Henry Antes in a letter to Spangenberg noted that because of the heat and hard physical labor most of the Brethren required three to four shirts a year.[36] It is certain that in these pioneering years none of the members received more than a minimum of clothing, yet outsiders never failed to comment on the personal neatness of the Moravians. The tannery provided the necessary leather for the footwear of the community. The many shoemakers were kept busy making and repairing the boots and shoes of the Brethren and Sisters. In the period between October and December of 1747 alone they produced 145 pairs of shoes and eleven pairs of boots in addition to repairing 272 pairs of footwear.[37]

The need for adequate shelter from the elements was the most costly to meet since the rapidly expanding population was constantly making new demands for more housing. The Moravians themselves had almost no capital to invest in extensive building programs, most of their money having been used up in the purchase of land. Yet only five years after the founding of the community substantial choir houses had been built for the Single Brethren's and Single Sisters' choirs. The Married Persons' choir also had found a home, either in the Bell House, where most of them took meals, or in a number of smaller buildings which were temporarily used to care for the overflow. Sawmills and smithies enabled the Moravians to provide many of the basic construction materials for their buildings. At the smithies, for example, most of the tools of the community were made, together with all ironware required for the various mills of the community. This again saved Bethlehem from a major capital outlay. The sawmills converted the valuable assets of forestland into planks of timber from which many of the early buildings were constructed. During these early years in Bethlehem the first bookstore in the whole of the Lehigh Valley was built. A tavern, the old Gasthaus zur Krone, provided lodgings for itinerant Moravians as well as for curious visitors from other parts of Pennsylvania, New Jersey, and New York.[38] Bethlehem thus had taken great strides in creating on the deserted Whitefield tract not simply a way station for itinerant missionaries but a flourishing economy capable of meeting most of the needs of over 1,300 persons.

IX. PROCESSES OF ECONOMIC DIVERSIFICATION

IN DESCRIBING the development of the occupational structures of Herrnhut and Bethlehem we have put to one side the problems encountered by the Moravians in their attempt to create a diversified economic system. Many of their most persistent economic difficulties during the second half of the eighteenth century may be traced to three areas: agriculture, industry, and commerce. An examination of the relative success or failure of the Moravians' ventures in these fields will serve to clarify the patterns of economic development in the settlements.

Difficulties in Agriculture

Any community aspiring to a high degree of autonomy and independence from the outside world must of necessity strive to develop a self-sufficient economic system in which agricultural production plays a vital role. Given the Moravians' desire to achieve such independence it seems surprising that agriculture was almost entirely absent from Herrnhut and played a secondary role in Bethlehem. Clearly, factors other than the goal of economic self-sufficiency helped to shape the role agriculture was to play in the lives of the eighteenth-century Moravians. One of the most crucial of these factors was that Zinzendorf himself had strong misgivings about the compatibility of the peasant role with the Moravian way of life:

If the community could propagate itself in such a way that one could be sure that one would raise only children of God and that these in turn would raise children of God, then the agricultural way of life would be admirable. But since what becomes of one's offspring is an exceedingly dubious and uncertain matter . . . I have observed that the preservation of the community is best assured through a process of continuous change.[1]

The Count had apparently decided that the religious goals of the Moravians could not readily be preserved in a community whose members developed strong ties to the land.

Several impediments to the development of agriculture among the Moravians can be specified more precisely. In the first place, the peasant was both less willing and less able to leave his occupation from one day to the next in order to take up a call to missionary service. Unlike the skilled craftsman he could not hope to find work readily available elsewhere. The inevitable ties of the peasant to his land thus conflicted with the Moravians' requirement for considerable occupational mobility in order that the missionary goals of the community might be met. The occupational status of the agricultural worker was also felt to conflict with the requirements of choir living.[2] The principle of segregation according to sex which was inherent to the choirs was difficult enough to apply to skilled crafts; in agriculture its adoption was patently impossible.

It has sometimes been argued that the Moravians did not participate in agriculture because there was no land available, the community having been established on swamps and hills highly unsuitable for cultivation.[3] Yet the fact remains that Zinzendorf, who permitted the Moravians to settle at the foot of the Hutberg, also possessed a large estate given almost entirely to agricultural production. Indeed, it was only thanks to the existence of Zinzendorf's manorial estates in Hennersdorf and Berthelsdorf, tilled by non-Moravian hands, that the Unity was able to weather the financial crises of the second half of the eighteenth century.[4]

The very fact that Herrnhut had to introduce specific legislation to prohibit the pursuit of agricultural occupations indicates that it was not the absence of available land which prevented this development.[5] In a memorandum delineating the borders between Herrnhut and Berthelsdorf the following remark appears: "The residents of Herrnhut will use from the land allotted to them only what is considered to be absolutely necessary, and leave the remainder to the manor, since extensive farming is not merely unbecoming but detrimental to the plain and simple life." [6]

Why then were the Moravians in Bethlehem permitted to engage in agriculture, while their fellow Brethren in Herrnhut were being thus restrained? Quite simply, because in Pennsylvania there was no one else to do this work for them, no manorial estates of aristocrats favorably disposed toward them, no neighboring peasantry willing to till the fields in return for a wage, and no nearby community willing or able to trade much of its own agricultural surplus for other commodities.[7] It was this inability to rely upon the labor of others which had forced Bethlehem to establish an agriculture of its own and to develop what came to be referred to as the "Patriarchal Economy" of Nazareth and the Upper Places.

Yet even in Bethlehem the Moravians had constant problems in trying to recruit persons for agricultural occupations. A leading Moravian noted regretfully that "the hearts of the Brethren do not in the least incline toward farming." [8] The Brethren were loathe to take up an occupation which would virtually exclude them from the pursuit of missionary activities. As a result, less than twenty per cent of the community's labor force was engaged in agriculture.

Yet their output was considerable. By 1756, 1,800 acres had been cleared and put under cultivation. In 1759 this figure rose to 2,454 acres.[9] During this same period the total value of the agricultural products of the Moravians rose consistently to a high of £5814/—/10 sterling during the last year of the General Economy.[10] The rise in the number of livestock attests to a similar increase in prosperity. By 1759 there were 761 head of cattle, 377 sheep, seventy-eight horses, fifty-one pigs, and innumerable chickens.[11] The Bethlehem General Economy had within the short span of a decade developed to such an extent that not only had almost 2,500 acres of wilderness been cleared and cultivated, but the yield of agricultural produce was satisfying close to half the demand for such products made by a population which had by then grown to approximately 1,300 persons.

The purchase of additional meats and grain constituted the major items of expenditure.[12] This productivity would appear to be no mean feat for a community in which agricultural labor was generally regarded with disdain and was considered to be at best an unfortunate necessity for preserving the exclusiveness of the religious settlement.

Problems of Industrialization and Commerce

The history of the Moravians' attempts to develop industries along capitalistic lines provides some penetrating insights into the interplay of religious and economic values within the communities of Herrnhut and Bethlehem. The nature of the resolution of conflicts between these disparate sets of ethical values played a vital role in the development of the two communities.

Zinzendorf's own attitudes toward the establishment of industries among the Brethren were for the most part negative. As early as 1746 he insisted that the Saviour wanted no industries among the Moravians in order to keep profiteering from being turned into a sacred cause in His name. Wealth could better be obtained through the simple, innocent *Commercio* which developed out of the Brethren's lack of concern with material self-improvement.[13] At other times the Count's aversion to industrialization was based upon the questionable assumption that one factory simply ruined another.[14] Although he admitted to almost total ignorance in economic matters, his views were not always inaccurate. For instance, he foresaw very clearly that industrialization would threaten the social structure of the community in at least two different ways: first, it would jeopardize the choirs by necessitating the establishment of places of work outside the choir houses, thereby severing crucial ties of the economy to the socioreligious life of the Moravians; second, and even more important, it would seriously hamper missionary activities since a factory worker clearly could not find employment away from home as easily as could a skilled craftsman. To practice his trade the latter needed but a few tools, whereas the former was dependent upon the physical and social structures of a whole factory.[15]

The Count's unwillingness to permit the development of industry did much to hamper such a trend, but it could not prevent it altogether. The men to whom Zinzendorf had entrusted most of the economic cares of the community, men like von Damnitz and de Watteville, because they understood these matters better than he, were insisting that the community had to explore every opportunity for gainful employment, including that of industrialization. They argued that unless more employment opportunities were created the choirs would crumble, the missionary activities collapse, and the religious goals come to naught.[16] While Zinzendorf continued to give absolute priority to the missionary goals of the community, von Damnitz and de Watteville held that there were times when the economic needs of the Moravians must be given first consideration. The serious financial straits in which the Unity found itself by the end of the time of the Sifting had made at least some of the Moravians aware that economic issues could not be ignored forever.

The first attempt to develop an industry in Herrnhut was made in the early seventeen-forties, when a textile factory was started. This venture failed, not for lack of capital, for there were at that time many well-to-do fellow Moravians willing to lend sums of money to the community, but because there were no personnel experienced in running such an enterprise. The raw materials were bought at exorbitant prices, and there was too much of one type of yarn and far too little of another. After only four years the whole enterprise had to be liquidated.[17]

Other attempts to develop a textile industry during this period failed similarly. Meanwhile the linen weavers continued to lack both the necessary capital to purchase yarn in large quantities and the vital knowledge of the availability of markets for their products. Merchants and businessmen outside Herrnhut were unlikely to be attracted to ply their trades in a community so openly hostile to the ethics of sound business. What was missing was a competent businessman in whom investors and buyers could have faith, a man not likely to be found in Herrnhut where the required occupational skills were held in low esteem.

Such a businessman was, however, found in the person of Abraham Dürninger. Born in 1706, he was the son of a successful textile and tobacco merchant in Strasbourg. Though his education included traineeships to commercial firms in London, Amsterdam, and Basle, his mother's intensely pious convictions had helped to generate in young Abraham a conscience which found it increasingly difficult to reconcile his economic activities with his religious ethics.[18] In his search for a resolution of this conflict Dürninger first became acquainted with the Brethren in Herrnhaag, Wetteravia, in 1741. After an extended visit to the same community in 1743 he settled there in 1744. From 1745 to 1747 he was an accountant at Zinzendorf's theological seminary in Lindheim. In 1747 he was sent to manage the community store in Herrnhut, and in accordance with Moravian tradition he married before taking over his new post so that a helpmeet should complement his work in the community. Between 1747, when Dürninger first took over the community store, and 1773, the year he died, he managed not only to turn the store into a highly profitable wholesale and retail establishment but also to develop a textile-printing establishment, a local industry for the manufacture and world-wide export of linen, and a number of other economic enterprises.

How, then, was it possible that as a Moravian Dürninger was able to reconcile his business activities with his religious ethics, while as a young man he had consistently failed to do so? According to Dürninger himself, it was not until 1747 that he finally became convinced, after much soul searching, that it was possible to be a Christian merchant and businessman, that one could indeed "live a devout life in any occupation as long as the sufferings of our Lord Jesus Christ constitute the sole object of our love." [19] The religious imperative underlying all his economic actions derived from his belief that the Lord had entrusted him with a very special mission: the

ethical but sound conduct of a business enterprise. His aim, therefore, was not to accumulate personal wealth but to give service in
the name of the Lord and to provide employment opportunities for
persons sharing his religious convictions. A testimony to the success
with which Dürninger pursued his business calling in accordance
with religious values is to be found in his epitaph:

> Es ist wohl schwer, doch geht es an,
> Dass ein Kauf und Handelsmann,
> Selig werden kann.[20]

Dürninger's conception of his business vocation as a personal calling from God helped also to shape his relationships both to the
Herrnhuters and to non-Moravians. He was convinced that fundamentally he was responsible to Jesus alone for the conduct of his
business affairs. He stated emphatically that "the Firm [A. Dürninger and Co.] belongs neither to the Unity as a whole nor to the
community of Herrnhut, nor to myself, but to our dear Saviour."[21]
Nevertheless, Dürninger was sufficiently shrewd as a businessman
to recognize that in order to maximize his credit standing among
non-Moravians it was essential that he have his business bear his
own name and that it be clearly separated from the economic ventures of the Unity, which at that time were in precarious financial
straits. Dürninger had also, as early as 1752, secretly signed a legal
document according to which all business conducted in his name
belonged in fact to the community of Herrnhut.[22] Although the
Moravians were reasonably sure that Abraham Dürninger would
not misuse any company profits, they wanted to make certain that
any possible heirs might not be tempted by the prospect of making
rapid profits for themselves. As to his relations with men in the outside world, Dürninger followed the Brethren's precept of rendering
unto Caesar what was Caesar's. He maintained excellent relations
with the political authorities of Saxony, as well as with the merchants of the Six Towns' Federation, in spite of the fact that the
former were trying to tax him to the utmost and the latter to thwart
his business ventures altogether.[23]

Dürninger's conception of his business as a special mission entrusted to him by the Saviour enabled him to retain a considerable degree of independence and personal freedom in the conduct of his business affairs. Yet he remained, in spite of his excellent training in the field of commerce, a man only sporadically committed to rational principles of business management. He was never, in fact, fully able to reconcile his business interests with his religious interests. On the one hand we have Dürninger the businessman, persuasively arguing with the Herrnhuters that he cannot run a business as long as his best weavers are taken away from him on one day's notice to follow a call for missionary service.[24] Similarly, he argued that he could not make any profits for the community if he was obliged to pay the high wages demanded by the Brethren. In spite of his very real desire to provide employment for the Brethren, he recruited about three fourths of his employees from neighboring communities, people who were willing to work for the wages he offered.[25]

But there was also another Dürninger, a man who was convinced that whenever he attended a country fair he went there "in the company of the dear little angels"[26] and who fully concurred with Zinzendorf's belief that childlike innocence and simplicity constituted the major virtues toward which all should strive. Although Dürninger was far more a rational businessman than any of his fellow believers in Herrnhut, he retained a hankering for metaphysical speculation and introspection. As Hammer indicated: ". . . throughout his life there runs, like a red thread, an unusually pronounced bias toward metaphysical reflection which threatens to veil everything real and rational in an irrational fog."[27]

When Dürninger first took over the Herrnhut local store in 1747, both he and his wife used to take turns behind the counter. His immediate task was to diversify the goods sold and to build the little country store into a profitable wholesale and retail trade operation. By 1754 his store inventory listed a vast array of foodstuffs, tobacco, assorted cloth goods, and items of clothing, as well as

"pocket knives, toothbrushes, and bedsprings."[28] In addition
Dürninger was importing metal and pig iron from Leipzig, furs
and animal skins from New York, and children's toys from the
Riesengebirge. When he became its proprietor the store's total goods
in stock were valued at 2,856 talers. By 1762 the goods imported during that year alone were worth 103,000 talers.[29]

Dürninger's desire to improve the living conditions of the Moravians by providing more opportunities for employment soon led
him to open up other enterprises, the most important of which was
concerned with the manufacturing and export of linen. Spinning
and weaving had come to Herrnhut with its earliest Moravian settlers, but their economic position remained precarious because wool
and flax were bought by each individual separately and the cloth
produced was generally sold by the Brethren and Sisters who had
made it. Dürninger was the first to recognize that the community
needed someone to organize the weavers so that the raw materials
they required could be purchased wholesale, and the goods produced be exported in large quantities far beyond the boundaries of
Upper Lusatia.

The growth of the linen-export business can best be seen from a
list of the places to which these goods were being sent. In 1753
Dürninger was already shipping goods to Hamburg, Amsterdam,
Utrecht, London, Cadiz, Bayonne, Leghorn, Basle, and Berne. By
1770 his exports were going as far as New York, Jamaica, Buenos
Aires, Carthage, Curaçao, and St. Petersburg.[30] Dürninger had become the largest exporter of linen in the whole of the Oberlausitz,
having successfully competed against the merchants of the neighboring towns.

Information on the number of weavers employed by Dürninger
is not readily available. Initially he had wanted to give as much employment as possible to the Moravians in Herrnhut; but statistics on
the number of looms being worked in his employment indicate
clearly that the surrounding countryside came to provide a larger
and larger share of his labor force. In 1756, for instance, Dürninger

had twenty-two looms in Herrnhut and thirty-eight in the surrounding countryside: ten years later there were only eighteen looms left in Herrnhut, whereas the number in neighboring communities had risen to 111.[31] Dürninger had come to recognize that if he was going to be able to run a successful business and help the Moravians financially, he could not continue to employ so many of the Brethren, since their wage scales were considerably higher than those of nearby communities. To compete successfully with the merchants of the Oberlausitz, Dürninger was forced to pay only the wages which they were paying.

The expansion of the linen trade led Dürninger to branch out in a number of directions. The volume of his trade in cloth goods made it advisable for him to import his own yarn and thread, and he soon expanded this import into a wholesale operation for the whole of the Oberlausitz.[32] He also developed his own bleachery, even though the terrain along the Petersbach was none too suitable. The bleachery showed a deficit in its early years, but after 1774 it began to accumulate a small margin of profit.[33]

Dürninger's first real factory developed out of his experiments in chintz and calico printing.[34] As the fame of his prints spread it became necessary for all the textile printers to be housed under one roof, and in 1752 the first building designed specifically for the production of textile printing was constructed. An early inventory of the print patterns of the Dürninger factory listed the following: six designs for bedspreads, forty-five designs for handkerchiefs and scarves, and 461 patterns for "assorted" purposes.[35] The amount of cloth printed gives some indication of the volume of this business. During the year 1762, 898 shocks were printed.[36] The volume increased gradually to a high of 1,047 shocks in 1767, but thereafter declined steadily until the business collapsed altogether a few years after Dürninger's death.[37] This venture had been successful in the beginning primarily because Dürninger had managed to get hold of a secret formula for a permanent blue dye and because he had encountered no competition from the rest of the Oberlausitz. Its ultimate failure can be traced to the emergence of textile-printing plants in such nearby cities as Löbau and Zittau, which enjoyed special governmental tax privileges, and to the development of protectionist tariff policies in England, Spain, and Portugal which virtually halted the export of chintz and printed calico to those countries.[38]

Two other Dürninger enterprises deserve mention, the manufacture of tobacco and the production of sealing wax. Neither of these yielded great profits, but they did provide additional employment opportunities for the Moravians. Tobacco had always been sold in the communal store, but it was Dürninger's brother Johannes, also a resident of Herrnhut, who perfected a snuff tobacco which came to be known throughout Saxony as "genuine Herrnhuter Rappé." [39] The sealing-wax business remained small because the demand for it was never very great.

The financial success of Dürninger's ventures can best be gauged by a comparison of his assets at the time he took over the community store in 1747 with his holdings at the time of his death. In 1747 the store was in debt for a total of 651 talers although the goods in stock were valued at 2,856 talers.[40] At the time of his death his assets were as follows:

		Talers
Capital of the firm Abraham Dürninger and Co.		277,000
Estimated value of buildings of the firm		39,000
Donations (mostly to the Unity)		78,770
Total assets [41]		394,770

In addition Dürninger had during his lifetime donated to Herrnhut, to the Unity, and to various missionary efforts of the Moravians a sum amounting to 131,914 talers.[42] If we bear in mind that during the early years Dürninger had to pay high interest rates for borrowed money, it becomes clear that the net earnings of his firm during his lifetime must have totaled well over half a million talers.

Dürninger's will failed to specify clearly whether the firm was communal or private property and merely appointed two of his employees, Gambs and Hoozena, to carry on the enterprise. After a considerable amount of haggling among Herrnhut, the Unity, and Gambs and Hoozema it was finally agreed that the firm belonged neither to Herrnhut nor to the Unity but to the appointed directors.[43] It was argued that just as the firm had once belonged to Dürninger, who had in fact been considered the real owner as a result of the directorship entrusted to him by the community, so it should now belong to the new generation of directors. It was, however, agreed that henceforth the Elders Conference of Herrnhut should have the right to appoint the directors of the firm. This important provision, by severely restricting the ability of a director to choose his successor, prevented the emergence of a family-controlled firm.

The firm continued to expand and prosper to such an extent that by 1800 the net annual profits amounted to around 100,000 talers, whereas in Dürninger's lifetime the net annual profits had never risen above 55,000.[44] The firm's major business was centered on the manufacturing and export of linen, the wholesale grocery import and export, and the manufacturing and export of tobacco. In the nineteenth century the firm suffered some serious setbacks due primarily to its tardiness in introducing new machinery. But the belated introduction of mechanized spindles and looms enabled the firm to continue its business to this day, even though now it no longer ranks as one of the major linen-export houses of Europe.[45]

The religious values of the Moravians, their attitudes toward economic development, and their choir system with its strains toward egalitarianism had made it very difficult for an industrialized economy to take root in their midst. Most Moravians were exceedingly hostile toward any attempt to force them into the employer-employee relationship typical of capitalistic enterprises. As members of the Single Brethren's choir were quick to point out, it was a fact that no matter how much money Dürninger bequeathed to the Unity he nevertheless became rich while the weavers working for him remained poor.[46] Dürninger's devotion to the religious ideals of the Moravians and his consequent generosity toward them mitigated the circumstances but did not alter the fundamental inequality inherent in the relations between those who owned the means of production and those who labored for them. The firm of Dürninger and Co. succeeded only insofar as it was able to free itself from the religious and social ethics of the Moravians. Dürninger himself has all too often been portrayed as the Christian capitalist par excellence, as though his Christianity somehow made him a better businessman. In fact, however, it is clear that Dürninger's firm would have prospered even further and developed far more rapidly had it not been for his bent toward religious mysticism and the partiality he showed to the religious and social goals of Herrnhut.

In eighteenth-century Bethlehem there were a number of conditions favorable to industrialization. Perhaps the single most important one was the positive challenge of the New World to introduce new forms of social and economic organization, unencumbered by the rigidities so characteristic of much of the social structure of Western Europe during the eighteenth century. It was this impetus to innovation which created in Bethlehem strong pressures for large-scale industrial enterprises in a community which had been intended primarily as a self-contained agricultural center with only limited crafts. The development of an extensive linen-weaving enterprise, the emergence of a pottery whose wares were renowned as far as Philadelphia, and the establishment of a foundry which serviced not only Bethlehem but many of the neighboring communities may be cited as just a few examples of the way in which Bethlehem was developing along lines unplanned and unintended by Zinzendorf and his associates.[47] The absence of a guild system and of strongly entrenched and competently organized competitive economic interest groups in nearby communities also made it much easier for a growing business venture to succeed. The economic conspiracy of the Six Towns with which Dürninger had to contend constantly had no counterpart in eighteenth-century Pennsylvania.

The absence of available capital and the threat of a high labor turnover due to missionary callings were, however, as much of an impediment to industrialization in Bethlehem as they were in Herrnhut. But all in all, conditions in Bethlehem were more favorable to the development of large-scale industry than in Herrnhut. Why then was no such enterprise to be found in Bethlehem? Why was no young Dürninger attracted to the Moravians in Pennsylvania? The answer is to be found in British law, under which the Moravians were forbidden to engage in manufacturing pursuits on any large scale.[48] This prohibition must be considered the major barrier to the development of industry in Bethlehem. The very fact that the Moravians were running into trouble with the British over the volume of their linen and wool weaving as early as 1752 suggests that without such a regulation the Moravians would undoubtedly have enlarged and expanded their enterprises considerably.[49] By the time of the Revolution, when this ban was finally lifted, the community of Bethlehem was, for reasons which we shall explore below, no longer in a position to take full advantage of the new economic freedom. We are thus faced with the historical irony that industrialization, albeit on a limited scale, was achieved in Herrnhut, a community whose environment presented stubborn resistances to such a development, whereas it failed to take hold in eighteenth-century Bethlehem, whose social organization and local conditions were far more favorable to such a development.

Brief mention should finally be made of Bethlehem's activities in the field of commerce, which in their own way were expanding as rapidly as Dürninger's store in Herrnhut. The population growth of the community, combined with an increase in the demand for Moravian goods by neighboring communities, led in 1753 to the formation of a separate branch of the General Economy dealing with trade and commerce.[50] Spangenberg justified the expansion of these activities on the grounds that the community desperately needed cash to purchase such items as iron, gunpowder, glass, and salt, and thus could not afford to let its neighbors purchase wares in Philadelphia when they could more readily obtain them from the Moravians.[51] In 1753 the "Store-Haus" was completed and soon became an important meeting place for Moravians and non-Moravians alike. Its strategic status as a community resource is reflected in the fact that by 1758 there were over 250 separate items in stock.[52] At the same time three inns, the Crown, the Rose, and the Sun, provided food and lodging for visiting tradesmen and other persons. Provisions were also made to develop shipping facilities for the community so that goods could be transported via the Lehigh and Delaware Rivers to Philadelphia, Baltimore, and New York and thence across the Atlantic to and from Europe.[53] What had happened to the merchants of New England a century earlier had become the fate of the Moravian merchants in Bethlehem; they "had become, by virtue of the services they performed for the public, part of the separate, intractable world of Atlantic commerce." [54] And this occurred in spite of the fact that commerce was regarded by the Moravians as an occupation unsuitable for the Brethren "because sin adheres to it in the same way as a nail does to the wall." [55]

The justification used by the people in Bethlehem was that the store benefited only the General Economy. All profits had to be turned over to the central administration and all money needed to purchase goods had to be applied for. Furthermore, the daily activities of Moravian businessmen were subordinated to communal regulations designed to preserve the religious integrity of the settlement. Businessmen were admonished to practice brotherliness and to be guided by norms of Christian fairness, not by a concern for profit. Communal prices were fixed by the Trades Conferences and strictly observed; when outsiders came to Bethlehem to purchase goods no bargaining was possible.[56]

The diversification of the Moravian economy in Herrnhut and Bethlehem had thus proceeded along lines not clearly anticipated by the founders of the two communities. For better or for worse the Moravians were becoming more and more part of the outside world, to which they were tied as much by trade as by missionary expeditions. But the nature of this development differed significantly in the two communities. Herrnhut could continue to keep its Brethren largely untainted by the worldliness associated with industrial and commercial occupational statuses because it had been able to secure the services of one man who managed to develop his business largely by using non-Moravian labor, but who nevertheless was willing to turn over much of his profits to Herrnhut. The absence of any large-scale industry in Bethlehem during this same period was due, as we have seen, not to an unwillingness to become engaged in such activities but to the arbitrariness of a British law which effectively thwarted any attempts in this direction. In the field of commerce, where no such restrictive law operated to their disadvantage, the Moravians of Bethlehem had shown all too clearly that they were quite capable of expanding their economy to include trade and commerce with the outside world.

Economic Relations with non-Moravians [57]

In spite of their professed aspirations toward communal exclusivism, the Moravians could hardly ignore the outside world. Herrnhut's manifest goal of economic self-sufficiency was constantly threatened by the fact that it could not provide an adequate number of employment opportunities for its members. As a result many Moravians were forced, as we have seen, to seek employment in one or another of the neighboring communities of the Oberlausitz. The impossibility of providing full employment within Herrnhut prior to Zinzendorf's return from exile in 1747 was so obvious that no attempt was made to prohibit employment outside Herrnhut. During the seventeen-thirties a number of Herrnhuter carpenters had found employment in Oderwitz and Hennersdorf, while the services of Moravian masons were made use of in the construction of a school in Bernstadt. Some of the Moravian Sisters also found employment in Bernstadt, as well as in Ruppersdorf and Oderwitz, where they earned their livings by spinning wool.[58]

At the same time some attempts were made to limit the negative effects of exposure to the values of secular society. Thus Zinzendorf insisted that an employer in Oderwitz could employ ten Moravian Sisters only on condition that "no lewd or immoral word be spoken in their presence." [59] But such specifications in the employment contract were often a poor guarantee against contamination by worldly values. In 1734, for instance, the Judiciary Council severely reprimanded a number of carpenters who, while employed in neighboring communities, "had behaved like men of the world and incurred debts." [60] As early as 1732 the Communal Council ordered that, whenever feasible, Brethren and Sisters working outside Herrnhut should nevertheless return to Herrnhut for the night. Two years later the Council ruled that no one could accept employment outside Herrnhut without prior permission from the members of the Helpers Conference, and the Moravians were reminded that they had not come here "for the sake of occupational advantage but rather for the sake of their consciences and the welfare of their souls." [61] With the increased diversification of the Herrnhut economy, a deliberate attempt was made to restrict the amount of such outside employment.

The neighboring communities of Herrnhut, meanwhile, were not clamoring for a supply of Moravian labor. Although an occasional employer in Hennersdorf or Oderwitz might wish to employ a number of the Brethren, the majority of employers regarded Herrnhut as an additional and unwelcome competitor in an already highly competitive economy. Moravians were generally employed only when the demand for labor could not be met by the community concerned, and when, furthermore, no labor supply was forthcoming from other neighboring settlements. A few cryptic entries in the records of Herrnhut suggest that outside work was not always available. In 1731, for example, the trades masters reported that it would not be easy to find work in Bernstadt since the people of Bernstadt had let it be known that "they wanted to starve out the Herrnhuters once and for all." [62]

In the seventeen-forties, following Zinzendorf's tightening of the regulations regarding choir segregation, outside employment was discouraged more strongly than before. Such a rule could not have been enforced had it not been for three factors: the continued diversification of the Herrnhut economy which further reduced the ranks of those unemployable within the community; the increased opportunities for Moravians to find work in one of the communities overseas, especially in Bethlehem; and the increased resistance of neighboring communities to the employment of Herrnhuters. During the seventeen-fifties and sixties Herrnhut was for the first time forced to depend upon outside labor to meet some of its own occupational needs. The expansion of the community's building program required many carpenters and masons, of whom only a few could still be found in the ranks of the Brethren. In 1756 close to 100 non-Moravian carpenters and masons were employed in Herrnhut, but the men were forced to eat and sleep outside Herrnhut in nearby Berthelsdorf.[63]

The need for non-Moravian employers and employees constituted only one bond between Herrnhut and the neighboring communities of the Oberlausitz. An additional tie is to be found in the trade relations which linked the Moravians to the economy of Saxony. Here the antagonism of the neighboring communities toward Herrnhut's economic growth came sharply to the fore. Unlike Bethlehem, Herrnhut found itself in an environment unfavorable to economic development. During the eighteenth century, trade and commerce in Saxony were still regulated by institutions which had emerged in the Middle Ages. As early as 1346 six of the major towns of the Oberlausitz had banded together into the *Sechs Städte Bund* in an attempt to preserve their common economic interests.[64] The guilds of the Six Towns' Federation jealously guarded their virtual monopoly of occupational opportunities, rigidly controlling wages as well as standards of craftsmanship.

In the early years of Herrnhut the masons and carpenters, many of whom had acquired guild status prior to joining the community, had attempted to form guilds in Herrnhut.[65] This step was regarded unfavorably both by Zinzendorf, who feared that such groups might be overly concerned with worldly matters, and by the guild organizations of the Six Towns, who were afraid that such independent groups might jeopardize their own authority. As early as 1726 Zinzendorf complained to the authorities of Zittau that their hatmakers were putting pressure on the Herrnhut hatmaker to leave the community and that they were circulating rumors designed to cast aspersions upon the poor man's character.[66] A year later the members of the tanners' guild in Bautzen rejected the application of a Herrnhut tanner for guild membership because the tanner in question wished to continue to ply his trade in Herrnhut.[67] Members of the various textile guilds in Bernstadt similarly refused guild membership to weavers, tailors, and cloth cutters in Herrnhut. The Herrnhuters were refused permission to use such guild-controlled facilities as the fulling mill of Bernstadt. Attempts were also made to prohibit and prevent by force, if necessary, the sale of goods made by nonguild members. By 1728 Zinzendorf had decided to prohibit Moravian membership in guilds based outside Herrnhut. During the same period guilds still existing in Herrnhut were gradually transformed into quasi-religious organizations and stripped of their original economic functions. Guild meetings continued to take place in Herrnhut but were devoted for the most part to love feasts in which hymn singing, prayer, and other forms of religious devotion constituted the main order of business.

The economic development of Herrnhut was fought continually by the Six Towns' Federation. In 1762 the Federation lodged a formal complaint with the Saxon Government. They complained that the village of Herrnhut had been paying disproportionately low taxes since it was still considered a rural area, that it had not created new economic opportunities but merely usurped existing ones of the towns, that its emphasis on communal property gave it unfair advantage in the accumulation of capital which did not exist in the towns where everyone abided by the laws of private property, that it was undercutting the price and wage regulations of the guilds of the towns, and that the frequent absence of members of the community abroad prevented them from doing their military service.[68] The government failed, however, to take any action on these petitions. Undoubtedly Herrnhut was not alone in threatening the economic powers of the Six Towns' Federation; a number of other "new" towns were also helping to undermine the position of the Federation.[69]

Although the Oberlausitz presented a highly competitive economy in which economic privileges gained centuries earlier were bitterly defended, Pennsylvania in the first half of the eighteenth century presented an economy which by comparison was still highly flexible and in which there was far more room for communities to prosper without necessarily stealing one another's markets. As a result Bethlehem's relations with neighboring communities in the Lehigh Valley were generally good. Levering reports that these communities "did not seem to take a sinister view of the prosperous advance made by the intelligent and united industry of the Moravians, or to become much excited by the bugaboo of peril to Protestant government through their presence and activities. . . ."[70]

Occasionally the evident prosperity of Bethlehem aroused the resentment of less thriving neighbors, particularly of those who also harbored antagonism to the religious values of the Moravians. For example, in 1746 a constable from one of the so-called Irish settlements to the north of Bethlehem lodged a formal complaint against the Moravians as "Sabbath breakers" for having cut grain on Sunday. It was not a general custom for Moravians to work on Sunday, but because of a very wet summer in which the first dry day in a long time happened to be a Sabbath, they had decided that such work in the fields was a necessity if they were not to starve the following winter. Thanks largely to the counsel and intervention of their own Justice of the Peace, Henry Antes, the whole matter was solved without any of the Moravians having to go to jail.[71]

The absence of deeply entrenched economic-interest groups in Pennsylvania thus facilitated Bethlehem's relations with non-

Moravians, whereas Herrnhut's relations with the Oberlausitz were constantly threatened by the hostile attitudes of the guilds and the Six Towns' Federation. These differences in the economic environment of the two communities played a crucial role in the subsequent development of Bethlehem and Herrnhut, enhancing adaptation to the secular world in one, but retarding it in the other.

X. FINANCIAL GROWTH
OF THE COMMUNITY

THE FINANCIAL TRANSACTIONS of the Moravians in Herrnhut were, as we have noted, subjected to detailed communal regulations during the early decades of the eighteenth century; no one could lend or borrow even a small sum of money without first obtaining permission from the Elders Conference. During the Sifting Period most of these controls were ignored. Indifference to financial matters came to be valued as an intrinsic good: "The whole of human creation thinks along materialistic lines, and only the favorites of the Saviour are able to do otherwise." [1] The conviction that "God will take care of his own" [2] was held so firmly that the Moravians gladly left all material concerns in the hands of their Saviour. This relaxation of controls had an adverse effect on the finances of the Brethren.

The financial situation was further aggravated during this period by the fact that the emphasis on the good religious life in turn made the Moravians far less willing to defer gratifications in other spheres of their daily activities. As a result the Herrnhut economy was forced to bear somehow the spiraling costs of a higher standard of living. Items which had once been considered luxuries now appeared on the Moravians' tables almost daily. "Ordinary people of this world eat white rolls and cakes only three or four times a year, whereas with us they appear on the table three or four times a week." [3] Expensive wines, coffee, tea, chocolate, and whipped cream, as well as a vast variety of spices and costly tobaccos came to figure prominently in the daily expenditures of the community.

Ostentatiousness was not restricted to food and drink alone; the choice of clothing underwent some striking changes during this period. Previously the women's clothing had been characterized by simplicity. The same dark dresses and snipe-bill shaped bonnets were worn by all. Only the color of the ribbons used to fasten their bonnets varied according to their respective choir affiliation: scarlet for the little children, crimson for the older girls, pink for the Single Sisters, light blue for married women, and white for the widowed. But during the time of the Sifting women began to appear in a great variety of dresses, petticoats, and bonnets frequently adorned with frills and intricate lace designs. The immigrants of humbler origin, having been daily reminded of the essential equality of all Brethren before God, were apparently no longer willing to dress in garments inferior to those of their aristocratic fellow worshippers. The religious excesses thus had been accompanied by a similar loosening of controls in the economic sphere. Patterns of conspicuous consumption were indulged in with little thought as to how the community could finance this new style of living. Zinzendorf aptly summarized the ethos of that period: "Our ethic was that of Mary Magdalene and we had not yet learnt how to play the role of Martha and deal with the world outside." [4]

In order to finance their extravagances the Moravians borrowed heavily with little regard as to how they might repay the interest incurred, let alone the principal.[5] Unfortunately the Moravians' penchant for detail and exactitude in the keeping of records was similarly disrupted during these years, so that it is impossible to gain any details on just how extensive the liabilities of the Moravians had become. Hamilton estimated that by the end of the time of the Sifting the Moravians had outstanding debts amounting to at least 300,000 florins.[6] This figure refers not just to Herrnhut but to the Unity as a whole; in the second half of the eighteenth century it becomes impossible to separate the financial histories of the two.

In the seventeen-fifties the Herrnhuters were in a precarious financial situation which had been worsened by the collapse of the settlement of Herrnhaag, founded by the Brethren during the early years of the Sifting. Repayment of the large debts they had incurred was out of the question; they had difficulty enough in finding the necessary funds to meet the interest due on the loans granted by various persons in Germany, Holland, and England.[7] Yet during this same period some funds were apparently still available for the support of an extensive building program. A house for the Widowers' choir was built in 1754, an annex to the Single Brethren's choir was completed in 1755, and the following year the Single Sisters were able to move into entirely new quarters of their own. The year 1757 saw the completion of a large building to be used for communal functions; two years later the new home of the Widows' choir was completed, while yet another building was added to those of the Single Brethren's choir in 1764.[8] The funds for this extensive building program were for the most part advanced by wealthy friends and benefactors, many of whom were willing to accept interest rates as low as one or even one-half per cent.[9] Since many of the new buildings provided for a much lower ratio of persons per room, the cause of this real-estate boom cannot be attributed simply to the needs of a growing population. Clearly the Moravians remained optimistic that the economic situation would soon improve and continued to depend more upon the goodness and wisdom of God than upon their own economic efforts.

No review of the financial history of the Brethren in Herrnhut can afford to ignore the role of the aristocracy in the Moravian economy. In addition to financing the building program, they played a crucial role in helping Herrnhut to weather the financial crises of the Sifting Period. Paulus Weiss contributed 40,000 talers in 1743; Dinah von Layrisch offered a similar amount in 1754; while in the same year Count von Gersdorf bequeathed his estates to the Moravian Church.[10] The von Damnitz, von Schachman, and von Wiedebach families all donated considerable sums of money and, in many cases, property to help pay off debts.

The number of persons residing in Herrnhut who could claim to be part of the nobility was never very large. In 1748, for example, there were eighty-seven such persons in a total population of 800.[11]

By 1759 there were 164 members of the aristocracy in a total population of 1,605 persons.[12] The fact that during these years the aristocracy constituted approximately ten per cent of the population of Herrnhut might not have been of such significance had it not been for the fact that these men and women, by virtue of their social position, were, as we have seen, frequently given important positions of leadership. They, therefore, found themselves in situations in which they could readily impress their values, ideals, and modes of conduct upon others.

The members of this class influenced the economic development of Herrnhut in a number of ways. On the positive side, their presence in the community helped to raise the overall standard of living. Accustomed to various social amenities, they saw to it that many of these were included in the life of Herrnhut. The roads of Herrnhut were paved, elm trees were planted alongside the highway leading to the Hutberg, and the water and sewage systems were improved. In the choir houses the arrival of new members of the nobility was frequently followed by improvements in the daily diet as well as in interior decorating.[13] This improvement in the standard of living in turn provided an outlet for a more varied pattern of production and consumption. The diversification of food and dress created a demand for new products and assured a ready market for such innovations.

Another consequence favorable to the economic development of the community was that members of the nobility created additional employment opportunities for the unskilled. The Brothers and Sisters employed by them as servants, most of whom had no skills, would not have been able to find employment readily elsewhere. But the most important contribution of this class to Herrnhut's economy was its provision of most of the community's capital. Without their support, Herrnhut could never have survived the hardships of its earliest years or the financial crises of the Sifting Period.[14]

The impact of the aristocracy upon the communal economy was

not always advantageous. Although they undoubtedly helped to raise the standard of living, at times they raised the patterns of consumption to heights that bore no relationship to what the community could afford. The enthusiasm with which, during the latter part of the seventeen-forties, the Sisters emulated their social betters turned out to have been a costly adventure which neither the individuals nor the community could subsequently find revenues to pay for.[15] An even more serious impediment to the economy was that the aristocracy was indirectly to blame for the shortage of certain skilled trades in the community. The educational system of the Moravians, which espoused and propagated many of the values typical of the nobility, was not one to encourage the young generation of Herrnhut to take up manual work. Recruitment of non-Moravians was complicated by the fact that Herrnhut "had become too aristocratic a place for many trades, so that the immigration of masons and carpenters declined because such persons could no longer fit readily into the social strata of the community." [16]

Finally, mention should be made of a factor whose influence was less easy to perceive but which ultimately had a far more adverse effect upon the economy than all the above mentioned. We refer here to the emotional and sensual character of their "Lebensgefühl" —the strong feudal elements in the aristocratic value system and the penchant for religious mysticism—which impeded the development of a rational attitude toward economic activity.[17]

The aristocrats' propagation of values inimical to economic development unquestionably had an adverse effect upon the economy of Herrnhut.[18] Yet, ironically, it was this same group who, more than any other, helped to restore financial life to the economy of Herrnhut after Zinzendorf's death, when clamoring creditors threatened bankruptcy proceedings. Strategic though their role was on the financial balance sheet of Herrnhut during the eighteenth century, the aristocrats' ultimate impact upon this little economy cannot be gauged in talers and pfennigs. It rests rather in the direction which they, as leaders of the community, gave not only to the economy but to the development of the Herrnhut community as a whole.

The time of the Sifting had left the Moravians in Herrnhut, as we have seen, with considerable financial liabilities which all but destroyed the economic assets so diligently accumulated during the pioneering years of the community. Moreover, Zinzendorf's refusal to hand over full responsibility for the financial affairs of Herrnhut even to such trusted aristocratic friends as de Watteville or von Damnitz meant that these affairs remained in a state approximating chaos until after his death in 1760.

One of the most critical issues discussed at the Synod of Marienborn, convened four years later, concerned the financial affairs of the Unity. At his death Zinzendorf had bequeathed his properties, including the estates of Berthelsdorf and Hennersdorf, to his three surviving daughters and one nephew. Yet it was equally clear that these same properties had already been pledged to meet the debts of the Church. In the end the situation was resolved by the Brethren paying a sum of 120,000 talers to Zinzendorf's heirs. The Moravians thus became the owners of the estate and at the same time assumed responsibility for all debts contracted by the Count in his furtherance of the Moravian cause, a debt which amounted to over one million talers.[19] Small wonder that Dürninger had refused to be held liable for the debts of either the Moravians in Herrnhut or those of the Unity as a whole.

In a desperate move to extricate themselves from these financial difficulties, the Moravians resorted to a number of devices to meet their obligations to their creditors. During the seventeen-sixties and seventies a number of attempts were made to socialize the industries of Herrnhut. In theory the private owner of such an enterprise was to receive one half the estimated value of his business, in return for which he pledged himself to hand over all future profits to the community. In practice, however, the financial difficulties in which Herrnhut found itself made it impossible to raise the capital necessary for communal acquisition of such enterprises. Had it not been for the good faith of the private-business owners, who for the sake of their religious convictions were willing to hand over their profits to the community, these attempts at socialization of the economy could never have taken place. Even so, the number of enterprises taken over by the community was small.[20] The fact that the community failed to play any part in the organization or supervision of the industries it had acquired would seem to corroborate our view that the Moravians were guided by motives of expedience rather than principle; at this point they were ready to use any means which might help to weather the financial straits in which they found themselves.

Five years later, at the Synod of 1769, further solutions to the debt problem were proposed. It was agreed that as a matter of principle the members of the Moravian Church "were morally bound to personally and individually stand for the debt." This decision proved difficult to enforce since many members felt that the Synod did not in fact have the power to dispose of an individual's property in such a manner. It was decided also to divest the Unity of property holdings against which heavy debts were laid and turn these over to individual settlements or private persons in an attempt to force them to shoulder these financial obligations.[21]

The problem of the Unity debt remained. A proposal to divide the debt among the various congregations, each to be responsible for its own share, was strongly opposed in Herrnhut. Even the modified proposal that the local congregations be held responsible not for the capital indebtedness but only for a share of the annual interest outstanding was resisted by the Herrnhuters to such a degree that Spangenberg and Reichel, both members of the newly created Unity Elders Conference, were assigned the task of persuading the members of the Herrnhut congregation to drop their resistance.[22] The Moravians in Herrnhut felt that they had already contributed to the best of their abilities to the finances of the Unity, and while they were willing to continue to stand for the debts of their own local congregation, they did not see why they should be taxed so heavily for debts incurred by the Unity as a whole. No immediate change of heart took place.

But two years later, in September, 1772, at an emotionally charged celebration of the fiftieth anniversary of the founding of Herrnhut, the Single Sisters took the first step toward recognizing the Unity debt as their own. Their statement stands as a testament to the resurgence of a spirit of religious dedication in which personal interests were clearly subordinated:

After weighing how we might be able in proportion to our slender means to contribute something towards lessening the debt of the Unity, i.e., our own debt, we agreed cheerfully to sacrifice and to dispose of all unnecessary articles, such as gold and silver plate, watches, snuffboxes, rings, trinkets and jewelry of every kind for the purpose of establishing a sinking fund, on condition that not only the church at Herrnhut, but all the members of the Church everywhere, rich and poor, old and young, assent to this proposal. This agreement, however, is not binding on those individuals who can contribute in other ways. Therefore, dearest Brethren and Sisters, let us not delay, but united in love, as one person, let us take the work in hand with courage and faith, either in the manner proposed now or in any other which may be deemed more eligible, and let us not be the last to show love and faithfulness to our Lord and His cause.[23]

As a result of this appeal the Herrnhuters' contributions grew to over 22,000 talers by the end of the same year.[24] For the time being the threat of bankruptcy was lifted.

Bethlehem, owing in part to the absence of any aristocracy, had not been exposed to the religious and economic excesses of the Sifting to the same degree as Herrnhut. Even Cammerhoff's attempts to introduce a more lavish style of living in matters of food and clothing were of short duration and met only limited approval. The financial transactions of the community were, even during the time of the Sifting, recorded with much more care, exactitude, and regularity than in Herrnhut. The Moravians in Pennsylvania were apparently less ready to entrust conduct of their finances to the Lord; the numerous account books stored in the Archives attest to their diligence in the keeping of accounts.[25] Even during the earliest years of the community every trade, agricultural division, business, and industry were required to and did in fact keep detailed accounts of their economic transactions. Thanks largely to the skills of Christian Örter, who combined the occupations of communal accountant and organist, these individual lists of raw materials and products were then entered onto monthly and annual balance sheets which provide a detailed picture of the financial state of affairs in Bethlehem at that time.

By 1761 the land owned by the Moravians, the value of which had been greatly enhanced by the agricultural efforts of the Brethren, was estimated to be worth over £12,000, Pennsylvania currency.[26] Only twenty years earlier the Moravians had paid less than a quarter of this sum for the purchase of the original 500 acres of the Allen tract in the forks of the Delaware and the 5,000 acres of the Whitefield tract, frequently referred to as the Barony of Nazareth.[27] The buildings, every one of which was constructed during this same period, were valued at £22,209/17/2. In addition to real estate, the General Economy in 1761 had in hand stock from the trades, the commercial enterprises, and the agricultural undertakings amounting to close to £10,000, almost one-half of which was derived from the products of the skilled craftsmen of the community. The total assets of the General Economy were valued at £50,486/10/8¾. It is typical of the American Moravians' concern for exactitude that not one farthing was omitted from this account.

During the same year the liabilities which the General Economy had incurred amounted to £20,114/6/11¼, three quarters of which consisted of borrowed capital. The net balance of assets over liabilities thus amounted to over £30,000. But it must be remembered that these £30,000 existed only in the account books of the Moravians; being intricately bound up with the real estate of the Brethren, they did not constitute a readily available fund of cash.

The English economic laws impeded the financial transactions of the Moravians as much as they hampered those of the American colonies as a whole. Spangenberg once remarked bitterly:

America is being sucked dry by England. Invariably more goods come here from the old countries than can be remitted from this side. As a result the local merchants are forced to go into debt and in the end to become bankrupt, or they are impelled to settle in cash. But from where are they going to obtain this cash? Formerly they got it through trade with the Spanish. But now the Spanish coasts are being so closely guarded and the ships of the English [colonists from America] can no longer slip through. As a result there is a shortage of cash everywhere, and the distress is heightened because paper currency is no longer to be permitted. That's how things are in the country, in New York as in Pennsylvania.[28]

During the year, May, 1760 to May, 1761, the income from the commercial enterprises of the General Economy, notably the inn, the country store, and the drugstore, totaled £1,173/10/4½. The trades brought in £1,819/15/5 and the agricultural products, including those of the mills, were assessed at £1,945/16/9½. The General Economy thus experienced an intake in one year of close to £5,000. At the same time the Moravians in Bethlehem were forced to spend £2,927/9/4¼ for food and clothing that could not be produced by the General Economy. The maintenance of the educational institutions of the community and support of those too old, too young, or too sick to work cost them an additional £5,567/11/5. It is clear that at this rate the community could never accumulate the necessary capital to repay debts already incurred, let alone to finance any major economic innovations in the future.

The Moravians, in Herrnhut as in Bethlehem spurred by their devotion to religious ideals, had clearly expended great effort in the development of communal economies that attained a considerable degree of self-sufficiency. In particular the industrial enterprises of the seventeen-fifties showed great promise. Why, then, did they fail to continue to develop along these lines? The reasons, which we shall examine later, are complex, but for the present one major factor may be singled out: the absence of any significant amount of capital formation in both communities.[29] The lack of such capital must be attributed largely to the ambivalence inherent in the religious ethics of the Moravians toward the accumulation of such funds. Zinzendorf, who had always regarded trade and commerce with suspicion, stated flatly that the Brethren's aim should be "to be reasonably well off but not rich, to be supported by diligence, industry, sensible institutions and luck, but never capital." [30] He was convinced that a concern with the accumulation of profits "rests assuredly not under divine providence, but under the direction of Satan." [31] At the Synod of Marienborn it was decreed that "the principle that all savings are held in trust for the Saviour should be deeply imprinted in the heart of all the Brethren." [32] This latter point of view did not, however, benefit the economic enterprises of the Brethren, since it was generally felt that all profits could best serve the work of the Lord by being donated directly to the support of missionary activities. Dürninger alone was enough of a businessman to see that if such profits were ploughed back into business they could then provide much greater financial support for missionary enterprises in the future, but his views failed to find support among the Brethren.

The missionary efforts of the Moravians thus tended to absorb what capital might otherwise have been used to further their economic ventures. It should be remembered, moreover, that Bethlehem's financial situation in 1760 reflected the work of only about 500 persons, who in turn had to support the other 800 so that they might be free to devote themselves on a full-time basis to the conversion of the heathen.[33] Given this loss of potential manpower, the community was severely hampered in accumulating any significant amount of capital.

XI. THE COMMUNAL ECONOMY ON TRIAL

BY THE SEVENTEEN-SEVENTIES the economic systems of Bethlehem and Herrnhut had come a long way. The array of occupations had become more diversified, the varieties of trades and industries pursued had multiplied greatly, and financial assets had also increased. The religious enthusiasm which had inspired so much of this devotion to work had at the same time greatly enhanced the financial standing of these communities. Were the Moravians now confronted with the same paradox already noted by their English friend John Wesley?

I fear that wherever riches have increased, the essence of religion has decreased in the same proportion. Therefore, I do not see how it is possible, in the nature of things, for any revival of true religion to continue long. For religion must of necessity produce both industry and frugality, and these cannot but produce riches. But as riches increase, so will pride, anger, and love of the world in all its branches.[1]

Evidence of the increased wealth of the two communities has been presented in preceding chapters. In both Herrnhut and Bethlehem one finds also a corresponding decline in the saliency of religious ethics. In Bethlehem a group of workers had noted in 1765 that:

(1) Our Saviour observes, that we have left our primitive simplicity. (2) That much conformity to worldly values has gradually insinuated itself into the conduct of our Congregation. (3) That in the way of our trade and business *profit is made a main matter and that in consideration thereof the Congregation principles are neglected.* (4) *That we study more how to get money and profit, than how to save our souls.*[2] [Italics mine.]

In Herrnhut a similar state of affairs had developed. The attainment of an adequate standard of living was becoming a prime concern, and the Synod of 1775 was forced to conclude that: "Nothing offends the authority of our dear Saviour in the community of the Brethren so much, as the bourgeois notion, that the attainment of a good police force and a high standard of living . . . constitute the raison d'être of our system."[3] The achievement of economic success was thus no longer a means toward the furtherance of the religious goals of the community; it was pursued as an end in itself. These secularizing influences of wealth might well have made themselves felt even earlier had it not been for the vast missionary and educational enterprises of the Moravians which severely restricted the possibility of individual or communal accumulation of capital. In order to understand more fully the manner in which such secular influences were infiltrated into these communities it becomes necessary to analyze separately the crises of maturity besetting Bethlehem and Herrnhut.

Pressures for Abrogation of the General Economy of Bethlehem

We have seen how, in spite of occasional setbacks, the General Economy of Bethlehem had by 1760 developed into a complex economic unit capable of sustaining over 1,300 persons in addition to supporting many missionary enterprises among the Indians. Yet only two years later this same economic system was no longer in existence. The communal aspects, which had been characteristic of this economic system for two decades, had vanished. The determinants of these changes were manifold.

One might hypothesize that the breakdown of the General Economy was likely to have been caused by the failure of this system to meet the economic needs of the community. Yet our data on the output of the economy have already indicated a considerable diversification of labor, industries, and products, and the analysis of financial statistics shows that the net assets of the community continued to grow. The annual balance of income over expenditures showed a deficit in 1759 only, a result of extensive building operations during that year, and indicated profits in both 1760 and 1761, the very time when the abrogation of this economy was being considered. That the community did not begin to go into debt until some years after the economy had been completely reorganized suggests even more strongly that the failure of the General Economy to meet the needs of the community cannot have been a cause of the changes that took place in 1762.[4]

Certain other economic factors did, however, contribute to the breakdown of this system. For example, the rate of economic growth fostered an increasing sense of wealth and prosperity among the members of the community. Sessler clearly recognized the importance of this prosperity factor as a cause of the ultimate breakdown of the General Economy when he stated that, "increasing prosperity was accompanied by a growing feeling of self-sufficiency and a waning sense of dependence upon the Economy for every enjoyment."[5] As a result some Moravians, more particularly those engaged in trade and commerce, had begun to resent some of the economic constraints put upon them by a communal economy. This does not necessarily imply that such persons had become more materialistic at the expense of their religious vocation, for most of them were convinced that they could better provide material support for the work of the missions by establishing independent businesses of their own. In K. G. Hamilton's opinion, even a religious community could not eradicate the profit motive permanently.[6] Sessler supported this viewpoint by pointing out that: "With the first measure of success, their individual instincts to appropriate, to hold, to possess and to dispense their profits according to their pleasure, asserted themselves."[7] Although other communities, notably those of the Hutterites and the Amish, have been far more successful than the Moravians in suppressing the profit motive, it would seem that such suppression is far more likely to create economic conflicts in nonagrarian communities which cannot readily isolate themselves from the outside world.

Certain inequities inherent in the occupational structure of Bethlehem also contributed to the abrogation of the General Economy. Frictions and dissatisfactions developed as a result of inequalities created under a system in which a relatively small core of craftsmen and agricultural workers was expected to support itself and also provide for the many missionaries and other members of the pilgrim congregation. Such grievances had been voiced as early as 1754.[8] Hostilities between the French and the British from 1755 to 1757 temporarily smothered most of this discontent. Unrest in Pennsylvania and distrustful attitudes toward the Moravians, who had refused to take part in the war, served indirectly to intensify the internal cohesion of the community. But when the hostilities came to an end and the community returned to a way of life no longer endangered by imminent military clashes, the same dissatisfactions that had been silenced for so long came once more to the fore.

Despite the Moravians' explicit emphasis on the dignity of all types of work, it was inevitable that in a community dedicated to the pursuit of missionary goals those occupations concerned directly with these ends carried greater prestige than those that supplied their material basis. In the early years of the community the situation was still sufficiently flexible to permit a considerable interchange of personnel, so that missionaries sent into the field would then return to pursue a trade in Bethlehem, and other artisans or even farmers might in turn leave their handicrafts to preach for a time in some distant community. But with the expansion of the economy and the greater diversification of labor interchanges became less and less desirable from a purely economic standpoint. Missionary work began to be assigned to professionals, and the craftsmen and agricultural workers in Bethlehem saw their own chances of carrying out such missions decline steadily. The economically productive workers, therefore, found themselves in a situation in which they had to provide for the economic support of persons whose jobs they aspired to but could rarely attain. Small wonder that some of them became discontented.

The growth of Bethlehem had brought with it a gradual decentralization of authority and a corresponding increase in the degree of autonomy of action granted to the economic branches. This freed the businessmen in particular from some of the earlier immediacy of religious sanctions and enabled them to consider issues from a more practical point of view. But it also intensified conflicts within the community as long as the leadership of Bethlehem remained convinced that economic issues must invariably be subordinated to the religious goals of the Moravians. Thus there had developed within the economic institutions of Bethlehem several important sources of strain and conflict. By themselves, these cannot, of course, explain the abolition of the economic system, but in conjunction with other factors they may well have accelerated such a change.

The choir system attenuated many of these conflicts. With the growing prosperity of the community, the Moravians in Bethlehem began to chafe more and more under the restrictions against independent action imposed upon them by the choir system. In the early years, when the men could not afford to house themselves, let alone their families, in separate dwellings, they welcomed the choir arrangement as an excellent solution to their problems. Now that the community was prospering they felt that they could begin to strike out on their own and provide homes for their families. There is no doubt that dissatisfaction with the choir arrangements soon began to color their attitudes toward the economic practices of the community, and thereby initiated further pressures for change of the status quo. The failure of the choirs, moreover, to socialize adequately the second generation to the ideals which had inspired their parents meant that there was growing up in Bethlehem a generation of young people who did not identify themselves with all the values cherished by their parents and who regarded many of the economic arrangements of the community as outmoded. Religious values do not appear to have played a crucial role in the breakdown of the General Economy. Although the religious spirit of the community had been declining, there was no abrupt change but a very gradual relaxation of the crusading enthusiasm of the early years, conditioned by economic and demographic developments of the past decade.

Pressures for the abrogation of the Bethlehem General Economy thus came from many sources. Changes in the social and economic structure of the community, many of which were the direct outcome of increasing prosperity, had created individual discontent with the status quo, and the religious enthusiasm of the early years had begun to wane. But these factors alone would not have created the necessary impetus for a total reorganization of the community. The catalytic element was Herrnhut's insistence in 1761 upon closer supervision and control of the financial, social, and religious affairs of Bethlehem, an insistence analyzed earlier as being engendered partly by the Germans' fear of secularization of the American community. In part, too, Herrnhut's action arose from the infiltration of a secular spirit into its own ranks, as a result of which Bethlehem was viewed not so much as a missionary center but as an important source of revenue for the Unity as a whole.

Some Moravians have argued that the abrogation of the General Economy can be explained quite simply by the fact that it was never intended to survive for very long, being conceived at the outset as a temporary expedient to cope with pioneer conditions in Pennsylvania. Yet our analysis of the documents relating to the early years of Bethlehem leads us to believe otherwise. The purpose of this community was to provide a missionary center for the activities of the Moravians, and this missionary goal was neither completely achieved nor abandoned after a period of only twenty years. The characterization of the General Economy as an interim measure thus appears to be an ex post facto rationalization. Certainly one

finds no evidence of the prevalence of such a viewpoint prior to
1759.

The argument that, had the General Economy been intended as a
permanent arrangement it would surely also have been introduced
into other Moravian settlements, is similarly unconvincing. It ignores the fact that the Moravians never did develop a single plan to
cover all their settlements. The plan for the General Economy was
clearly intended to cope with the special conditions of eighteenth-
century Pennsylvania; its abrogation, however, cannot be attributed
to a radical change in conditions in the American colony. The only
major alteration which occurred was the sudden change of heart in
the ranks of the German leaders of the Unity. In view of this it is
almost ironic that the final ratification of the plan to abolish the
General Economy of Bethlehem was left not to men but to God.
Recourse was made to the lot, which validated the proposal.[9]

The Reign of Exclusivism

The year 1762 marked a major turning point in the economic history of Bethlehem, for it brought with it the abrogation of the General Economy and the introduction of a system of enforced exclusivism which lasted for over eighty years. The alteration of the existing
economic structures centered on reallocation of property, decentralization of the financial organization, and redefinition of the limits of
communal responsibility for the support of missionary work.

The most radical changes concerned the reallocation of property,
under which private property once more took the place of communal ownership. In order, however, to enable the community to
meet its financial obligations for the support of education and of social welfare for the destitute, a number of economic enterprises, including agriculture, were retained by the community. They constituted in effect a modified form of socialized economy:

All the agricultural branches deliver their produce of grain, livestock,
butter, eggs, flax, hemp, etc., to meet the daily needs of the children's
institutions and the workers and pilgrims. The same holds true for the

baker, the miller, the clothmaker, the potter, the soapmaker, the drug-
gist, as well as supplies of sugar, coffee, tea and similar items provided
by the store. The nailsmith contributes nails, the farrier lends his skills,
the forester a cord of wood and the builders their due in wood and
planks.[10]

Although agriculture, the mills, the communal stores, and the inns
remained socialized for some years to come, most of the trades appear to have been taken over by individuals who simply contributed
a certain amount of their products to the community.[11]

In most cases the master craftsmen had the option of acquiring
the capital assets of the trade venture, including house, fixtures, and
tools. Occasionally they were also able to obtain a small amount of
capital on which they paid interest to the community. But whereas
capital had been in short supply under the General Economy, it became even more scarce under a system of private enterprise where
each business needed separate funds. The land on which these properties were situated continued to belong to the community, which
held it in trust for the Unity lest private ownership of land might
encourage speculation and profiteering, thereby endangering the religious ideals of the Moravians.[12] Under the new system persons
working in the socialized branches of the economy or employed by
master craftsmen in private business became wage earners. Those
who continued to reside in the choirs had now to pay for their bed
and board.

With regard to property and capital accumulated during the years
of the General Economy, it was decided by the members of the
newly constituted Economic Conference, most of whom were residents of Herrnhut, that there could be no reimbursement or compensation for individual members of the General Economy. Under
the Brotherly Agreement, signed by all members in 1754, it was concluded that all property belonged to the Unity as a whole, "as
worldly attorneys for the Saviour." [13] Neither the individual nor the
community of Bethlehem, therefore, had any right to such property,
or for that matter to any capital compensation for services rendered

during this period.[14] Individual capital deposited in the community fund could of course be reclaimed as before. But now the community had to pay interest on capital not immediately retrieved.

Under the new financial arrangements for the first time the community granted financial autonomy to the individual trades, the different branches of the socialized industries, and the choirs, all of which had now to render separate financial statements. Moreover, the economic and financial affairs of Bethlehem were separated completely from those of Nazareth and the Upper Places.[15] Missionary work was organized and financed primarily from the Unity in Herrnhut. The return to the family meant that the educational institutions of Bethlehem no longer had to provide free education, care, or food to the children of the community. Those who made use of the existing schools were expected to pay for them. These changes in the missionary and educational functions of Bethlehem significantly reduced the economic obligations of the community.

The individual was thus once again granted the right to the fruits of his labor and in return had to pay for whatever social services he required. There was no major property revolution for the simple reason that the only significant type of property in Bethlehem at that time, namely land, remained, as before, in the hands of the Unity. But once the individual had been given the right to a wage or a salary the opportunity to accumulate wages and to acquire capital presented itself to him for the first time. The community had hoped that by socializing some of the major economic enterprises it could assure itself of an income adequate to cover the expenses incurred in providing necessary social services for its members. Yet throughout the ensuing decade expenditures generally exceeded income, and the total assets of the community were more than offset by liabilities.[16] Consequently, Bethlehem was in no position to increase its contribution to the amelioration of the Unity's debt, as the German Moravians had so fervently hoped it would.

The financial difficulties encountered by Bethlehem in the second

half of the eighteenth century had clearly not been anticipated by
von Marschall and his colleagues. Many of the changes which
sounded reasonable enough on paper broke down in practice. Thus,
although the Church decreed that the Moravians in Bethlehem, who
were now wage earners, must pay for their children's educations, it
turned out that many parents simply could not afford to do so. The
Elders had failed similarly to gauge the extent to which Bethlehem
would be severely hampered by a shortage of cash. Since the community could not sell the most valuable asset it had—land—and the
socialized industries were unable to make a profit, the community
was forced to borrow capital in order to pay off its immediate debts
as well as provide the salaries of Brethren working in the direct employment of the community.[17] The situation was further aggravated by the fact that even the borrowing of capital had become a
difficult venture. In part, this may be attributed to the general political unrest in Pennsylvania, but it was undoubtedly complicated still
further by the fact that the people in Pennsylvania, puzzled by the
recent changes in Bethlehem's economy, frequently preferred to
withhold loans until there was evidence of greater stability.[18]

Underlying these specific economic problems was a far deeper
crisis. What distinguishes this new period from the time of the
General Economy is the decline in the willingness of the individual
to contribute to the community above and beyond what he was
legally required to do. The Brother or Sister no longer felt under an
obligation to contribute to the economic welfare of the community,
since the community in turn had abrogated most of its original obligations for the welfare of the individual. The days of religious zeal
and devotion to a common cause were gone. Instead there emerged
more and more clearly a spirit of rational calculation of economic
rights and obligations. Religion was being gradually relegated to a
separate sphere in which man's beliefs no longer had an immediate
impact upon his economic actions.

The very fact that during the seventeen-sixties the private industries fared far better than those still under communal control gives

some indication of the extent to which the religious enthusiasm which had inspired the great economic output of the General Economy had now ceased to play a significant role in the life of the worker.[19] Those remaining in the socialized economic enterprises felt less and less incentive to work hard. Those working for themselves at least were able to substitute a desire for personal profit in place of the original religious goals, but those working for the community had no such incentive.

The leaders of the Unity were thus forced to recognize, belatedly, that the community could no longer hope to make a profit out of enterprises run along socialized lines. In 1766 most of the remaining branches under this type of control were handed over to private citizens. The farms were leased to individual tenants. Only the commercial establishments, the store, and the inns remained under direct communal ownership.[20] Finally, as a result of deliberations at the Constitutional Synod of 1769, it was decided to abolish all remaining communal ownership of economic enterprises. More importantly, the property of the Unity was from this time on clearly separated from that of the community of Bethlehem. The communal authorities constituted a "congregational diacony," which purchased from the "general diacony" of the Unity approximately 4,000 acres of land, as well as all buildings and industries formerly owned by the Unity, for a total purchase price of £29,000, Pennsylvania currency.[21] Since Bethlehem was in no position to make such payment in cash immediately, the arrangement in effect meant that Bethlehem simply assumed these £29,000 as its share of the Unity's debt. The fact that the land was not sold to Bethlehem outright, but under a perpetual lease arrangement, meant that the Unity continued to exert important control over the manner in which such land could be used, let, or disposed of.

Within a decade of the initial steps taken to terminate the communal economy of Bethlehem, the reorganization of the community had progressed so far that not a single industry was left in the hands of the community. Private enterprises were beginning to show profits, and the Church Elders in Germany were hopeful that Bethlehem would soon be able to make a significant financial contribution to ameliorate the economic plight of the Unity as a whole.

Throughout this process of reorganization a deliberate attempt had been made to regulate and restrict the actions of the residents in Bethlehem in such a way as to eliminate any further secularization or Americanization of the community. The right to settlement in Bethlehem continued to be granted exclusively to members of the Moravian Church. No one was permitted to leave the settlement without first obtaining permission from the communal authorities, and the community retained the right to force undesirable members to leave, as well as to refuse new members.

Even more significant were the rules adopted by the members in 1771, which explicitly restricted the economic freedom of the individual.[22] No business could be started, no industry expanded, or subsidiary enterprise developed without the consent of the Moravian authorities. Apprentices could not be hired or fired without the consent of the Church. The same restrictions applied to the borrowing or lending of capital. Finally, any tendencies toward monopoly of trade or business were explicitly discouraged as not befitting the Christian ideal of doing unto others as you would have done unto yourself. Under the perpetual-lease system anyone buying a house had, in the name of himself and his future heirs, to reserve for all time the right of the owner of the land; the Unity had to approve or disapprove any sale, lease, mortgage, or gift of such property. Bond had to be deposited by all buyers of property, which would be forfeited should this agreement ever be broken. Furthermore, the leases contained a "limitation" clause under which the owner of the building who, for one reason or another, was forced to sell back the property to the administration of Bethlehem, was obliged in cases of disagreement about the selling price to accept the valuation made by an independent committee. This valuation, however, could not exceed a maximum-sale price fixed in the original lease. In this way the Church hoped to discourage its members from participating in any real-estate speculation.[23]

In their zeal to keep Bethlehem free from the taints of the secular world, the authorities in Germany had endeavored to combat these dangers by enforcing a rigorous system of exclusivism under which economic activity in Bethlehem, although in private hands, was nonetheless to be subjected to severe communal controls. What the authorities failed to realize was that this system could hope to function effectively only as long as certain values and norms were adhered to by the members. Once this ceased to be the case for a significant number of persons, the system lost its raison d'être. Thus the authorities, by enforcing a system which became more and more alien to the Bethlehem residents' way of life, helped to precipitate the very outcome they had so desperately tried to forestall—the transformation of a self-sufficient religious community into an American town, a place in which the hallmark of the community was to be found in business and commerce and not in religion or in missionary enterprises.

These changes did not occur overnight. Indeed, the system of exclusivism was retained, as we have seen, until well into the nineteenth century. The majority of Moravians, although not particularly pleased with the new arrangements, had no clear vision of an alternative solution, and so preferred to accept the status quo, albeit with grumbling. At the same time the community was already beginning to lose a significant part of its population, men and women who found the institutions of Bethlehem too restrictive and who preferred to seek a living elsewhere. Evidence of this trend is to be found in the population statistics which document the stagnation of the community. At the height of the General Economy Bethlehem numbered over 1,300 persons; by 1765 this population had shrunk to 593 persons. In 1771 there were only 560 persons, and this figure rarely rose above 600 throughout the remainder of the eighteenth century.[24] The system of exclusivism was being maintained only at the price of communal vitality and growth.

Even before the end of the century other forces of change were beginning to make themselves felt within the invisible walls of Bethlehem. The struggle for the political independence of the colonies was not a matter in which the Moravians played a leading part, but at the same time they could not cut themselves off from the revolutionary ideas about man's freedom and right to social and economic equality which were being discussed even in the rural backwaters of Pennsylvania:

A supplement of the newspaper was handed to us and it was desired that we read it publicly: It is an address of the Congress to the people. We were disturbed by the fact that we would have to impart such things to our Brothers and Sisters in the congregation, things in which after all we have no part, nor do we care to have a part.[25]

The people of Bethlehem were, therefore, forced to re-examine many of the values they had for so long taken for granted.

Even before any new movement toward modification of the policy of exclusivism, by now so patently out of step with the tide of events in Pennsylvania, could take root, the overseers of the Unity in Europe decided once more to intervene and thwart any such movement. John F. Reichel was asked to undertake an official visit to Pennsylvania to "help guide the affairs" of Bethlehem during these turbulent years.[26] This guidance took the form of a considerable tightening and centralization of the authority structure of the community. The Church Elders were convinced that they were merely taking necessary precautions, "making things fast and going into snug winter quarters for the vicissitudes of an inclement season." [27]

By the beginning of the nineteenth century economic conditions in Pennsylvania were improving rapidly. Now that the political future of the nation had been assured, there developed a renewed vigor in economic activities: merchants and businessmen could at last plan ahead with a considerable degree of confidence in the future. Yet in Bethlehem the rigid rules governing the expansion of any economic enterprise were still being enforced. But whereas the younger men and women of the congregation had in the seventeen-eighties and nineties accepted the economic status quo, even though they chafed under some of the regulations, the new generation was rapidly exhausting its level of tolerance and actively clamoring for a revision of the old arrangements. These demands for change might well have gone unheeded for some time had it not been that the financial conditions of the community were deteriorating rapidly. The first two decades of the nineteenth century witnessed not merely stagnation, but decline in the economic system of the community. The choirs had long ceased to be economically self-sufficient, and those communal enterprises leased out to individuals showed heavy losses. By 1815 the community's debts totaled more than $42,000.[28]

In 1818 the Church Elders were finally forced to concede defeat and to embark upon the gradual abrogation of the system of exclusivism.[29] The economic restrictions upon private enterprise were among the first to be lifted. These developments were soon followed by a remarkable increase in economic activity and success in the community. Businessmen realized that the system of exclusivism was doomed at last, and that it was merely a matter of a few years before other regulations, including those governing the lease or sale of property, would similarly be abolished. In 1844 the lease system was indeed terminated; as a result property could for the first time be sold to both Moravians and non-Moravians. The period of exclusivism was at an end. Where one hundred years earlier militant religious immigrants from Germany had willingly subordinated all economic interests to shared religious goals, American businessmen, industrialists, and laborers, dedicated to the values of private enterprise, were now laying the foundations for a capitalist giant of the steel industry.

Pressures for Modification of the Economic Structure of Herrnhut

After Zinzendorf's death the leaders of Herrnhut had decided, as we have seen, to socialize the major branches of industry, trade, and commerce so that all economic profits could be made immediately available to the community as a whole. A number of factors prevented the full-scale socialization of the Herrnhut economy. In the first place the community did not have the necessary capital to buy such industries or trades from individuals; most of this socialization of the economy could, therefore, take place only as long as Moravians, motivated by their religious values, were willing to hand over their businesses to the community. The Moravian leaders would appear also to have failed to realize that such a total reorganization of the economy would require a considerable degree of bureaucratization if businesses were to be run efficiently. But instead of recruiting and training administrative personnel for such posts, they merely reiterated their belief in the fundamental efficacy of the norms of brotherly love, trustworthiness, and honesty as the best means to sound business practice.

By 1769 it was clear that the drive to socialize the economy had failed to provide the expected increase in revenue. Not only had it yielded no financial benefits, but it had apparently brought in its wake a number of other negative consequences. In the General Synod of 1769 the following faults of the system were singled out for special mention: a tendency to laziness, lack of thrift, and non-attention to detail, excessive expenditures on building, too costly expansion of plant facilities, and, finally, excessive concern for the provision of employment for all and sundry without due regard to the efficiency of the enterprises involved. The Synod concluded:

The workers came to shun real work and in matters of food, drink and clothing they behaved in a manner inconsistent with their origins. . . . *That we now live in palaces instead of huts, that we have become a secular body of the State instead of obtaining our inspiration from the Cross, is not to our credit but to our ruin.*[30] [Italics mine.]

The tendencies to ape the aristocracy without regard to the economic feasibility of such a step, so prominent during the years of the Sifting, had apparently still not been fully eliminated. The imposition of a socialist organization on the economy during the seventeen-sixties had failed to take into account the fact that such communal socialism can function effectively only as long as the members are fully committed to the communal goals. But the religious enthusiasm which might have provided such a unity of purpose was no longer as militant as it had been in the pioneering years of Herrnhut. Under these circumstances it was inevitable that most of the workers should take more than they contributed and should accept the social and economic benefits of the community without feeling obligated to return any favors.

The Synod of 1769, therefore, decided to reverse its earlier position and to place all economic enterprises in private hands. This was to extend also to the choir industries which, until that time, had never paid any salaries to their workers. Under this new arrangement the members of the community would thus have "the privilege of contributing to the needs of the community and the Unity as a whole out of their very own purse." [31] The manifest reason for this return to private enterprise would appear to have been the failure of the socialized industries to yield adequate revenues. A less obvious but nevertheless important incentive was provided by the fact that communal ownership of property had begun to create a number of tax problems with the Saxon government. Since the community was in no position to raise additional revenue for tax purposes, it may well have been convenient simply to return these industries to private control.

By returning to the individual his freedom in economic enterprise it was hoped that Herrnhut could once again recapture the spirit of simplicity, thrift, and self-sacrificing devotion to religious ideals so characteristic of the community in its earliest years. But such wishful thinking failed to take into account that during the past few decades the social structure of Herrnhut had changed drastically. The band of devout immigrants who had freely chosen to work together under the charismatic leadership of Zinzendorf was no more. In their stead now stood a second and even third generation whose membership in the Herrnhut community had been an accident of birth, and they could look forward to earning their livings with a degree of security unknown to their forefathers. The leaders of the Synod of Marienborn failed to realize that these young people demanded greater economic freedom not to serve better the religious goals of the community, but for its own sake. The clock, in short, could not be turned back.

By 1775 it was clear that the economy of Herrnhut, freed from communal constraints, was in an even worse position than before. Most of the private enterprises were in financial straits, and the community, shorn of any income sources of its own, was in no position to provide assistance. Meanwhile the debts of the community continued to increase.[32] Not only were the Moravians without any capital to tide them over lean years, but they lacked the necessary experience to run businesses of their own.[33] Most of them had grown up under the choir system, and, as a result, their experience in the conduct of economic affairs had been minimal. Certainly they were no match for craftsmen and merchants of the Oberlausitz, who from earliest childhood had been exposed to the realities of a highly competitive economy. True, these same men had only a few years earlier been demanding greater economic independence, but their ardor for the values of private enterprise cooled all too rapidly once they had become aware that enthusiasm alone could guarantee economic solvency, let alone success.

As a result of the deliberations of the Synod of 1775, the economy of Herrnhut was transformed into a loosely knit federation of communal and choir "diaconies," each with its own treasury.[34] The Proceedings of this Synod make it clear that the impetus for federation of these separate economic units was a purely religious one. The aim was to provide mutual brotherly assistance so that if one trade or choir suffered great losses it could, nevertheless, be carried by those economic branches which had managed to accumulate some profits. Any attempt at rationalization of the economic or financial structure of the community on economic grounds was absent. Under this system the individual was once again assured social and economic security in return for his or her labor for the benefit of the whole community.

Not only was this economic system still intact at the end of the eighteenth century, but it continued unchanged until 1893, at which time some attempt was made to provide for a less centralized system of economic control.[35] Such an economic system, in which the religious norms of brotherly love and helpfulness overruled all considerations of economic efficiency or utility, could be maintained only as long as the members of the community continued to uphold the religious values underlying the system. The longevity of this economic regime is a testament to the continued dominance of the sacred over the secular among the Moravians of the Oberlausitz.

We have seen how the economic systems of the two communities developed, expanded, and battled for survival. In both the religious enthusiasm which had inspired so much activity in the earliest years of the communities declined somewhat after the first few decades. After a brief and unsuccessful trial, private property in Herrnhut was once more subordinated to strong religious and social controls. The primacy given to the religious and social goals of the community effectively thwarted any secularization of the German settlement. But in Bethlehem prosperity attained under a communal economy merely accentuated the desire for personal autonomy in economic affairs. Private businesses were soon flourishing, while the communal economy was going into debt. Imperceptibly the Moravians in Bethlehem had come to separate their economic and social roles from their religious role. By the mid-nineteenth century Bethlehem was a prospering American city, many of whose citizens happened to subscribe to the Moravian religion, whereas Herrnhut was still a Moravian community, whose religious character continued to be reflected in its social and economic organization. Its economy was as different from the rest of the Oberlausitz as it was from the economic system of its sister community of Bethlehem, whose organization had once so closely mirrored its own.

CONCLUSION

IN THE PRECEDING chapters the changing institutions of Herrnhut and Bethlehem have been portrayed in some detail. We have shown that in the middle of the eighteenth century the religious values and imperatives of the Moravians dominated all the structures of the community. The central emphasis placed upon the cultivation of personal piety had led to the development of a vast body of ethical precepts which spelled out in detail the conduct deemed appropriate to any given situation.

The social institutions of the two communities centered around the choirs, which provided their members with communal living quarters, food, clothing, and employment, and shouldered full responsibility for the care and education of the members' children. The choirs had largely taken over all functions traditionally associated with the nuclear family. The explicit subordination of family loyalties to those of the choirs bears ample testimony to the degree to which the concern with religious goals dominated and overruled all other considerations.

The penetration of religious values into the economy of Herrnhut and Bethlehem significantly shaped the course of economic development. Christ was regarded as the sole owner of man's possessions, and the community and the choirs were mere administrators of God's wealth. The community, moreover, had the right to determine what occupation a man should pursue. In theory the Moravians upheld the sanctity of private property, and technically never appropriated the worldly goods of their members. But in Bethlehem the concepts of a Christian communitarianism were for a time interpreted literally and led to a communal sharing in production as well as consumption. The community took care of all material needs of a member in return for his labor and the fruits of his labor. By effectively preventing the immigrant from making use of the few possessions he had brought with him, the Moravians destroyed the foundations upon which a system of private property could be meaningfully built. The occupational structures of the two communities were dominated by skilled craftsmen. The social structure of Herrnhut differed from that of Bethlehem in one important respect: it included a small but significant number of individuals from the ranks of the German aristocracy.

In the middle of the eighteenth century the political institutions of the Moravians showed no clear line of demarcation between sacred and secular authority. The functions of decision-making were diffused among the various institutions of the community, and little structural differentiation of authority was to be found either in Herrnhut or Bethlehem. Theoretically, Christ, as Chief Elder of the community, had supreme authority over secular and sacred affairs. In practice, the extensive use of the lot to ascertain the Saviour's will on a given issue gave a central place to theocratic authority in communal affairs and acted as an important check on the development of democratic rule in Bethlehem and autocratic rule in Herrnhut.

A hundred years later, the overwhelming majority of the citizens of Herrnhut and Bethlehem still adhered to the same religious beliefs and ethics which had been such a source of strength to the founders of these settlements. But in every other respect the two communities of 1850 bore little resemblance to their eighteenth-century antecedents and even less to one another. In Herrnhut the choir system had been preserved, but membership in the choir was now based upon voluntary acceptance of such an arrangement. The choirs had shed most of their social and economic functions, and responsibility for the care and education of the community's children had reverted to the family. Although the total membership of the choirs represented a minority of the people in the community as a whole, they formed a religious elite which continued to play a central role in the activities of Herrnhut. In Bethlehem the choirs had vanished altogether, bequeathing to posterity only a Widows' Pension Society and a group of handsome and unusually large buildings, ill suited to the housing needs of the nineteenth-century residents of the community.

The economic institutions of Herrnhut had been transformed into a loosely knit federation of communal and choir "diaconies," each with its own treasury, but pledged to provide mutual assistance. The norms of Christian brotherliness rather than the pursuit of profit continued to guide economic conduct. The economic institutions of Bethlehem, on the other hand, had shed all traces of religious communitarianism. They were now guided exclusively by the norms of American capitalism. In 1850 the government of Herrnhut rested in the hands of a religious elite, most of whom also held leading positions on the executive council of the Moravian Church. In Bethlehem local government was entrusted to a burgess and nine councilmen, all of whom were elected by the voting citizens of the community, whether or not they happened to adhere to the Moravian faith. And the lot was still being used in Herrnhut at a time when it had been all but abandoned in Bethlehem.

In short, whereas the institutions which had once attested to the dominance of the religious factor in both communities—the choirs, the communal economy, and the rule of Christ through the lot— had persisted in Herrnhut, they had ceased to exist in Bethlehem, being replaced by economic, political, and social institutions of a purely secular character. Not that Herrnhut was static: on the contrary, we have documented numerous instances of changes taking place in this community. But none of these changes seriously threatened the dominant value system of the community or succeeded in transforming the major social, political, or economic institutions of the settlement. In Bethlehem they did just that.

These changes in the value system and social structures of Herrnhut and Bethlehem reflect as a common trend the gradual secularization of these Moravian settlements. Having separated the various dimensions of social change with which this study deals, we now find it possible to define secularization more precisely. From a sociological perspective, secularization may refer to one or more of the following: a decline in the salience of religious ideas and a corresponding rise in the importance of economic, social, or political ideas as determinants of the content of the communal value system; a rationalization of conduct with reference to nonreligious values; a process of status and role differentiation whereby the religious status is broken down into three or four statuses and roles so that it becomes but one segment of an individual's status set; a structural differentiation of institutions, involving a reallocation of functions once subsumed under the dominant religious institution to separate economic, social, or political organizations; a reallocation and redistribution of social resources with reference to nonreligious values; a realignment of personal motivations and interests toward nonreligious ends. In sum, secularization involves a redefinition of the domain of the sacred and a consequent delimitation of the role of religion as a determinant of a society's cultural values, its social structure, and the personality characteristics of its members.

In order to define the process of social change more precisely one needs to identify not only the polarities but the specific sequence of events that occurred between 1750 and 1850. From one perspective the interplay among various components of social structure and culture may be seen as a continual process. Yet it is possible to isolate certain analytically significant sequences within this broader system of interdependent relationships, and to show their workings in greater detail.[1] We will limit ourselves in this context to a review of the major determinants of the differing rates of secularization observed in the two communities.

The central clue to the differences in the rates of secularization is to be found in the interaction between religion and the economic, political, and social conditions of the two communities. Religious beliefs and ethics alone fail to yield an adequate explanation as to why social change was so much more pronounced in Bethlehem than in Herrnhut. For in neither community did the content of these religious values change significantly. Deets, in his study of social change among the Hutterites, claimed that the main clue to the persistence of the social order was to be found in the persistence of beliefs.[2] Clearly this generalization does not apply to the Moravians, whose social structures changed even though their religious beliefs remained the same.

Moreover, since the religious norms of the Moravians did not endorse a single and consistent mode of ethical conduct, even the direction of change cannot be properly explained with reference to religion per se. The very selection of a particular religious ethic justifying one mode of human conduct rather than another—diligent pursuit of economic activities rather than subordination of work in favor of passive contemplation of the glories of salvation—was made on other than religious grounds. The fact that the Protestant ethic gained at best an ambivalent foothold in Herrnhut while it flourished in Bethlehem cannot be attributed to differences in the religious ideas or values of these two communities. It was a consequence of differences in their class structure, differences which made such a work ethic far more palatable to the skilled craftsmen of Bethlehem aspiring to middle-class status (if they had not already attained it) than to the aristocracy of Herrnhut. Where individuals are offered a choice of ideologies, or of ethical interpretations of an ideology, they will tend to identify themselves with those values which conflict least with their existing value commitments.

Max Weber, unlike Marx, was convinced that religious ideology did not derive directly from class position, but that it was a means of interpreting that position.[3] The same may be said of the religious ideology of the Moravians. Yet when Weber examined their ideology by reading only sources dealing with Herrnhut, he failed to recognize that the absence of a religious ethic congruent with a rational orientation toward economic action was not peculiar to Moravian religious beliefs as such, but was a reflection rather of the class composition of the leadership of Herrnhut at that time.

The presence of an aristocracy in Herrnhut and its virtual absence from Bethlehem were strategic in that the aristocracy tended to identify itself with an interpretation of the religious ideology of the Moravians not generally subscribed to by members of the other social classes. The aristocracy provided economic support for the communal enterprises of Herrnhut without which the community could not have survived; and the influence of the members of the aristocracy in the affairs of Herrnhut was magnified through their role as formal leaders of the community. Thus differences in the systems of social stratification of the two communities, due in large measure of Zinzendorf's policy of selective migration, were one strategic determinant of the differences in the rates of social change observed.

Nor did the aims of the religious interests of the Moravians necessarily coincide with their objective consequences. The interaction between the work ethic and practices prescribed by religion and the underlying economic potentials produced sharply different results in the two communities. In Bethlehem the Brethren's devotion to religious goals enhanced not only their spiritual welfare but, given the generally favorable economic conditions, also their material welfare. The accumulation of wealth thus became objectively possible and represented an alternative interest in guiding the conduct of the Moravians. Once the accumulation of wealth became not a means to the furtherance of the religious goals of the community but an end in itself it threatened the very values without which it could not have arisen.[4] The actions of the Moravians arising from their orientation toward religious goals thus in turn created economic processes which reacted so as to alter the very values which had precipitated them.[5]

In Herrnhut, because of relatively unfavorable economic conditions, the secularizing effects of wealth were never experienced to the same degree as in Bethlehem. The Protestant ethic, even if it had been adhered to in Herrnhut as rigidly as it was in Bethlehem, could not alter this basic difference between the two communities. Under such conditions hard work could not produce wealth in

Herrnhut and could hardly fail to produce riches in Bethlehem. This major difference in the character of social change in the two communities must, therefore, be attributed not to their religion as such, but to the interplay between religiously motivated actions and underlying differences in the prevailing economic conditions.

Finally, Herrnhut and Bethlehem were, as a result of their emphasis on missionary work, exposed to the secular influences of the outside world. Indeed, so fundamental was the Moravians' devotion to missionary interests that they ignored the fact that members were thereby being exposed to secular values for considerable periods of time. Indeed, the more active their missionary enterprises the more they were exposed to the values of the secular world. Under such circumstances their attempts to create religiously exclusive communities could never be wholly successful, for, unlike the Hutterites or the Mennonites, their very adherence to their religious goals prevented them from withdrawing into a self-contained little society, and so evade the dangers of competing value systems.

In Bethlehem the American Revolution places the Moravians in the center of political action, not only intensifying their contacts with the world beyond the walls of Bethlehem but exposing them to values diametrically opposed to their own. In Herrnhut the political values of the larger society to which the Moravians were exposed offered no such threat to the religious values of their community. On the contrary, by their overall emphasis on the sanctity of tradition and loyalty to the past, they merely endorsed the Moravians' commitment to the status quo. These differences in the political environment to which members of the two communities were exposed thus constitute another determinant of the different rates of secularization observed.

Although unanticipated and unintended consequences of interests are to be found in all societies, the Moravians seem to have been the victims of more than their share of such "sociological blindness." This blindness appears to have operated primarily in connection with the identification of consequences of religious interests for other aspects of the social structure of their communities. In part it may be attributed to the fact that the Moravians' religious values explicitly enjoined them from any concerns with the objective consequences of their actions for their material well-being. It may be attributed also to the fact that their exclusive concern with religious ends tended to distort their analysis of the conditions and means whereby such ends could be achieved. True, seen from the point of the religious values basic to their dominant interests, their actions even during the Sifting Period were rational in the sense that they represented a straining toward consistency in the relation of action to values.[6] But their actions were nonrational when viewed with reference to the requirements of the community as a whole. They frequently obstructed the realization of economic and social goals, which, though not paramount at the time, nevertheless had to be realized if the community was to survive.

Herrnhut's far more pronounced failure to anticipate the objective consequences of action must be attributed to the fact that in the American community, primarily because of differences in economic and social conditions, the Moravians' commitment to religious values was never so exclusive or absolute as in Herrnhut. The less exclusive men's commitment to religious ends, the more likely are they to perceive the latent consequences of adherence to such values for the achievement of nonreligious ends.

It has been noted that to the extent to which an ideology fails to meet the interests of categories of individuals in the society it will generate conflicts which, when not resolved by mechanisms of social control, will lead to changes in the social structure, or even the value system of the community. Our examination of differences in the social change of Herrnhut and Bethlehem leads us to posit further that it is not enough that the interests of individuals fail to be met satisfactorily, for in both communities the Moravians found that many of their interests—for social intercourse, for economic reward, or for social prestige—were not being satisfied. The difference thus lies not in the extent to which individual interests failed to be realized, but in the fact that in Bethlehem people had a considerable objective opportunity to change the situation, and perceived that they did, whereas in Herrnhut they had little such chance. It was thus much easier for forces of social control to be effective in checking personal discontent in Herrnhut than in Bethlehem. One can conclude that neither the social structure nor the value system of the society is likely to change unless there are actual or perceived conflicts between its component elements and there exist, objectively as well as subjectively, the facilities to resolve these conflicts.

Our study of the secularization of these communities leads us to conclude that it is not possible to single out either economic or religious determinants of social change as having what Weber termed "a law of development and a compelling force entirely their own." [7] At any given point one institutional order may have greater primacy in determining changes in the social structures than the other institutional orders. In Herrnhut the religious institutions had and were able to retain such primacy for nearly two centuries; in Bethlehem primacy shifted from the religious to the economic institutions in less than a hundred years. But this was a product of the interaction of concrete social structures and specific historical circumstances, not of any inherent tendencies in the institutional factor as such. In tracing the historical development of the institutions of Herrnhut and Bethlehem, we have tried always to document the nature of the interdependence among their structural attributes and processes, not to take these characteristics of specific institutional orders as given. By analyzing the social processes responsible for the occurrence of specific connections between the structural attributes of these institutions, we have attempted to account for the patterns of secularization observed in these Moravian settlements. Differences in the antecedent and concomitant economic, political, and social conditions of the two communities thus altered the consequences of the religious values of the Moravians for conduct in such a way as to promote the secularization of the American community while retarding it in the German one.

Zinzendorf, after his temporary exile from Herrnhut in 1736, is said to have exclaimed, echoing Archimedes: "Da mihi locum et movebo mundum." [8] (Give me a place and I will stir the world.) He was given a place—Bethlehem—only it did not stir the world in quite the manner the Count had anticipated, being known to us today primarily for its steel industry rather than its missionary enterprises. To this day at Christmas time a giant star is erected to shine down on this town, illuminating a massive complex of steel mills, in the shadow of which still stand the choir houses of the Brethren in silent testimony to the religious enthusiasm of a bygone age. Five thousand miles to the east, Herrnhut, all but forgotten and ignored by the twentieth-century world, was able to perpetuate until the first World War the kind of religious community the Count had striven so hard to realize in Pennsylvania.

NOTES

THIS BOOK is based on my doctoral dissertation ("Communal Pietism and the Secular Drift: A Comparative Study of Social Change in the Moravian Communities of Bethlehem, Pennsylvania, and Herrnhut, Saxony, in the Eighteenth and Early Nineteenth Centuries," Columbia University, 1965). Printing costs and the reader's convenience have, however, necessitated a considerable reduction in its annotation and documentation. Reference has occasionally been made to the Dissertation Copy, which may be consulted in the Columbia University Library or through the Microfilm Services of Ann Arbor, Michigan.

Abbreviations Used in the Notes

MA Beth   Moravian Archives, Bethlehem, Pennsylvania
MA Hh   Moravian Archives, Herrnhut, Saxony
TMHS   *Transactions of the Moravian Historical Society*

Introduction

1. See Peters, *All Things Common: The Hutterian Way of Life;* and Hostetler, *Amish Society.*

2. See Bestor, *Backwoods Utopias;* and Vallier, "Production Imperatives in Communal Systems" (unpublished Ph.D. dissertation, Harvard University, Cambridge, Mass., 1959).

3. Weber, *The Protestant Ethic,* pp. 131, 135, 248.

4. For an elaboration of my primary sources see the Introduction to the Bibliography.

5. The concept of social system, following Parsons, refers to any system generated by a process of interaction between two or more actors. The actors may be individuals, or they may consist of collectives. They interact as role players whose orientation to each other is defined with

reference to their shared norms. Talcott Parsons and Neil J. Smelser, *Economy and Society* (Glencoe, Illinois, The Free Press, 1956).

6. For a more detailed discussion of the concepts of values and social structures see Talcott Parsons and Edward A. Shils, *Toward a General Theory of Social Action* (Cambridge, Harvard University Press, 1951), pp. 114–50, 159–89. The concept of institution is used here to refer to a complex of norms and values which have been institutionalized into regulatory patterns governing a particular substructure of the community: social, economic, political, or religious. In this sense institutions may be said to refer both to the normative and the structural elements of a given subsystem of the community. In this particular usage of the term we depart from Parsons, who has generally restricted the concept of institutions to refer only to the complex of norms and not the corresponding substructure within which these norms are incorporated.

7. For a more detailed discussion of the early history of the Moravian Brethren see Brock, *The Political and Social Doctrines of the Unity of the Czech Brethren;* and Müller, *Geschichte der Böhmischen Brüder,* Vols. I–III.

8. Zinzendorf, a member of the high nobility of Saxony, was born in 1700 and raised by his grandmother, the Countess of Gersdorf, whose salon was a frequent meeting place for the leaders of German Pietism. In 1722 he married Erdmuthe Dorothea, Countess of Reuss, who bore him twelve children. Christian Renatus, his only son to reach maturity, succumbed to a lung ailment at the age of twenty-five. Zinzendorf died in 1760. For a detailed biography of this complex man see Beyreuther, *Der junge Zinzendorf, Zinzendorf und die sich allhier beisammen finden,* and *Zinzendorf und die Christenheit.*

9. For an account of the years immediately preceding the founding of Bethlehem see Hellmuth Erbe, *Bethlehem,* pp. 11–18; and Johannes Plitt, Denwürdigkeiten aus der Geschichte der Brüder Unität, Vol. III (unpaginated MS), MA Beth.

Chapter I: Beliefs and Practices

1. Since our central purpose is to define the implications of religious beliefs and practices for human conduct we shall not attempt here to

provide a theological interpretation of their doctrine or a history of the development of their dogma. For examples of such histories see de Schweinitz, *History of the Unitas Fratrum;* Cranz, *Alte und neue Brüder-Historie.* Theological treatises include Betterman's *Theologie und Sprache bei Zinzendorf* and Sawyer's *The Religious Experience of the Colonial American Moravians.* For an elaboration of the sociological perspective see Weber, *The Protestant Ethic,* pp. 97–98.

2. Hutton, *History of the Moravian Church,* p. 483.

3. For a more detailed discussion of the religious beliefs of the *Unitas Fratrum* see Brock, *Political and Social Doctrines,* pp. 84–97.

4. Schwarze, *John Hus,* p. 148.

5. de Schweinitz, *The Moravian Manual,* p. 97.

6. Zinzendorf, having discovered Comenius's *Ratio Disciplinae,* is said to have remarked, "I could not peruse the lamentations of the old Comenius . . . without adopting the resolution: I will, as far as I can, help to bring about this revival . . . though I have to sacrifice my earthly possessions, my honors, my life. . . ." Quoted in de Schweinitz, *History of the Unitas Fratrum,* p. 605.

7. Quoted in Herpel, *Zinzendorf über Glaube und Leben,* p. 34.

8. Jüngerhaus Diarium, April 4, 1758, MA Hh, quoted in Uttendörfer, *Zinzendorf's religiöse Grundgedanken,* p. 10.

9. Jüngerhaus Diarium, May 25, 1759, MA Hh, quoted in Uttendörfer, *Zinzendorf's religiöse Grundgedanken,* p. 93.

10. Sawyer, *The Religious Experience,* p. 28.

11. Quoted in Betterman, *Theologie und Sprache,* p. 12.

12. Much has been written about the Sifting Period by both Moravians and non-Moravians, but whereas most Moravian historians tend to belittle, gloss over, and underestimate its importance (see the works of Cranz, J. T. Hamilton, Hutton, Levering, and Uttendörfer), non-Moravian scholars have tended instead to exaggerate its significance by assuming that the values manifested during the Sifting Period were characteristic of the Moravians throughout the eighteenth century. Ritschl, upon whose work Weber relied almost exclusively in his interpretation of the religious ethic of the Moravians, is especially guilty of taking a part for the whole. But others, including Knox, Sessler—and even Sawyer, who makes much of his objectivity while at the same time referring to events of the Sifting Period as "shocking," "distasteful,"

"unseemly," and "disgraceful"—show similar tendencies to let value judgments pass for historical fact. Beyreuther, who provides one of the most objective appraisals of the Sifting Period, makes it clear that its adequate evaluation can probably never be made since the Moravians systematically destroyed many of the documents crucial to the time of the Sifting. Beyreuther, *Zinzendorf und die Christenheit,* p. 230.

13. Zinzendorf's Berliner Reden an die Frauen, April 27, 1738, MA Hh, quoted in Uttendörfer, *Zinzendorf's religiöse Grundegedanken,* p. 104.

14. Hutton, *History of the Moravian Church,* p. 274.

15. Cammerhoff's "Epistola" (fifteenth letter) to Zinzendorf, MA Hh, quoted in Sessler, *Communal Pietism,* p. 163.

16. Herrnhaag, founded by the Moravians in Wetteravia in 1738, was constructed on a lavish scale. But the luxurious style of life pursued by the members of this community was short-lived. Only twelve years after its founding, Herrnhaag suffered a total financial collapse. J. T. Hamilton, *A History of the Church,* pp. 119–27; Sessler, *Communal Pietism,* pp. 156–81.

17. Sessler, *Communal Pietism,* p. 163.

18. "Litaney zu den Wunden des Mannes," reproduced in Sessler, *Communal Pietism,* pp. 235–38.

19. *Ibid.*   20. *Ibid.,* p. 235.

21. Date recorded was July 26, 1745 as quoted in Uttendörfer, *Zinzendorf's religiöse Grundgedanken,* p. 105.

22. Sawyer, *The Religious Experience,* p. 143.

23. Uttendörfer, *Zinzendorf's religiöse Grundgedanken,* p. 151.

24. Synodal Verlass, December 6, 1740, p. 18 as quoted in Uttendörfer, *ibid.,* p. 152.

25. Sawyer, *The Religious Experience,* pp. 127–29. When the adoration of Christ reached its peak during the Sifting time, Christ came to be spoken of as a father as well, and God retreated into the background as a kind of grandfather.

26. For a perceptive biography of this Moravian leader see Gerhard Reichel's *August Gottlieb Spangenberg, Bischof der Brüderkirchen.*

27. J. T. Hamilton, *A History of the Church,* p. 4.

28. For a more detailed discussion of Zinzendorf's role in the Pennsylvania Synods see Sessler, *Communal Pietism,* pp. 20–71.

29. *Ibid.*, p. 220.

30. J. T. Hamilton, *A History of the Church*, pp. 220–21.

31. *Ibid.*, p. 337.

32. See Weber, *The Protestant Ethic*, p. 313, where he argues that the striving for enjoyment of salvation in this world "meant a weakening of the inhibitions which protected the rational personality of the Calvinist from his passions."

33. Knox, *Enthusiasm*, p. 410.

34. Uttendörfer, *Zinzendorf's Weltbetrachtung*, pp. 36–37.

35. Wagner, *Die Handlung Dürninger*, p. 21.

36. Zinzendorf's Eventual Testament, December 27, 1738, quoted in J. Plitt, Denkwürdigkeiten, Vol. I (unpaginated MS), MA Beth.

37. Hermann Plitt, *Zinzendorf's Theologie*, p. 381.

38. See Uttendörfer, *Wirtschaftsgeist*, p. 477, footnote 151.

39. Sessler, *Communal Pietism*, pp. 100–20.

40. H. Erbe, *Bethlehem*, pp. 91–92.

41. de Schweinitz, *The Moravian Manual*, p. 97.

42. Emile Durkheim in *The Elementary Forms of the Religious Life* (London, George Allen and Unwin, Ltd., 1915), p. 226, has advanced the thesis that religious rituals, although "their apparent function is to strengthen the bonds attaching the believer to his God, at the same time really strengthen the bonds attaching the individual to the society of which he is a member, since the God is only a figurative expression of society." One does not have to accept his view that God is "only" a figurative expression of society to uphold his thesis concerning the social function of religious ritual.

43. Such "Memorial days" included August 13, the day on which a "Baptism of the Spirit" led to a new covenant of peace and the signing of the statutes of Herrnhut in 1727; and November 13, the day on which in 1741 Christ accepted the Chief Eldership of the Church. See de Schweinitz, *The Moravian Manual*, pp. 119–44.

Chapter II: The Emergence of Communal Government

1. J. T. Hamilton, *A History of the Church*, pp. 30–31.

2. *Ibid.*, p. 31.   3. *Ibid.*, pp. 35–36.

4. Letter of Johann von Zeschwitsch to Zinzendorf, May 3, 1725, MA Hh, quoted in Uttendörfer, *Alt-Herrnhut,* pp. 16–17.

5. J. T. Hamilton, *A History of the Church,* pp. 36–37.

6. Dober, *Beschreibung und zuverlässige Nachricht,* pp. 11–22.

7. For details of the Brotherly Agreement and the Precepts and Prohibitions see Müller, *Zinzendorf als Erneuerer der Brüderkirche,* pp. 97–118, where the two documents are reproduced in full.

8. Uttendörfer, *Alt-Herrnhut,* p. 27.

9. Müller, *Zinzendorf,* pp. 3–4.

10. Seigneurial Precepts and Prohibitions, Nos. 4, 17–19, 33; Statutes of the Brotherly Agreement, Nos. 12, 20, 37; MA Hh, quoted in Müller, *Zinzendorf,* pp. 97–116.

11. Uttendörfer, *Alt-Herrnhut,* p. 27. The status of Elder, as perceived by Zinzendorf at that time, constituted a position of secular authority and was modeled far more closely after that of the common village Elder, typical of local government in rural Saxony, than after any ancient Christian conception of this role.

12. "Verlass der weltlichen Direktion des Ortes Herrnhut," April, 1728, MA Hh, quoted in Uttendörfer, *Alt-Herrnhut,* p. 26.

13. Dober, *Beschreibung und zuverlässige Nachricht,* p. 29.

14. Herrnhut Diarium, September 22, 1734, MA Hh, quoted in Uttendörfer, *Alt-Herrnhut,* pp. 31–32. The proceedings of the meetings of the Judiciary Council, 1729–1740, have been preserved in the Herrnhut Archives.

15. Uttendörfer, *Alt-Herrnhut,* p. 31.

16. *Ibid.,* p. 32.   17. *Ibid.,* pp. 64–65.

18. Memorandum of Moscherosch to Zinzendorf, February 3, 1743, MA Hh, quoted in Uttendörfer, *Alt-Herrnhut,* p. 60.

19. The failure to develop an autonomous economic administration had one decided advantage. It greatly facilitated the subordination of economic activities to the dominant religious goals of the community by leaving the ultimate powers of decision-making in economic affairs in the hands of the men who were also most instrumental in formulating the overall policies for the community as a whole.

20. Uttendörfer, *Alt-Herrnhut,* p. 29.   21. *Ibid.*   22. *Ibid.*

23. Müller, *Zinzendorf,* pp. 7–8.

24. J. Plitt, Denkwürdigkeiten, MA Beth.

25. Renkewitz, *Zinzendorf*, pp. 71–73; J. T. Hamilton, *A History of the Church*, pp. 97–98. No official minutes of the proceedings of this conference appear to have been kept. Although a number of eye-witness accounts have been preserved, including those of Zinzendorf and Spangenberg, none of these gives a detailed factual account of the events of the day, most of them being devoted to expressions of amazement and gratitude that Christ should have permitted his election to this office.

26. Brock, *The Political and Social Doctrines*, p. 79.

27. For an excellent historical account of the status of Bishop in the Moravian Church see Kenneth G. Hamilton, "The Office of the Bishop in the Renewed Moravian Church," TMHS, XVI, Part I (1953), pp. 30–58. My discussion draws heavily on this article.

28. *Ibid.*, p. 34.   29. *Ibid.*, p. 36.   30. *Ibid.*, p. 44.

31. J. T. Hamilton, *A History of the Church*, p. 76.

32. *Ibid.*, p. 98.   33. *Ibid.*, p. 112.

34. For an elaboration of his views on this point see the Proceedings of the Seven Pennsylvania Union Synods, MA Beth, Vol. I (1742).

35. J. T. Hamilton, *A History of the Church*, p. 114.

36. *Ibid.*, p. 152.   37. Burkhardt, *Die Brüdergemeine*, pp. 80–81.

38. J. T. Hamilton, *A History of the Church*, p. 153.

39. Quoted in *ibid.*, p. 157.   40. *Ibid.*, p. 159.

41. See Uttendörfer, *Alt-Herrnhut*, pp. 27–32.

42. Sessler, *Communal Pietism*, pp. 156–57.

43. Members of the aristocracy held positions of secular power in the community far out of proportion to their percentage of the total population. In part, this is simply a reflection of the number of offices held by the Count himself. But even when one excludes Zinzendorf, one finds that members of the aristocracy held up to fifty per cent of the positions on the Judiciary Council, as many as thirty-five per cent of the offices of the Helpers Conference, and up to eighty-five per cent of the positions on the Board of Administrators and the Board of Directors. Yet, during this same period the aristocracy never accounted for more than ten per cent of the total population of Herrnhut. Although Uttendörfer gives no tabulation of such statistics per se, he does bring together inventories of the membership of the various committees, indicating name, occupation, and social position of these persons. It becomes possible, therefore, to de-

termine the representation of various groups among the power-holders of the community. Cf. Uttendörfer, *Alt-Herrnhut,* pp. 27, 29, 30, 32; Uttendörfer, *Wirtschaftsgeist,* p. 12. Moreover, Bötticher's history of the aristocracy of Upper Lusatia makes it possible to trace the history of every member of the aristocracy who resided in Herrnhut during the eighteenth century. Bötticher, *Geschichte des Oberlausitzer Adels,* Vol. III.

44. "Report of Count Max von Zinzendorf upon his visit to Herrnhut in 1748," MA Hh, quoted in Uttendörfer, *Wirtschaftsgeist,* pp. 15–16.

45. Uttendörfer, *Alt-Herrnhut,* pp. 173–74.

46. For an excellent discussion of the character of the aristocracy of Herrnhut see Beyreuther, *Der junge Zinzendorf,* pp. 9–43.

47. Uttendörfer, *Wirtschaftsgeist,* p. 266.

48. Gerth and Mills (eds.), *From Max Weber,* p. 296. My classification of types of authority is based upon Weber's threefold conception of such types.

49. J. T. Hamilton, *A History of the Church,* p. 200.

50. *Ibid.,* p. 202.   51. *Ibid.*

52. *Ibid.,* p. 203. Hamilton elaborates upon the deliberations of this Synod in considerable detail. See especially pp. 200–15.

53. *Ibid.,* p. 204.

54. *Ibid.,* pp. 218–19; K. G. Hamilton, *John Ettwein,* p. 5.

55. J. T. Hamilton, *A History of the Church,* pp. 218–19; Burkhardt, *Die Brüdergemeine,* pp. 83–101.

56. J. T. Hamilton, *A History of the Church,* p. 218.

57. Sessler, *Communal Pietism,* p. 79.

58. *Büdingische Sammlung,* Vol. III, p. 235.

59. "Diarium seit der arrivée der See—und Pilgergemeine in Bethlehem am 21. Juni 1742," MA Hh, quoted in H. Erbe, *Bethlehem,* p. 19.

60. Bethlehem Diarium, June 25, 1742, MA Beth.

61. H. Erbe, *Bethlehem,* p. 30.

62. Letter of Spangenberg to Zinzendorf, October 8, 1755, copy in MA Beth.

63. Levering, *A History of Bethlehem,* p. 182.

64. H. Erbe, *Bethlehem,* p. 34.

65. According to entries in the Communal Diary of Bethlehem the Communal Council met weekly, whereas Uttendörfer in *Alt-Herrnhut,*

p. 29, notes that the Communal Council of Herrnhut met only when the need arose, which was at best sporadically.

66. H. Erbe, *Bethlehem*, p. 31.

67. Sessler, *Communal Pietism*, pp. 20–71.

68. As Vicar General of the Bishops the occupant of this office had the authority to ordain Bishops from any one of the three tropes, Moravian, Lutheran, and Reformed, which formed part of Zinzendorf's Church of God in the Spirit. As Vicar of the Eldership for America he was also the chief spiritual leader of Moravians in America. Levering, *A History of Bethlehem*, p. 177. The term "Oekonomus" was more frequently used to describe the office of the Chief Supervisor of Bethlehem than was the aforementioned official episcopal title, which fell into disuse after Zinzendorf's failure to unite Lutherans, Reformed, and Moravians into one church in Pennsylvania.

69. Levering, *A History of Bethlehem*, pp. 175–77.

70. Peter Böhler to Zinzendorf, March 9, 1759, MA Hh, quoted in H. Erbe, *Bethlehem*, p. 31.

71. H. Erbe, *Bethlehem*, p. 31.

72. The Diarium Bethlehem as well as the Choir Diaries frequently refer to Spangenberg as Joseph.

73. Moravian historians vary considerably in their interpretation of this step; some have argued that Spangenberg himself had requested that he be returned to Germany for health reasons, others have regarded it as a triumph of the leaders supporting extreme emotionalism in Herrnhut, who found in Cammerhoff a man who, unlike Spangenberg, shared their values and gloried in the bloodiness of the Saviour's wounds. Having been unable to find a single letter in which Spangenberg requests a transfer, even though it is true that his wife, but not he, had been seriously ill, I tend to agree with Erbe that Cammerhoff's appointment was carried out at the insistence of Zinzendorf and had nothing to do with Spangenberg's own desires in the matter. H. Erbe, *Bethlehem*, p. 33; cf. Levering, *A History of Bethlehem*, p. 185; Sessler, *Communal Pietism*, p. 183; G. Reichel, *Spangenberg*, Chapter XI.

74. H. Erbe, *Bethlehem*, pp. 97–103; Levering, *A History of Bethlehem*, pp. 223–24.

75. H. Erbe, *Bethlehem*, p. 98.

76. Gerth and Mills, *From Max Weber*, p. 297.

77. "Resolutiones und Verfügungen an das Bethlehemer Oekonomat, vom 2. April 1761," MA Beth.

78. That this fear was not altogether unjustified is borne out by the fact that Spangenberg's initial reaction to the need for the drastic changes suggested by German Moravians, like Köber, was to insist that Bethlehem must remain true to its original missionary goals even if this had to be at the expense of certain economic considerations. See Spangenberg's reply to the London Conference, dated November 11, 1760, quoted in H. Erbe, *Bethlehem*, pp. 128–29.

79. H. Erbe, *Bethlehem*, pp. 136–43.

80. Levering, *A History of Bethlehem*, p. 418.

81. *Ibid.*, pp. 419–20.

82. J. T. Hamilton, *A History of the Church*, p. 219.

83. K. G. Hamilton, *Ettwein*, p. 84.   84. *Ibid.*, p. 85.

85. Levering, *A History of Bethlehem*, pp. 680–81.

86. *Ibid.*, p. 681.

Chapter III: The Use of The Lot

1. This was true not only of critical tracts written to discredit the Moravians, such as (Anonymous) *Haupt-Schlüssel zum Herrnhuterischen Ehe-Sacrament;* Finley, *Satan Stripped of His Angelick Robe;* but also of discussions supposedly favorable to the Moravians, such as Mortimer's *Marrying by Lot: A Tale of the Primitive Moravians.*

2. For an interesting discussion of the use of the lot and other chance devices in various societies see Vilhelm Aubert, "Chance in Social Affairs," *Inquiry,* II (1959), pp. 1–24. The Old and the New Testaments contain several references to the practice of the lot: Joshua 10:13–21, dealing with the division of land among the tribes of Israel according to the lot; II Samuel 2:1, where David seeks the Lord's guidance as to whether he should go into the land of Judea, and if so, to which city; Proverbs 16:33, "The lot is cast in the lap, but the whole disposing thereof is of the Lord;" Proverbs 18:18, "The lot causeth contentions to cease and parteth between the mighty;" Acts 1:23–26, "And they gave forth their lots; and the lot fell upon Mathias, and he was numbered with the twelve apostles."

3. For other cross-cultural references to the use of the lot see Gataker, *Of the Nature and Use of Lots;* Huizinga, *Homo Ludens;* Cohen, *Chance, Skill and Luck.*

4. Verlass der Interims-Arrangement Konferenz vom 14. Juni 1762, MA Beth.

5. de Schweinitz, *The Moravian Manual,* p. 97.

6. Cranz, *Alte und neue Brüder-Historie,* Part XI.

7. Hutton, *A History of the Moravian Church,* p. 178.

8. Edward Rondthaler, "The Use of the Lot in the Moravian Church" (Paper read before the Wachovia Historical Society, MA Beth), p. 3.

9. J. T. Hamilton, *A History of the Church,* pp. 2–6.

10. The history of the local government of the Oberlausitz fails to provide evidence of resort to the lot, with the exception of its occasional usage in the selection of persons to some minor office such as secretary of a local guild. See Pescheck, *Geschichte der Industrie und des Handels in der Oberlausitz;* Knothe, *Urkundliche Grundlagen zu einer Rechtsgeschichte der Oberlausitz;* Jecht, *Untersuchungen zur Gründungsgeschichte der Stadt Görlitz.*

11. In the period under consideration the lot came to be used with such frequency that it becomes virtually impossible to compile any statistics on its use. The records of councils and committees cannot always be relied upon to make due note of the use of the lot. Thus a check of the material in the Bethlehem Archives revealed that in cases where the lot had apparently been employed this fact might be recorded in one source but not in another dealing with the same event. Proceedings of the Helpers Conference during the seventeen-fifties, for example, frequently refer to a use of the lot; this is not mentioned in either the Bethlehem Diarium or the Choir Diaries, which leads one to suspect that in other instances a specific use of the lot may not have been recorded at all. But even if one were to take the available information on such usage as reliable, the sheer task of tabulating the information would take months, if not years, to complete. In the Bethlehem Archives recorders generally indicated the employment of the use of the lot by an asterisk. But even with this shorthand designation the task of sifting all the available material for references to the use of the lot would take more time than the reliability of the information thus obtained would seem to warrant.

12. Letter of Grassmann to the Brethren in Pennsylvania, December 6,

1742, MA Hh, quoted in Uttendörfer, *Alt-Herrnhut,* pp. 174–75.

13. Uttendörfer, *Wirtschaftsgeist,* p. 250.

14. The nature of the Moravian choir system is examined in detail in Chapters IV–V.

15. Minutes of the Helpers Conference, January 10–11, 1752, MA Beth.

16. Verlass der Ältesten Konferenz, June 15, 1754, MA Hh, cited in Uttendörfer, *Wirtschaftsgeist,* p. 214. In Bethlehem the separation of the community into pilgrim and local settlements, which in effect determined whether an individual was to be a missionary or merely to support a missionary by means of his trade or agricultural skills, was in many cases determined by the lot. H. Erbe, *Bethlehem,* pp. 23, 30.

17. Protocolle des Gemeinrats 1730–1735, MA Hh, *passim,* quoted in Uttendörfer, *Alt-Herrnhut,* p. 29; Rondthaler, "The Use of the Lot," p. 5, MA Beth; H. Erbe, *Bethlehem,* p. 24; J. T. Hamilton, *A History of the Church,* p. 69; de Schweinitz, *The Moravian Manual,* pp. 107–8.

18. The site for Bethlehem was ratified by the lot. See Levering, *A History of Bethlehem,* p. 61. The decision to abandon the General Economy of Bethlehem was similarly validated by the lot. H. Erbe, *Bethlehem,* p. 134. The erection of a large new house for the Single Sisters in Herrnhut took so many years because in the beginning the lot rejected each proposal. Verlass der Ältesten Konferenz, May 1 and 13, 1743, MA Hh, cited in Uttendörfer, *Alt-Herrnhut,* p. 93; H. Erbe, *Bethlehem,* p. 30; Sessler, *Communal Pietism,* p. 143; K. G. Hamilton, *Ettwein,* p. 63.

19. Uttendörfer, *Alt-Herrnhut,* p. 100; see especially the minutes of the *Richter's Kolleg* in the Herrnhut Archives; Burkhardt, *Die Brüdergemeine,* Part II, Chapter 6; also Proceedings of the various General Synods, especially those of 1764 and 1769, MA Beth.

20. Ritter, *History of the Moravian Church,* p. 118.

21. J. T. Hamilton, *A History of the Church,* p. 116; Uttendörfer, *Wirtschaftsgeist,* p. 250.

22. G. Reichel, *Spangenberg,* pp. 67–68; H. Erbe, *Bethlehem,* p. 30; see also the Minutes of the Helpers Conference and of the various economic committees during the seventeen-fifties, MA Beth.

23. Protokolle der Interims-Arrangement Konferenz vom 6. Juli 1772, MA Beth.

24. *Büdingische Sammlung,* Vol. I, p. 521.

25. *Ibid.,* Vol. II, pp. 783, 802.

26. My purpose here is not to malign the character of the Count or to denigrate the leadership of Herrnhut or Bethlehem but merely to indicate that what was manifestly regarded as an expression of divine will nevertheless was open to human manipulation.

27. Only very rarely was the "preliminary" question of whether or not a given problem should be put to the lot submitted to the lot in the eighteenth century. Nor can it be argued that a blank at this time left God the option to say nothing at all. For in such a case the Lord's silence on a given matter was in itself an answer, generally interpreted as a sanction for doing nothing at the present, and, therefore, quite distinct from a situation in which a question was not put to the lot at all.

28. Letter of Ettwein to Nathaniel Seidel, May 24, 1772. Ettwein Papers No. 1145, MA Beth, quoted in K. G. Hamilton, *Ettwein,* p. 73.

29. In one case concerning the election of two candidates to the Helpers Conference in Herrnhut in 1734 only three names were submitted along with *nine* blanks. Zinzendorf is known to have opposed the candidacy of two of the three persons nominated. The lot's verdict: two blanks. Uttendörfer, *Alt-Herrnhut,* pp. 29–30.

30. I am not implying that the Moravian use of the lot was in itself a submission of communal decisions to a game of chance. For it is clear that the Moravians adhered to this practice only as long as they were convinced that it was a genuine expression of God's will. I do believe, however, that the interpretation of this expression of God's will left considerable room for human manipulation.

31. K. G. Hamilton, *Ettwein,* pp. 73–74.

32. Letter of Ettwein to John de Watteville, Ettwein Papers No. 1216, MA Beth, quoted in K. G. Hamilton, *Ettwein,* p. 75.

33. Wagner, *Die Handlung Dürninger,* pp. 21–22.

34. Frohberger, *Briefe über Herrnhut,* p. 111.

35. If there was a strong social consensus in the community that supported the personal beliefs of a Brother he was more likely to ignore the verdict of the lot. Thus Immanuel Nitschmann felt free to "decline wedded bliss at this time" because the members of the Bethlehem community were fully aware of the fact that he could not support a family at this time, nor was there room for additional married couples; K. G. Hamilton, *Ettwein,* p. 81. In the case of Zinzendorf's daughter's selection

as a missionary familial obligation was sufficient to bolster her refusal. "She did not have Mama's permission," Sessler, *Communal Pietism*, p. 46. Only a very few persons had the independence of spirit to overrule the lot when the general consensus in the community supported the lot's verdict. Dürninger for one, was able to overrule the lot successfully in a number of cases in which he regarded the employment of the lot as an unwarranted infringement of the freedom necessary to the conduct of his economic enterprises; Wagner, *Die Handlung Dürninger*, p. 92.

36. Robert K. Merton, "Social Structure and Anomie," *Social Theory and Social Structure* (rev. ed., Free Press, 1957), p. 148.

37. For a detailed functional analysis of the lot see the Dissertation Copy, pp. 550–55.

38. A comparison of the minutes of the Helpers Conference during the seventeen-fifties and sixties gives indication of the magnitude of this change, Protokolle der Helfers Conferenz, 1752–69. See also Levering's notebook "Organisation and Administration, January 1752—October 1764," MA Beth.

39. K. G. Hamilton, *Ettwein*, pp. 75–76.

40. de Schweinitz, *The Moravian Manual*, p. 106.

41. J. T. Hamilton, *A History of the Church*, pp. 202–3, 217.

42. K. G. Hamilton, *Ettwein*, p. 76.   43. *Ibid.*, p. 77.

44. *Ibid.*, p. 78.   45. *Ibid.*, pp. 100, 260, 269.

46. Letter of Ettwein to the Unitäts Ältesten Conferenz (undated). Ettwein Papers No. 870, MA Beth, quoted in K. G. Hamilton, *Ettwein*, p. 85.

47. K. G. Hamilton, *Ettwein*, p. 85.

48. Proceedings of the General Synod, MA Beth, 1782.

49. *Ibid.*, 1782, 1789, 1801.

50. Quoted in German by J. T. Hamilton, *A History of the Church*, p. 319.

51. *Ibid.*

52. Proceedings of the General Synod of 1818, MA Beth.

53. J. T. Hamilton, *A History of the Church*, p. 334.

54. *Ibid.*, p. 336.

55. Synodal Verlasz, 1867, MA Beth.

56. J. T. Hamilton, *A History of the Church*, p. 472.

57. Rondthaler, "The Use of the Lot," p. 7, MA Beth.

Chapter IV: The Development of the Choir System

1. See Lewis A. Coser, "Political Functions of Eunuchism," *American Sociological Review*, XXIX (December, 1964), 880–85 for an interesting discussion of alternate ways of dealing with this problem.

2. Protocolle der Synode in Gotha, June 16, 1840, MA Hh, cited by Uttendörfer, *Zinzendorf und die Jugend*, p. 82.

3. J. Plitt, Denkwürdigkeiten, Vol. II, Sec. 143, July 2, 1727, MA Beth.

4. Herrnhut Diarium, December 31, 1734, MA Hh, quoted in Uttendörfer, *Alt-Herrnhut*, p. 82.

5. J. T. Hamilton, *A History of the Church*, p. 42; Sessler, *Communal Pietism*, pp. 96–97.

6. At the same time the distinction between bands and choirs should not be drawn too rigidly. Both terms refer to the same social structure, except that the term *Banden* has traditionally been reserved for characterization of the exclusively religious groups of the early years of Herrnhut, whereas the term "choir" is used to designate these same groups at a later stage of development.

7. Protocolle der Synode in Gotha, June 16, 1740, MA Hh, quoted in Uttendörfer, *Zinzendorf und die Jugend*, p. 82.

8. Brüderlicher Verein und Willkür in Herrnhut, June 15, 1727, MA Hh, reproduced in Müller, *Zinzendorf*, pp. 106–10.

9. Diarium seit der Arrivée der See-und Pilgergemeine in Bethlehem, am 21. Juni, 1742, MA Hh, quoted in H. Erbe, *Bethlehem*, p. 40.

10. Verlass der Amerikanischen Provinzial Synode zu Lititz, April 17–19, 1765, MA Beth.

11. Letter of Zinzendorf to Captain Garrison, October, 1752, MA Hh, quoted in H. Erbe, *Bethlehem*, p. 28.

12. Diarium der Gemeine Herrnhut, MA Hh, quoted in Uttendörfer, *Alt-Herrnhut*, p. 83.

13. Dober, *Beschreibung und zuverlässige Nachricht*, p. 13.

14. The Constitution and Regulations of the Brethren in the Inn, February 29, 1736, MA Hh, quoted in Uttendörfer, *Alt-Herrnhut*, pp. 85–86.

15. Uttendörfer, *Alt-Herrnhut*, p. 87.

16. There was no systematic recording of population statistics of

Herrnhut during these years. Some demographic information is, however, to be found in the choir and community diaries, which generally recorded membership figures every few years. For detailed references to these population statistics see the Dissertation Copy, pp. 53–54.

17. Diarium der Gemeine Herrnhut, December 1, 1741, MA Hh, quoted in Uttendörfer, *Alt-Herrnhut,* p. 89. Any portrayal of the growth of the Single Brethren's choir which relies primarily on catalogues of population and housing statistics is likely to be misleading in at least one respect: these tabulations ignore the constant flow of population in and out of the Brethren's choir. For example, in the year 1743 eighteen new members came to the Single Brethren's choir from other Moravian communities, seventy-five new members came from the "world outside," thirty-six were sent abroad on missionary activities, and thirty-four were either ordered to leave or left of their own accord. Uttendörfer, *Alt-Herrnhut,* p. 92.

18. Dober, *Beschreibung und zuverlässige Nachricht,* p. 19.

19. For detailed footnote references to the population statistics see the Dissertation Copy.

20. Protocolle der Ältesten Konferenz, May 1 and May 13, 1743, MA Hh, quoted in Uttendörfer, *Alt-Herrnhut,* p. 93.

21. Protocolle des Richterkolleg, August 29, 1736, and Verlass der Ältesten Konferenz, July 28, 1742, MA Hh, quoted in Uttendörfer, *Alt-Herrnhut,* p. 95.

22. Uttendörfer, *Wirtschaftsgeist,* p. 289.

23. Uttendörfer, *Alt-Herrnhut,* p. 95.

24. Protocolle des Richterkolleg, May 28, 1743, MA Hh, quoted in Uttendörfer, *Alt-Herrnhut,* p. 96.

25. Diarium der Gemeine Herrnhut, December, 1744, MA Hh, quoted in Uttendörfer, *Alt-Herrnhut,* p. 96.

26. Uttendörfer, *Alt-Herrnhut,* p. 97.

27. The very fact that Bethlehem was not founded until 1740, that is, until almost the end of the period of choir growth which we have just sketched for Herrnhut, had important consequences for the manner in which the choir system evolved in this transatlantic Moravian settlement. For it was to the Herrnhut of the early seventeen-forties, and not of the seventeen-twenties, that the first Moravian immigrants, the majority of whom had spent a number of years either in Herrnhut or in one of the

other German settlements, looked for guidance and suggestions in the forming of their own communal structures. The transition from band to choir was thus achieved far more rapidly in Bethlehem than in Herrnhut.

28. Diarium Bethlehem, June 25, 1742, MA Beth.

29. Quoted in Levering, *A History of Bethlehem,* p. 178. Levering himself notes that although the choir principle is clearly stated, the scheduling of events is still very tentative.

30. Des Ledigen Schwestern Chores in Bethlehem Diarii, December 30, 1748, MA Beth. The "young Maidens" generally included girls from seventeen to twenty years of age.

31. Address of the community of Bethlehem to the Governor and Assembly of Pennsylvania, June, 1743, MA Beth.

32. See Diarium des Ledigen Brüder Chors, Vol. I, 1742–1762; Des Ledigen Schwestern Chores in Bethlehem Diarii, Vol. I, 1748–1756, MA Beth.

33. Levering, *A History of Bethlehem,* p. 142.

34. P. J. Acrelius, "A visit to the American Cloister at Bethlehem, June, 1754," *A History of New Sweden,* pp. 403–4.

35. See Wagner, *Die Handlung Dürninger,* pp. 38–77, for examples of such introduction of machinery.

36. H. Erbe, *Bethlehem,* pp. 41–42.

37. Altesten Konferenz, May 21, 1743, MA Hh, quoted in Uttendörfer, *Alt-Herrnhut,* p. 95.

38. Verlass des Richterkolleg, August 29, 1736, MA Hh, quoted in Uttendörfer, *Alt-Herrnhut,* p. 96.

39. Verlass des Richterkolleg, February 11, 1737, MA Hh, quoted in Uttendörfer, *Alt-Herrnhut,* p. 88.

40. "Lebenslauf der Anna Nitschmann," *Der Brüder Bote,* VIII (August, 1857), pp. 179–85.

41. For an elaboration of these functions see the Dissertation Copy, pp. 75–76.

42. See Chapter VII for details of the economic organization of Bethlehem.

43. H. Erbe, *Bethlehem,* p. 41.

44. Some historians have, however, tended to confuse consequence with cause. Thus I cannot agree with Sessler that "the reasons of econ-

omy for which it [the choir] was instituted in Europe were even stronger in America." Sessler, *Communal Pietism,* p. 97. Both in Europe and America the original motives underlying the establishment of choirs were clearly of a religious nature. It is only by tracing the gradual accretion of economic functions by the choirs that one comes to gain a proper historical perspective of the development of this institution.

45. In separating the discussion of economic functions fulfilled by the choirs from the analysis of social functions, I was guided primarily by the analytical advantages of such a procedure. To treat this analytical distinction as a historical fact would be to misinterpret the sequence of historical events. It is, therefore, essential to keep the empirical interdependence of the economic and social factors constantly in mind.

46. Jüngerhaus Diarium, September 19, 1755, MA Hh, quoted in Uttendörfer, *Zinzendorf und die Jugend,* p. 85.

47. Letter of Maria Spangenberg to Zinzendorf, April 21, 1746, MA Hh, quoted in H. Erbe, *Bethlehem,* p. 44.

48. See Uttendörfer, *Zinzendorf und die Jugend,* p. 84.

49. *Ibid.,* pp. 85–86.

50. Quoted in Uttendörfer, *Zinzendorf und die Jugend,* p. 79.

51. Jüngerhaus Diarium, November 11, 1750, MA Hh, quoted in Uttendörfer, *Zinzendorf und die Jugend,* p. 71.

52. Letter of Maria Spangenberg to Zinzendorf, April 21, 1746, MA Hh, quoted in H. Erbe, *Bethlehem,* p. 44.

53. See the Protocolle der Kinder-Conferenz, 1756–1759, MA Beth, which deal with matters regarding the content of education, how to bring up children, how to administer discipline, etc. The Kinder-chor Memorabilia, especially for the years 1753, 1759, and 1761, contain similar materials.

54. Haller, "Moravian Influence on Higher Education in Colonial America," *Pennsylvania Historical Quarterly,* III (1958), 10.

55. *Ibid.,* p. 11. For a comprehensive history of Moravian education in America see Haller's *Early Moravian Education in Pennsylvania.*

56. H. Erbe, *Bethlehem,* p. 46.

57. Jüngerhaus Diarium, November 12, 1750, MA Hh, quoted in Uttendörfer, *Zinzendorf und die Jugend,* p. 101.

58. Zinzendorf himself preferred at that time to permit single rather than married persons to settle in Herrnhut. He was convinced that mar-

ried persons were more likely to cause trouble since their allegiances to other persons and places would tend to be greater and thus more difficult to sever. A listing of the reasons for accepting or refusing admission to persons during this period, often annotated by Zinzendorf's comments, clearly illustrates the Count's viewpoint. See Diarium der Gemeine Herrnhut, 1730–1736, MA Hh.

59. H. Erbe, *Bethlehem,* pp. 39–40.

60. Uttendörfer, *Alt-Herrnhut,* pp. 188–89.

61. Frohberger, *Briefe über Herrnhut,* p. 97.

62. Clarence E. Beckel, "Early Marriage Customs of the Moravian Congregation in Bethlehem, Pa.," *Pennsylvania-German Folklore Society,* III (1938), 5. An indirect measure of the extent of such total segregation of the spouses can be found in the fluctuations of the birthrate of the community. An analysis of the birth statistics available for this period proved, however, only one thing concretely: namely, that procreation did not cease. It is true that the net reproduction rate for the period of the General Economy is indeed somewhat lower than during the seventeen-sixties and seventies, but to attribute this difference solely or even primarily to choir segregation would be to ignore the importance of other variables. Also, given the high degree of geographic mobility of the community, and the constant migration to and from Europe, it becomes very difficult to establish a meaningful demographic picture of the community at any one time. All attempts at construction of net reproduction rates can, therefore, at best present only very crude approximations of reality.

63. Levering, *A History of Bethlehem,* p. 410.

64. Uttendörfer, *Wirtschaftsgeist,* pp. 318–19.

65. See Henry, *Sketches of Moravian Life and Character,* pp. 297–98; Ritschl, *Geschichte des Pietismus,* pp. 377–78; Mortimer, *Marriage by Lot, passim.*

66. Uttendörfer, *Zinzendorf und die Jugend,* p. 83.

67. Verlass des Richterkolleg, MA Hh, in Uttendörfer, *Alt-Herrnhut,* p. 100.

68. Uttendörfer, *Alt-Herrnhut,* p. 101.

69. Verlass des Richterkolleg, January 1, 1735, MA Hh, cited in Uttendörfer, *Alt-Herrnhut,* p. 100.

70. Verlass des Richterkolleg, May 20, 1735, MA Hh, cited in Uttendörfer, *Alt-Herrnhut,* p. 100.

71. Verlass des Richterkolleg, November 20, 1736, MA Hh, cited in Uttendörfer, *Alt-Herrnhut,* pp. 102–3.

72. Verlass der Nazarether Conferenz, August, 1758, MA Beth.

73. Diarium des Ledigen Brüder Chores, December 7, 1744, MA Beth.

74. Letter of Maria Spangenberg to Zinzendorf, April 17, 1746, quoted in H. Erbe, *Bethlehem,* pp. 42–43, MA Hh.

75. Peter Böhler in a memorandum to Spangenberg upon the latter's arrival in May, 1754, MA Hh, quoted in H. Erbe, *Bethlehem,* p. 43. Concerning the choir of the "embryos," Zinzendorf had decreed that "When the marriage has been consecrated to the Lord, and the mother lives in constant association with the Lord, then the children in the mother's womb already constitute a choir of their own. . . . ," Jüngerhaus Diarium, September 19, 1755, MA Hh, quoted in Uttendörfer, *Zinzendorf und die Jugend,* p. 85.

76. A number of historians have insisted that the choir as family surrogate was at all times regarded as a temporary expedient to be removed as soon as the social and economic conditions of the community improved. See Sessler, *Communal Pietism,* pp. 96–97; Burkhardt, *Die Brüdergemeine,* pp. 5–7. But contemporary records fail to substantiate this assertion. It was only after the choir institutions already succeeded in making important inroads into the family structure that a few persons voiced concern about the possible outcome of such developments. Even von Damnitz, the earliest and the most outspoken critic of the choir system, never regarded this aspect of choir expansion as a "temporary expedient." It was only after the choir system had failed that such rationalizations came to be made.

Chapter V: Modification and Decline of the Choirs

1. See *Alter und Neuer Brüder Gesang,* 2 vols. (1753). Later editions of this hymnal deleted many of the sensory images of the first edition.

2. Uttendörfer, *Wirtschaftsgeist,* pp. 250, 274.

3. *The Litany Book,* p. 190.   4. *Ibid.,* Appendix.

5. Uttendörfer, *Wirtschaftsgeist,* pp. 202–3.

6. See Hans Walther Erbe, "Zinzendorf und der fromme Adel seiner Zeit" (unpublished Ph.D. dissertation, Leipzig, 1928,) pp. 60–78.

7. Ritschl, *Geschichte des Pietismus,* Vol. III, p. 381.

8. Uttendörfer, *Wirtschaftsgeist*, p. 253.

9. *Ibid.*, pp. 252–53. Although by the time Zinzendorf returned to Herrnhut the experiences of Herrnhaag had forced him to re-examine some of his ideas, he did not abandon the religious conceptions and imagery which had had such devastating consequences. Indeed, by placing most of the blame upon his young son, Christian Renatus, and publicly denouncing his offspring's excesses, his charismatic leadership remained largely untainted; and he was able to prolong in Herrnhut many of the emotional excesses which had first taken root in Herrnhaag.

10. In 1743 seventy-eight members of the "second sea congregation" had come directly from Herrnhaag. See "Namensverzeichniss der Geschwister so im Jahre 1743 auf dem Schiff Little Strength, nach Pennsylvanien gereiszt sind," MA Beth. A group of eighteen Moravians from Herrnhaag arrived in Bethlehem in 1748. See H. Erbe, *Bethlehem*, p. 98.

11. For a comparison of the occupational distributions of the communities see Chapters VIII and IX.

12. Sessler, *Communal Pietism*, p. 179.

13. Letter of Cammerhoff to Zinzendorf, June 20, 1747, MA Beth, quoted in Sessler, *Communal Pietism*, p. 171.

14. Letter of Maria Spangenberg to Zinzendorf, December 2, 1746, MA Hh, quoted in H. Erbe, *Bethlehem*, p. 44.

15. The Single Brethren's choir grew from fifty in 1744 to 312 in 1759. The Single Sisters increased their numbers from fifty in 1747 to 188 in 1762. The choir of the children expanded from twenty in 1746 to 349 in 1759. Data on the Married People's and Widows' choirs is not as readily available, but a catalog of the population of Bethlehem in 1756 lists 314 married persons, fourteen widows, and seventeen widowers. The high proportion of children and small size of the Widows' and Widowers' choirs reflects the age distribution characteristic of an immigrant population. See the Dissertation Copy, p. 113, for specification of the source material.

16. See especially Peter Böhler's extensive correspondence with Herrnhut, 1751–1754, MA Beth.

17. Die Projekte und Vorschläge zur künftigen Veränderung der Bethlehemischen Oekonomien spezie aber des ledigen Brüder Haus betreffend, December 16, 1761, MA Beth.

18. Spangenberg alone remonstrated that the community could not

afford to pay real wages. Memorandum von Spangenberg an die Brüder Unität, November 11, 1760, MA Beth.

19. Schreiben an das Unitäts Vosteher Collegium und Direktorium, August 27, 1764, MA Beth. The choir diaries of the Single Sisters contain numerous references to their inability to make ends meet. See especially the years 1769–1787.

20. See K. G. Hamilton, *Ettwein,* pp. 57–58, for an excellent discussion of this point, where Hamilton concludes that even in a religious community "the profit motive cannot be eradicated permanently."

21. Ettwein Papers No. 1336. Memorandum given to Bishop Seidel with reference to Questions submitted by the Bethlehem Board to the General Synod of 1769, MA Beth.

22. Ettwein Papers No. 867. Ettwein an die Ältesten Konferenz, 1775, cited in K. G. Hamilton, *Ettwein,* p. 58.

23. In 1781 the debts of the Single Brethren amounted to £46/1/3 and by 1797 they had risen to £701/17/1. Jahresrechnungen der Chordiaconie der Ledigen Brüder in Bethlehem, MA Beth.

24. See H. Erbe, *Bethlehem,* p. 126.

25. Köber, Resolutionen und Verfügungen an das Bethlehemer Oekonomat, April 2, 1761, MA Beth.

26. The official choir documents, as might be expected, failed to record the disenchantment of the choir members and the researcher has to rely for the most part on informal correspondence of members of the various choirs. The very fact that even the entries in the diaries lack the spontaneity and disarming frankness so characteristic of the wording in the earlier years suggests that toward the end of the eighteenth century the keeping of these diaries had become a mere ritual.

27. See K. G. Hamilton, *Ettwein,* pp. 57–58, 70–72.

28. The Widows' Society of Bethlehem was one of the first pension societies to be formed in the United States. For an account of the history of this society see Augustus H. Leibert, "Historical and Statistical Matters Relating to the Widows Society," TMHS, Vol. X, pp. 41–104.

29. K. G. Hamilton, *Ettwein,* pp. 67–68.

30. See Levering, *A History of Bethlehem,* pp. 522–25.

31. H. Erbe maintains that the Single Brethren's choir was disbanded in 1814 (*Bethlehem,* p. 154), but cites no evidence for this claim. The closing entry in the diary of the Single Brethren's choir is dated August 24, 1817 (Chor-Diarium der ledigen Brüder, Vol. V, MA Beth).

32. Chor-Diarium der ledigen Schwestern in Bethlehem, Vol. V, August 11, 1841, MA Beth.

33. Verlasz der Ältesten Conferenz, August 3, 1744, MA Hh, quoted in Uttendörfer, *Wirtschaftsgeist,* p. 189.

34. See Uttendörfer, *Wirtschaftsgeist,* pp. 243-44, which contains a detailed breakdown of finances for the years 1744-1776.

35. Köber, Proceedings of General Synod of Marienborn 1769, MA Beth.

36. Herrnhut Diarium, December 12, 1751, MA Hh, quoted in Uttendörfer, *Wirtschaftsgeist,* p. 202.

37. Brüder Haus Konferenz, February 11, 1861, MA Hh, quoted in Uttendörfer, *Wirtschaftsgeist,* p. 211.

38. In Bethlehem, because of the proximity of the missionary field work to their community, Moravians continued to be sent out to the neighboring Indians even for very brief periods of service.

39. Protokolle der Unitäts Direktion, 1765; Vol. III, pp. 555-56, MA Hh, quoted in Uttendörfer, *Wirtschaftsgeist,* pp. 87-88.

40. Schwestern Haus Diarium, October 19, 1744; April 28, 1745; February 8, 1746; March 4, 1755; MA Hh, cited in Uttendörfer, *Wirtschaftsgeist,* pp. 274, 278; Wagner, *Die Handlung Dürninger,* pp. 39-41.

41. Frederick de Watteville to Zinzendorf, June 21, 1754, MA Hh, quoted in Uttendörfer, *Wirtschaftsgeist,* pp. 19-20.

42. Figures on the number of persons in each choir are generally to be found in the last entry for a given year in the Herrnhut Diarium. The number of married persons rose from 194 in 1745 to 230 in 1760. In 1800 there were 232 married persons. See Uttendörfer, *Wirtschaftsgeist,* pp. 11-12.

43. Ältesten Konferenz, April 5, 15, and 26, 1746; May 10, 1746; July 29, 1746; October 27, 1746; MA Hh, cited in Uttendörfer, *Wirtschaftsgeist,* p. 290.

44. Jünger Haus Diarium, 1759, Beilage 18, 1; Helfers Konferenz, October 5, 1758, Ältesten Konferenz, April 8, 1768, MA Hh, quoted in Uttendörfer, *Wirtschaftsgeist,* p. 292.

45. Letter from Brother Thomas to the Ältesten Konferenz, June 12, 1766, Prediger Archiv, MA Hh, quoted in Uttendörfer, *Wirtschaftsgeist,* p. 307.

46. Wittwen Chor Diarium, November 3, 1746; August 30, 1751, MA Hh, cited in Uttendörfer, *Wirtschaftsgeist,* p. 318.

47. The Proceedings of the Vorsteher Collegium, for example, mention a gift of 1,386 talers which was bequeathed to the Single Sisters' choir in 1777 (Uttendörfer, *Wirtschaftsgeist,* pp. 288–89); see Hans Walther Erbe, "Zinzendorf," pp. 57–59; Gerhard Meyer, "Pietismus und Herrnhutertum in Niedersachsen im 18. Jahrhundert," *Niedersächsisches Jahrbuch,* XXIV (1952), 97–133.

48. Brüder Haus Diarium, October 10, 1765; Brüder Helfers Konferenz, February 18, 1761; March 3, 1761; July 8, 1761; MA Hh, cited in Uttendörfer, *Wirtschaftsgeist,* pp. 204–5.

49. Jünger Haus Diarium, September 3, 1752, MA Hh, quoted in Uttendörfer, *Wirtschaftsgeist,* p. 312.

50. See Uttendörfer, *Wirtschaftsgeist,* pp. 205, 404–5.

51. Helfers Konferenz, June 26, 1757, MA Hh, cited in Uttendörfer, *Wirtschaftsgeist,* pp. 99–100.

52. Oekonomats Konferenz, June 17, 1761, MA Hh, cited in Uttendörfer, *Wirtschaftsgeist,* p. 406.

53. Proceedings of the General Synod at Marienborn, 1769, MA Beth.

54. See Uttendörfer, *Wirtschaftsgeist,* pp. 294–95.

55. See Herrnhut Diarium, Memorabilia, 1746–1775, MA Hh.

56. Schriften Zinzendorf's, MA Hh, quoted in Uttendörfer, *Wirtschaftsgeist,* p. 340.

57. Synodal Verlasz zu Marienborn, 1764, MA Beth.

58. *Ibid.,* cf. Uttendörfer, *Wirtschaftsgeist,* pp. 342–46.

59. Uttendörfer, *Wirtschaftsgeist,* p. 347.

60. Uttendörfer, *Zinzendorf und die Jugend,* pp. 71–72.

61. Uttendörfer, *Wirtschaftsgeist,* p. 348.

62. This Synod marks the first real intervention of the bourgeoisie in matters of vital decision-making. Until then such matters had been left to Zinzendorf and to his predominantly aristocratic lieutenants.

63. Ältesten Konferenz, March 6, 1769, MA Hh, cited in Uttendörfer, *Wirtschaftsgeist,* p. 214.

64. Revision des Herrnhuter Wittwen Hauses, March 19, 1770, MA Hh, quoted in Uttendörfer, *Wirtschaftsgeist,* pp. 329–30.

65. Synodal Verlasz zu Barby, August 22, 1775, MA Beth.

66. Memorandum des Schwestern-kommitees, Synode zu Barby, 1775, MA Hh, quoted in Uttendörfer, *Wirtschaftsgeist,* p. 354.

67. Synodal Verlasz, 1775, MA Hh, cited in Uttendörfer, *Wirtschafts-geist*, p. 355.

Chapter VI: Marital Norms and Behavior

1. Zinzendorf, "Privat-Erklärung der von Gott selbst zusammen gebracht einfältigen Gemeine zu Herrnhuts, an einen Theologen der sie liebte," *Büdingische Sammlung,* Vol. I, Section VIII, p. 54. The Moravian view of marriage did not tally with the official Pietist doctrines of Spener and Francke. According to the Pietists, "Sexual intercourse was permitted, even within marriage, only as a means willed by God for the increase of His glory according to the commandment 'Be fruitful and multiply.' " Weber, *The Protestant Ethic,* p. 158.

2. H. Erbe, *Bethlehem,* p. 36.

3. Herbert Bemman, "Die Soziologische Struktur des Herrnhuter-tums" (unpublished Ph.D. dissertation, Heidelberg, 1921), pp. 116–17.

4. "Brüderlicher Verein und Wilkür" (1727), No. 20, MA Hh, reproduced in Müller, *Zinzendorf als Erneuerer der Brüderkirche,* p. 413.

5. Protokoll der Synode von 1769, p. 124, MA Beth.

6. Interim Arrangierte Konferenz, July 17, 1762, cited in H. Erbe, *Bethlehem,* p. 37.

7. Zinzendorf in a letter to the Supervisor of the Single Sisters' choir, September, 1752, MA Beth.

8. Memorandum from the American Conference in London, December 6, 1751, MA Beth.

9. *The Litany Book,* Appendix, quoted in Sessler, *Communal Pietism,* p. 117.

10. *A Collection of Hymns of the Children of God,* Part II, No. 372.

11. *Ibid.,* Part II, No. 377.

12. *Ibid.,* Part II, Nos. 268, 423. For a provocative discussion of the sexual themes inherent in the Moravians' theological speculations see Pfister, *Die Frömmigkeit des Grafen Ludwig von Zinzendorf.*

13. H. Erbe, *Bethlehem,* p. 183.

14. Herrnhut Diarium, December 31, 1753, MA Hh, cited in Uttendörfer, *Wirtschaftsgeist,* p. 11.

15. Spangenberg to Zinzendorf, December, 1754, MA Hh, quoted in H. Erbe, *Bethlehem,* p. 37.

16. Spangenberg to Zinzendorf, November, 1753, MA Hh, quoted in H Erbe, *Bethlehem,* pp. 37–38.

17. See Jordan, "Moravian Immigration to Pennsylvania," *Pennsylvania Magazine of History and Biography,* III (1879), 528–37.

18. Correspondence between Brother von Marshall and John Ettwein, Ettwein Papers No. 1101, MA Beth, cited in K. G. Hamilton, *Ettwein,* p. 81.

19. Konferenz des 9. März 1746. Unitäts Vorsteher Archiv I, 6, 4, MA Hh, cited in Uttendörfer, *Wirtschaftsgeist,* p. 371.

20. Synodal Verlasz zu Marienborn, 1769, MA Beth.

21. Schwestern Diarium, March 29, 1758, MA Hh, quoted in Uttendörfer, *Wirtschaftsgeist,* pp. 254–55.

22. Schwestern Diarium, October 15, 1743, MA Hh, quoted in Uttendörfer, *Wirtschaftsgeist,* p. 251.

23. Schwestern Diarium, July 4, 1744, MA Hh, quoted in Uttendörfer, *Wirtschaftsgeist,* p. 251.

24. Schwestern Diarium, July 7, 1745; June 25, 1745; September 5, 1746; MA Hh, cited in Uttendörfer, *Wirtschaftsgeist,* p. 252.

25. Verlass der Ältesten Konferenz, September 18, 1767, MA Hh, cited in Uttendörfer, *Wirtschaftsgeist,* p. 228.

26. Ältesten Konferenz, December 19, 1769, MA Hh, quoted in Uttendörfer, *Wirtschaftsgeist,* pp. 228–29.

27. Ältesten Konferenz, March 31, 1770, MA Hh, cited in Uttendörfer, *Wirtschaftsgeist,* p. 229.

28. Spangenberg to Zinzendorf, August 1755, MA Hh, quoted in H. Erbe, *Bethlehem,* p. 37.

29. Letter of Spangenberg to Johann de Watteville, March 5, 1762, MA Hh, quoted in H. Erbe, *Bethlehem,* p. 38.

30. Spangenberg to Zinzendorf, June 19, 1752, MA Hh, quoted in H. Erbe, *Bethlehem,* p. 37.

31. K. G. Hamilton, *Ettwein,* p. 83.

32. *Ibid.,* p. 82.

33. Ettwein Papers No. 859, MA Beth, quoted in K. G. Hamilton, *Ettwein,* p. 82.

34. See H. Erbe, *Bethlehem,* pp. 37–38.

35. The Moravians' penchant for meticulous record keeping is reflected in their marriage registers, which provide us with a detailed ac-

count of these events from the earliest days of the communities to the present day. For Bethlehem the Marriage Records of the Bethlehem Moravian Congregation, 1742–1892, have been edited and translated into English in an unpublished manuscript by Clarence Beckel, available in the Bethlehem Archives. These records of marriage include some important biographical information on the spouses. In most cases they include data on the following: (1) name, (2) date of birth, (3) place of birth, (4) names of parents, (5) chronology of residence, (6) occupation of father, (7) past and present occupation(s), (8) date of death, (9) place of death, (10) number of children, (11) race, and (12) details of previous or subsequent marriages. For Herrnhut our analysis has had to rely primarily upon statistics reported by Uttendörfer in his published histories of the community.

36. For a more detailed description of these events see Beckel, "Early Marriage Customs of the Moravian Congregation in Bethlehem, Pa.: The Use of the Lot in Relation to the Marriage Rites and Description of Some Notable Ceremonies," *Pennsylvania-German Folklore Society*, III, 1–32.

37. Marriage Records of the Bethlehem Congregation, Vol. I, MA Beth.

38. *Ibid.*

39. For details of these rates and the procedures used in computing them see the Dissertation Copy, p. 190.

40. *Ibid.,* pp. 190 91.

41. See Sessler, *Communal Pietism,* pp. 74–75.

42. Unfortunately the data on marriages in the Moravian Archives in Bethlehem do not contain adequate information of the age-sex distribution of the population to permit systematic control of these variables.

43. "Diarium seit der Arrivée der See-und Pilgergemeine in Bethlehem am 21. Juni, 1742," MA Hh, quoted in H. Erbe, *Bethlehem,* pp. 36, 183; Catalogus der Geschwister (1751), MA Beth.

44. K. G. Hamilton, *Ettwein,* pp. 52, 79.

45. *Ibid.,* p. 80.

46. Marriage Records of the Bethlehem Congregation, Vol. I, MA Beth.

47. *Ibid.*

48. These figures, based primarily upon data from the Herrnhut

Diarium, are analyzed in detail in the Dissertation Copy, pp. 195–96. The fact that the rate for Herrnhut decreased more sharply than that of Bethlehem may be attributed, in part, to the differences in the age distribution of the two communities. Whereas Bethlehem had a disproportionate number of its total population in age groups 20–40, Herrnhut, being a major center of emigration, tended to be underrepresented in these very groups. In addition, the tendency for the old, the infirm, and the retired missionaries to return to Herrnhut to spend the last years of their lives on German soil meant that the community had an even higher proportion of its population in the older age groups. It would seem very probable that were one able to control for differences in the age and structure of the two communities, the differences in the marriage rates would disappear.

49. *Ibid.*, pp. 196–97.

50. Frohberger, *Reise durch Kursachsen,* pp. 199–200.

51. Letter of Frederick de Watteville to Zinzendorf, June 24, 1754, MA Hh, quoted in Uttendörfer, *Wirtschaftsgeist,* pp. 25–26.

52. Frohberger, *Briefe über Herrnhut,* pp. 95–96.

53. Synodal Verlasz zu Barby, 1775, p. 352, MA Hh, cited in Uttendörfer, *Wirtschaftsgeist,* p. 411.

54. For a number of contemporary commentaries which attest to the material well-being of the community see Uttendörfer, *Wirtschaftsgeist,* pp. 418–19.

55. *Ibid.*, p. 418.

56. Konferenz der Deputierten der Unitäts Ältesten Konferenz mit der Herrnhut Ältesten Konferenz, July 14, 1786, MA Hh, quoted in Uttendörfer, *Wirtschaftsgeist,* p. 416.

Chapter VII: The Regulation of Property

1. Weber, *The Protestant Ethic,* p. 131.

2. "Precepts and Prohibitions," reproduced in Müller, *Zinzendorf,* pp. 105–6.

3. *Ibid.*, p. 107.

4. *Büdingische Sammlung,* Vol. III, p. 8.

5. Uttendörfer, *Alt-Herrnhut,* p. 108.

6. Thus Zinzendorf commented: "The natural caste remains as it is. If one wishes to make a gentleman out of someone who was born to be a peasant, one inflicts upon him a mask with a donkey's ears," quoted in Uttendörfer, *Alt-Herrnhut,* p. 79.

7. Uttendörfer, *Alt-Herrnhut,* pp. 125, 127, 129.

8. See Dissertation Copy, pp. 213–16.

9. Quoted in Uttendörfer, *Alt-Herrnhut,* p. 129.

10. "Concerning the New Innkeeper's Behaviour," January 30, 1727, MA Hh, quoted in Uttendörfer, *Alt-Herrnhut,* p. 130.

11. Herrnhut Diarium, February 15, 1731, MA Hh, quoted in Uttendörfer, *Alt-Herrnhut,* p. 131.

12. Herrnhut Diarium, April 29, 1731, cited in Uttendörfer, *Alt-Herrnhut,* p. 132.

13. Uttendörfer, *Alt-Herrnhut,* pp. 138–39.

14. Minutes of the Vorsteher Archiv, December 30, 1738, MA Hh, quoted in Uttendörfer, *Alt-Herrnhut,* p. 128.

15. "Inventory of the Drug Store," December 31, 1746, MA Hh, cited in Uttendörfer, *Alt-Herrnhut,* p. 129.

16. Herrnhut Diarium, December 22, 23, 1733, MA Hh, cited in Uttendörfer, *Alt-Herrnhut,* pp. 133–34.

17. *Ibid.,* p. 134.

18. For a more detailed account of this institution see Uttendörfer, *Das Erziehungswesen Zinzendorf's,* pp. 32–68.

19. Uttendörfer, *Alt-Herrnhut,* pp. 63–127.

20. "Verpflichtungsurkunde," August 17, 1746, MA Hh, quoted in Uttendörfer, *Wirtschaftsgeist,* p. 358.

21. December 21, 1747, Vorsteher Archiv, MA Hh, cited in Uttendörfer, *Wirtschaftsgeist,* p. 358. It seems unlikely that Zinzendorf would have been so ready to divest himself of these properties had it not been that he was himself in desperate need of cash to pay off some of his own creditors.

22. "Memorandum of von Damnitz," June 8, 1749, MA Hh, cited in Uttendörfer, *Wirtschaftsgeist,* p. 358.

23. "Memorandum of Zinzendorf," September 24, 1749, MA Hh, quoted in Uttendörfer, *Wirtschaftsgeist,* pp. 359–60.

24. Proceedings of the General Synod of Marienborn of 1764, MA Beth.

25. H. Erbe (*Bethlehem*, p. 23), basing his studies of Bethlehem on the records in the Herrnhut Archives, concluded that during the years 1742–1744 Bethlehem could best be characterized as practicing "a form of communism of love, as yet utterly untouched by economic or social considerations."

26. "General Plan for the Brethren's Economy at Bethlehem," 1744, MA Beth.

27. "John Ettwein to His Excellency General Washington," March 25, 1778, Letter No. 1203, MA Beth, quoted in K. G. Hamilton, *Ettwein*, p. 186.

28. "Brüderliches Einverständnis; einige zur Bethlehemschen und Nazaretschen Brüder Oekonomie gehörigen Momenta," Diarium Bethlehem, August, 1754, MA Beth (Tr., by Dr. W. N. Schwarze in Sessler, *Communal Pietism*, pp. 229–32).

29. "Die Gemeinorte oder Settlements der Brüder in Pennsylvanien, Bethlehem, Nazareth und Lititz," MA Beth.

30. Letter of Cammerhoff to Zinzendorf, June, 1747, MA Hh, quoted in H. Erbe, *Bethlehem*, p. 48. The Bethlehem Archives contain a whole shelf of documents detailing such transactions.

31. Letter of Cammerhoff to Zinzendorf, March 7, 1748, MA Hh, quoted in H. Erbe, *Bethlehem*, p. 49.

32. See L. T. Reichel, *The Early History of the Church*, p. 171.

33. "Account of the General Economy of Bethlehem, Nazareth . . . , June 1761 to May 1762," MA Beth. Although sums from this fund were occasionally used to defray a temporary expense of the community, no one had a legal right to dispose of this private capital.

34. "Brotherly Agreement," Paragraph 3, 1754, MA Beth.

35. "Draft of an Instrument to be signed by each one admitted into the Bethlehem Economy," 1754, MA Beth.

36. J. T. Hamilton, *A History of the Church*, p. 144.

37. "Brotherly Agreement," Paragraph 7, 1754, MA Beth.

38. Zinzendorf's Eventual Testament, December 27, 1738, quoted in J. Plitt, Denkwürdigkeiten, Part I, MA Beth.

39. Weber, *The Protestant Ethic*, p. 247.

40. Dober, *Beschreibung und zuverlässige Nachricht*, p. 133.

41. Quoted in English in Sessler, *Communal Pietism*, p. 103.

42. Composed in Bethlehem on October 27, 1745, quoted in L. T.

Reichel, *The Early History of the Church,* p. 174. Most of these hymns were, however, composed in German.

43. Letter of Spangenberg to Zinzendorf, April, 1746, MA Hh, quoted in Uttendörfer and Schmidt, *Die Brüder,* p. 106.

44. Spangenberg, "Gedanken über die General Oekonomie . . . ," March, 1751, MA Beth.

45. For a detailed description of the occasions upon which such love feasts took place see H. Erbe, *Bethlehem,* pp. 91–92. With the gradual secularization of the community these love feasts came to be observed only in connection with important church festivals, and the common meal assumed a symbolic meaning.

46. For a more systematic exposition and analysis of this problem with reference to the Kibbutz, Amana, and Hutterite communities see Ivan Vallier, "Production Imperatives in Communal Systems: A Comparative Study with Special Reference to the Kibbutz Crisis" (unpublished Ph.D. dissertation, Harvard University, Cambridge, Mass., 1959).

47. See Emile Durkheim, *The Division of Labor* (Glencoe, Ill.: Free Press, 1949), p. 353.

48. The choir system represented, as we have seen, an interesting experiment in the extension of the norms of religious equality to the social sphere. Yet even here, especially in Herrnhut, an attempt was made to separate the values of religious equality from the values of social differentiation. The history of the choir institutions illustrates the manner in which these two values continued to exist side by side in an admittedly uneasy truce.

49. Uttendörfer, *Wirtschaftsgeist,* p. 53.

50. "Der evangelischen Brüdergemeine zu Herrnhut, Brüderliches Einverständniss über derselben Ordnungen . . . ," MA Hh, quoted in Uttendörfer, *Wirtschaftsgeist,* p. 103.

51. "Verlass der oekonomischen Konferenz zu Nazareth," August, 1758, MA Beth.

Chapter VIII: The Division of Labor

1. For an elaboration of Zinzendorf's concept of religious exclusivism see Uttendörfer, *Alt-Herrnhut,* p. 192.

2. "General Plan for the Brethren's Economy at Bethlehem," 1744, papers concerning the early history of the Brethren in America, MA Beth. Important material on the General Economy is also to be found in "Bruder Ludwig's [Zinzendorf] Rede zum Abschied und Verlasz mit den Einländischen und Europäischen in Pennsylvanien zurückgelassenen Arbeitern, gehalten in Herrn Stephan Bennezet's House in Philadelphia am 29. Dez/9.Jan. 1742/43," MA Beth; "Special Plan vür Spangenberg mit welchem er anno 1744 nach America abgegangen," MA Beth. In discussing the economic system of Bethlehem during the period 1744–1762 it is impossible to separate the economic output of Bethlehem from that of the General Economy as a whole, particularly since all the financial transactions and accounts of that period treat Bethlehem and Nazareth as a single economic unit.

3. The Moravians compiled numerous statistics on the occupations of their members. For an elaboration of the distribution of occupations in Herrnhut and Bethlehem in the eighteenth century see Tables 1–6, pp. 280–87, 291–92, 303–8, 337–44, 347, 357–60 of the Dissertation Copy, which also indicates the specific source materials on which the tabulations were based. All the early statistics refer to the adult male population only.

4. See Dissertation Copy, pp. 281, 291.

5. It would seem rather unlikely that a young, struggling community could tolerate so many of its able-bodied men living off rents alone; this suggests that these people also pursued an additional occupation.

6. Bechler, *Ortsgeschichte,* p. 104.

7. "Inventory of Population and Occupational Pursuits," Herrnhut Diarium, April, 1727, MA Hh, quoted in Uttendörfer, *Alt-Herrnhut,* p. 10; "Catalogue of the Population of Herrnhut, 1745," MA Hh, quoted in Uttendörfer, *Wirtschaftsgeist,* p. 7.

8. Statistics on missionary activities are likely to have included only those on relatively short-term assignments. Those sent on longer missions were generally not included in the population registers of Herrnhut any longer. Since, moreover, emigrations of missionaries fluctuated considerably from year to year, these figures can only be taken as a very rough approximation of the facts themselves.

9. See Dissertation Copy, Table 4, pp. 337–44.

10. Verlass der Helfers Konferenz, November 28, 1764, MA Hh, cited

in Uttendörfer, *Wirtschaftsgeist*, p. 11. The emergence of semi-skilled workers as well as of commerce in Herrnhut is tied to the development of the textile industry by Dürninger. The importance of this man for the economic development of Herrnhut will be examined in the next chapter. Cf. Hammer, *Abraham Dürninger;* Wagner, *Die Handlung Dürninger.*

11. Wittwen Haus Diarium, May 1, 1758, MA Hh, cited in Uttendörfer, *Wirtschaftsgeist,* p. 322.

12. The percentage of unskilled laborers was greatest at the very time when the religious and emotional excesses of the Sifting Period were at their highest, a time in which little thought could have been spared for matters of vocational training.

13. J. E. Hutton, *History of Moravian Missions,* pp. 108–9.

14. Since many of these lists of occupations were originally compiled for tax purposes, only those aristocrats who owned no land in their own names would have been included. Members of the aristocracy who were property owners were exempt from taxation and thus presumably excluded from these communal inventories.

15. See Uttendörfer, *Wirtschaftsgeist,* p. 322.

16. According to a catalogue of 1764 the breakdown of the Single Brethren's choir according to type of employer was as follows: Employed by Single Brethren's choir, 114; employed by married master craftsmen, 67; employed by parents, 19; employed by Dürninger, 60; employed by the community or the Unity, 19; employed in Zinzendorf's household, 9; self-employed, 21, "Berufsliste des Ledigen Brüder Chors," June 17, 1764, MA Hh, quoted in Uttendörfer, *Wirtschaftsgeist,* pp. 196–97.

17. Report of Zinzendorf to the Communal Council, June 8, 1732, MA Hh, quoted in Uttendörfer, *Alt-Herrnhut,* p. 69.

18. "Inventory of Herrnhut Respectfully Submitted to the Governmental Commission of Saxony," May 14, 1736, MA Hh, quoted in Uttendörfer, *Alt-Herrnhut,* p. 82.

19. "Minutes of the Judiciary Council," October 25, 1740, MA Hh, cited in Uttendörfer, *Alt-Herrnhut,* p. 71.

20. Given the fact that the Moravians were extremely painstaking in their keeping of records, it seems likely that they also kept detailed accounts of economic production and financial transactions. Yet, Uttendörfer, in his compilation of documents relating primarily to the economic

history of the community, never once mentions the existence of such records.

21. For a detailed analysis of the occupational statistics of this period see the Dissertation Copy, Table 3, pp. 303–8.

22. "Vertheilung der Brüder in Nazareth in ihre verschiedene Handwerke," 1747, MA Beth.

23. See Cammerhoff's frequent request for more laborers to help build the houses of the General Economy. Cammerhoff's Epistola Tertia, 1747, MA Beth. Levering mentions that in order to speed up the construction of the Single Brethren's choir house four masons were hired "from elsewhere," *A History of Bethlehem*, p. 198.

24. Letter of Cammerhoff to Zinzendorf, March 17, 1748, MA Beth.

25. L. T. Reichel, *The Early History of the Church*, p. 166.

26. For a detailed breakdown of occupational data for 1759 see the Dissertation Copy, Table 6, pp. 357–60. In making comparisons with the earlier period it is important to bear in mind that the figures for 1747, 1750, and 1752 refer to the General Economy as a whole, whereas the data for 1759 refers only to the community of Bethlehem. Comparisons must, therefore, of necessity remain rather crude.

27. H. Erbe, *Bethlehem*, pp. 87–88, arrives at a similar conclusion after utilizing material on Bethlehem available in the Herrnhut Archives.

28. It becomes clear that even Bethlehem could afford such extensive missionary activities only as long as the ratio of the very young and the very old to those in the prime of life remained relatively low.

29. Levering, *A History of Bethlehem*, p. 198.

30. Verlass der Handwerker Konferenz zu Bethlehem, March, 1752, MA Beth.

31. "Letter of Cammerhoff to Zinzendorf," March, 1748, MA Beth. Sections of this very detailed account of the Bethlehem Economy have been abstracted by L. T. Reichel, *The Early History of the Church*, especially in Chapter III.

32. Letter of Spangenberg to Zinzendorf, June 17, 1752, MA Beth.

33. See comments of Thomas Penn and others in H. Erbe, *Bethlehem*, p. 59.

34. Letter of Cammerhoff to Zinzendorf, March 17, 1748, MA Beth.

35. *Ibid.*

36. Letter of Henry Antes to Spangenberg, 1744, MA Hh, quoted in
H. Erbe, *Bethlehem*, p. 61.

37. Cammerhoff to Zinzendorf, March 17, 1748, MA Beth.

38. The data on the early housing facilities of Bethlehem have been
taken from Levering, *A History of Bethlehem*, pp. 190–99.

Chapter IX: Processes of Economic Diversification

1. Jünger Haus Diarium, August 19, 1754, MA Hh, quoted in
Uttendörfer, *Wirtschaftsgeist*, p. 50.

2. Uttendörfer, *Wirtschaftsgeist*, p. 51.

3. Wagner, *Die Handlung Dürninger*, p. 27.

4. These estates, having been bequeathed to the Unity upon the death
of the Count, provided the security against which the Moravians were
able to borrow funds during the times of their greatest need. Uttendörfer, *Wirtschaftsgeist*, p. 51.

5. In 1758 a resolution was passed which insisted that the preoccupation of Moravians with agricultural concerns went against the basic plans
for the community. Memorandum des Direktorial Kolleg, July, 1758,
MA Hh, quoted in Uttendörfer, *Wirtschaftsgeist*, p. 51.

6. Memorandum des Aufseher Kollegium, September 3, 1766, MA
Hh, quoted in Uttendörfer, *Wirtschaftsgeist*, p. 51.

7. On the contrary, many neighbors depended upon Bethlehem to
supply their needs. See Spangenberg's letter to Graf Reuss, June 28,
1754, copy in MA Beth.

8. Letter of von Marschall to the Direktorial Kolleg, June 11, 1762,
MA Hh, quoted in H. Erbe, *Bethlehem*, p. 64.

9. Memorandum of Peter Böhler to Zinzendorf, June, 1756, MA Beth.
Sessler, *Communal Pietism*, p. 88.

10. Statement of account for the Bethlehem Economy, June, 1760, to
May, 1761, MA Beth.

11. Letter of von Marschall to the Direktorial Kolleg, June 1, 1759,
MA Hh, quoted in H. Erbe, *Bethlehem*, p. 59.

12. "Agricultural Receipts and Expenditures of the General Economy
of Bethlehem, Pennsylvania, June 1, 1758, to the end of May, 1759," MA
Beth.

13. Zeister Synode, May 24, 1746, MA Hh, cited in Uttendörfer, *Wirtschaftsgeist,* p. 36.

14. Oekonomats Konferenz, November 14, 1747, MA Hh, cited in Uttendörfer, *Wirtschaftsgeist,* p. 37. Some of the Brethren retorted that economic ruin was not due to the existence of other factories, but to prevailing conditions of monopoly.

15. Ältesten Conferenz, January 4, 1753, MA Hh, quoted in Uttendörfer, *Wirtschaftsgeist,* p. 39.

16. "Screiben des von Damnitz," October 16, 1750. Unitäts Vorsteher Colleg, MA Hh, quoted in Uttendörfer, *Wirtschaftsgeist,* pp. 38, 40.

17. For a more detailed history of this enterprise see Uttendörfer, *Alt-Herrnhut,* pp. 77–81.

18. The data concerning Dürninger's life history have been taken from Wagner, *Die Handlung Dürninger,* pp. 29–38.

19. Letter of Dürninger to French business associates, December 31, 1750, Copia Buch, Dürninger Archiv, Herrnhut, quoted in Uttendörfer, *Wirtschaftsgeist,* p. 157.

20. Quoted in Wagner, *Die Handlung Dürninger,* p. 112.

21. Uttendörfer, "Das Verhältniss der Dürningerschen Handlung zur Brüdergemeine Herrnhut und zur Unität bis zur dritten konstituierenden Synode der Brüderunität im Jahre 1775." MS (1923) Dürninger Archiv, Herrnhut, quoted in Wagner, *Die Handlung Dürninger,* p. 93.

22. Wagner, *Die Handlung Dürninger,* pp. 89–90.

23. *Ibid.,* pp. 101–4.

24. In the case of his employee Gambs, whose call to missionary service had been sanctioned by the lot, Dürninger managed to have the verdict of the lot reversed. See Dürninger Archiv Vol. 28. Autobiographical sketch of Gambs, cited in Wagner, *Die Handlung Dürninger,* p. 92.

25. Wagner, *Die Handlung Dürninger,* pp. 45–46, 91–92; see also the complaints voiced by many of the Brethren that they cannot make ends meet with the low wages offered by Dürninger, Verlass des Direktorium des Kommerzien Kommittees, Protokolle der Unitäts Direktion, 1765, MA Hh, cited in Uttendörfer, *Wirtschaftsgeist,* pp. 64–73.

26. Dürninger Archiv, Copia Buch, September 29, 1759, Herrnhut, quoted in Wagner, *Die Handlung Dürninger,* p. 95.

27. Hammer, *Abraham Dürninger,* pp. 7–8. Wagner denied that

there was anything irrational in Dürninger's conduct of his business affairs after 1747 but cites no evidence in support of his view.

28. Dürninger Archiv, Vol. 5, Materialwarenpreise, Herrnhut, quoted in full in Wagner, *Die Handlung Dürninger,* p. 78.

29. Uttendörfer, *Wirtschaftsgeist,* p. 143; Wagner, *Die Handlung Dürninger,* p. 80.

30. Wagner, *Die Handlung Dürninger,* pp. 43–45.

31. *Ibid.,* p. 46.

32. Uttendörfer, *Wirtschaftsgeist,* pp. 139–41.

33. Wagner, *Die Handlung Dürninger,* pp. 58–59.

34. *Ibid.,* pp. 60–64.

35. Verzeichnis der Druckformen, Dürninger Archiv, Vol. 4, Herrnhut, quoted in Wagner, *Die Handlung Dürninger,* p. 65.

36. A shock is defined in the Oxford English Dictionary as "a lot of sixty pieces." The length of the individual pieces, however, is not specified.

37. Druck Calculationes im Dürninger Archiv, Vol. 4, Herrnhut, cited in Wagner, *Die Handlung Dürninger,* p. 65.

38. Wagner, *Die Handlung Dürninger,* pp. 69–70.

39. *Ibid.,* pp. 70–71.

40. Uttendörfer, *Wirtschaftsgeist,* p. 143.

41. Status der Firma Abraham Dürninger und Co., December 31, 1773, Dürninger Archiv, Herrnhut, quoted in Uttendörfer, *Wirtschaftsgeist,* p. 143.

42. *Ibid.*

43. Wagner, *Die Handlung Dürninger,* pp. 120–23.

44. Bilanzen, Dürninger Archiv, Vol. 12, Herrnhut, quoted in Wagner, *Die Handlung Dürninger,* pp. 106, 175–76.

45. For a more detailed history of these enterprises during the nineteenth and twentieth centuries see Wagner, *Die Handlung Dürninger,* pp. 124–66; Wagner, *Abraham Dürninger & Co., 1747–1939* (Herrnhut: Abraham Dürninger Stiftung, 1940).

46. Uttendörfer, *Wirtschaftsgeist,* p. 152.

47. H. Erbe, *Bethlehem,* pp. 68–69.

48. "We cannot found factories in America, for it goes against British Law." Protokoll der Londoner Synode, 1753, MA Beth. See also Bining, *British Regulation of the Colonial Iron Industry.*

49. See Spangenberg's memorandum requesting Zinzendorf to intervene with the British Government on their behalf so that "the Commons in Old-England become not apprehensive," MA Hh, quoted in H. Erbe, *Bethlehem*, p. 71.

50. Spangenberg, "Gedanken die Gemeine und Pilgersache in Pennsylvanien betreffend—Die Oekonomie in Bethlehem," MA Beth.

51. Letter of Spangenberg to Zinzendorf, May 7, 1753, MA Beth, quoted in H. Erbe, *Bethlehem*, pp. 73–74.

52. "Status des Gemein-Store der Diakonie in Bethlehem," December 31, 1757, MA Beth.

53. One of these ships the "Little Irene," built by the Moravians, successfully completed its maiden voyage to Philadelphia but unfortunately was never able to complete the return trip because she had been found "too broad to be gotten upstream past the falls. . . ." Levering, *A History of Bethlehem*, pp. 287–88.

54. Bailyn, *The New England Merchants*, pp. 75–76.

55. Verlass der Interim Engen Conferenz, 1762, MA Hh, quoted in H. Erbe, *Bethlehem*, p. 77.

56. "Gedanken der Gemeinen und Pilgersache Pennsylvaniens betreffend," MA Beth. See also Sessler, *Communal Pietism*, p. 91.

57. Since most of our material deals with the world as seen by Moravians, our review of the economic relationships between the Brethren and their neighboring communities will of necessity be somewhat one-sided.

58. Writings of Zinzendorf, July 1, 1731, and March 4, 1734, MA Hh, cited in Uttendörfer, *Alt-Herrnhut*, pp. 71–72.

59. Herrnhut Diarium, August 1, 1733, MA Hh, cited in Uttendörfer, *Alt-Herrnhut*, p. 71.

60. Richterskolleg, September 27, 1734, MA Hh, quoted in Uttendörfer, *Alt-Herrnhut*, p. 71.

61. Minutes of the Communal Council, October 5, 1732, December 12, 1733, MA Hh, quoted in Uttendörfer, *Alt-Herrnhut*, p. 72.

62. Minutes of the Communal Council, November 17, 1731, MA Hh, quoted in Uttendörfer, *Alt-Herrnhut*, p. 70.

63. Minutes of the Helpers Conference, January 8, 12, 29, and February 26, 1756, MA Hh, cited in Uttendörfer, *Wirtschaftsgeist*, p. 222.

64. Wagner, *Die Handlung Dürninger*, p. 9; for an economic history of the Oberlausitz during the Middle Ages see Industrie und Handelskammer für die Preussische Oberlausitz, *Das wirtschaftliche Werden der Preussischen Oberlausitz*.

65. Herrnhut Diarium, January 2, 1742, MA Hh, cited in Uttendörfer, *Alt-Herrnhut*, p. 64.

66. Uttendörfer, *Alt-Herrnhut*, p. 79. During these years members of trade guilds in Saxony were supposed to practice their craft only in cities unless special permission had been granted by the guildmasters.

67. Letter of the Mayor of Bautzen to Zinzendorf, May 14, 1727, MA Hh, quoted in Uttendörfer, *Alt-Herrnhut*, p. 79.

68. Proceedings of the Unitäts Vorsteher Kollegium, June, 1762, MA Hh, cited in Uttendörfer, *Wirtschaftsgeist*, p. 422.

69. See Uttendörfer, *Alt-Herrnhut*, p. 80; *Wirtschaftsgeist*, p. 426.

70. Levering, *A History of Bethlehem*, p. 211.

71. *Ibid.*, pp. 211–12.

Chapter X: Financial Growth of the Community

1. Zinzendorf, Jünger Haus Diarium, August 27, 1750, MA Hh, quoted in Uttendörfer, *Wirtschaftsgeist*, p. 29.

2. Zinzendorf, Jünger Haus Diarium, February 5, 1753, MA Hh, quoted in Uttendörfer, *Wirtschaftsgeist*, p. 14.

3. "Memorandum des Herrn von Damnitz," Unitäts Vorsteher Collegium, June, 1754, quoted in Uttendörfer, *Wirtschaftsgeist*, p. 18.

4. Memorandum of Zinzendorf, September 26, 1755, MA Hh, quoted in Uttendörfer, *Wirtschaftsgeist*, p. 31. The Count's conduct of his personal financial affairs suggests strongly that he himself never learned to play the role of Martha. His attitude toward money matters continued to his death to be characterized by an almost total disregard for principles of economic rationality.

5. Sessler, *Communal Pietism*, p. 160.

6. J. T. Hamilton, *A History of the Church*, p. 148.

7. *Ibid.*, pp. 148–53.

8. Uttendörfer, *Wirtschaftsgeist*, pp. 12–13.

9. *Ibid.*, pp. 325–26.

10. J. T. Hamilton, *A History of the Church*, p. 229.

11. Bötticher, *Geschichte des Oberlausitzer Adels*, Vol. III. Bötticher makes it possible to trace the history of every member of the aristocracy who resided in Herrnhut during the eighteenth century. See also Bechler, *Ortsgeschichte*, pp. 74–75.

12. Verlass der Oekonomats Konferenz, 1759, MA Hh, cited in Uttendörfer, *Wirtschaftsgeist*, p. 12.

13. The role of aristocratic women in the Widows' choir appears to have been especially strategic for the economic development of that choir. Uttendörfer, *Wirtschaftsgeist*, pp. 322–23; Uttendörfer, *Alt-Herrnhut*, pp. 173–74; Bechler, *Ortsgeschichte*, p. 41.

14. Uttendörfer, *Alt-Herrnhut*, pp. 176–77.

15. *Ibid.*, pp. 40–44.

16. "Memorandum des Aufseher Kollegiums," March 18, 1767, MA Hh, quoted in Uttendörfer, *Wirtschaftsgeist*, p. 132.

17. See Hammer, *Abraham Dürninger*, p. 26. Redlich has argued that historians who studied the role of the German aristocracy of the eighteenth century tended to portray this class as one that lived a useless life. "European Aristocracy and Economic Development," *Explorations in Entrepreneurial History* (*1953*), VI, 78–91. Though Redlich never denied that there was an aristocratic way of life inimical to business activities, he was able to prove that quite a few members of this class did play important roles as innovators in various economic enterprises. Our study of the aristocrats of Herrnhut has, however, led us to conclude that, with the possible exception of one or two individuals, the members of this social elite did not manifest attitudes and values favorable to economic innovation and development.

18. Max Weber was never able to demonstrate that the Protestant ethic ever gained a foothold among members of the aristocracy, whether they were Calvinists, Lutherans, or Pietists.

19. E. W. Cröger, *Geschichte der erneuerten Brüderkirche*, III, 38. J. T. Hamilton, in *A History of the Church*, pp. 203–4, states the Unity's debts and obligations in American dollars. Since the first United States dollars were not minted until 1794 it is impossible to establish precisely the terms of Hamilton's exchange rates. The actual rates of ex-

change for the dollar varied from 1.25 talers in 1794 to 1.44 talers in 1874. A comparison of Hamilton's figures with those of Cröger suggests that Hamilton must have been using a rate of exchange of one dollar to 1.33 talers.

20. Verlass der Oekonomats Konferenz, February 4, 1763, MA Hh, quoted in Uttendörfer, *Wirtschaftsgeist,* pp. 373–74.

21. J. T. Hamilton, *A History of the Church,* pp. 218–19.

22. *Ibid.,* p. 227.

23. Translated from the German by J. T. Hamilton, in *A History of the Church,* p. 228.

24. J. H. Hamilton, *A History of the Church,* p. 229. Hamilton again quotes a dollar figure, which I have expressed in taler equivalents using an exchange rate of 1.33 talers to the dollar.

25. The Archives contain close to 1,200 separate account books, of which over fifty per cent relate to the eighteenth century. A systematic analysis of this material ought to provide some penetrating insights into the detailed operation of an eighteenth-century communal economy and should throw light on the question of the extent to which such economies were hampered by the colonial trade regulations of the day.

26. Unless otherwise indicated, the figures for 1760–1761 have all been taken from the financial statements of the assets, receipts, and expenditures of the General Economy, compiled by Christian Friedrich Örter for that year, MA Beth.

27. L. T. Reichel, *The Early History of the Church,* pp. 78–80, 87–89.

28. Memorandum Spangenberg's to Zinzendorf, June 4, 1754, MA Hh, quoted in H. Erbe, *Bethlehem,* p. 53.

29. The sole exception is to be found in the Dürninger enterprises, where, however, as we have already seen, it was only thanks to Dürninger's obstinate refusal to turn these profits over to the community that such capital could be accumulated.

30. Herrnhut Diarium, June 13, 1757, MA Hh, quoted by Uttendörfer, *Wirtschaftsgeist,* p. 49.

31. Herrnhut Diarium, December 30, 1745, MA Hh, quoted by Uttendörfer, *Wirtschaftsgeist,* p. 50.

32. 9. Erinnerung, Verlasz der Marienborn Synode von 1764, MA Beth.

33. "Gedanken des Herrn von Damnitz vom 8. Februar 1761," MA Hh, cited in H. Erbe, *Bethlehem*, pp. 88, 183.

Chapter XI: The Communal Economy on Trial

1. Quoted by Max Weber in *The Protestant Ethic*, p. 175.

2. "A short Relation and Abstract of the Conferences kept with all the laborers of the Pennsylvania Town and Country Congregations, assembled at Liditz from the 17th till the 19th of April 1765," MA Beth.

3. Synodal Verlasz zu Barby, 1775, pp. 155–56, MA Hh, quoted in Uttendörfer, *Wirtschaftsgeist*, p. 110.

4. H. Erbe, using evidence available on Bethlehem in the Herrnhut Archives, accumulated an array of data which similarly indicated that the economic situation around 1760 was by no means unfavorable, and concluded that internal economic factors could not, therefore, have initiated or even accelerated the abolition of this system (*Bethlehem*, pp. 123–26, 134). His final conclusion, however, ignores the operation of other economic factors which did contribute to the breakdown of the Economy.

5. Sessler, *Communal Pietism*, p. 188.

6. K. G. Hamilton, *Ettwein*, p. 58.

7. Sessler, *Communal Pietism*, p. 188.

8. Levering, *A History of Bethlehem*, p. 292.

9. H. Erbe, *Bethlehem*, p. 134.

10. Report of the Elders Conference of Bethlehem, May 31, 1766, MA Beth.

11. What was created was a form of taxation in kind rather than a type of socialized trade as suggested by H. Erbe, *Bethlehem*, pp. 141–42.

12. Levering, *A History of Bethlehem*, pp. 379–80.

13. "Brotherly Agreement," 1754, Paragraph 2, MA Beth.

14. It was to be expected that persons hostile to the Brethren and who had at one time lived in the General Economy might bring suit against the Moravians for having withheld from them the fruits of their labors. Levering reports one such test case in which a shoemaker who had left Bethlehem in 1759 and settled in Easton sued the Moravians for wages

owed to him, amounting to £525/13/9. The matter ultimately went to the Supreme Court of Pennsylvania, which in October, 1766, decided the case in favor of the Brethren. Levering, *A History of Bethlehem*, p. 380, footnote 17.

15. Sessler, *Communal Pietism*, pp. 195–96.

16. Statements of annual accounts of Bethlehem, Pennsylvania, 1762–1772, MA Beth.

17. "Bericht über den Status Oeconomicus von 1766," by Friedrich von Marschall, MA Hh, quoted in H. Erbe, *Bethlehem*, p. 146.

18. Letter of Marschall to J. P. Weiss, June, 1762, quoted in H. Erbe, *Bethlehem*, p. 146.

19. For a detailed comparison of the finances of the various enterprises during the seventeen-sixties see H. Erbe, *Bethlehem*, p. 147.

20. Levering, *A History of Bethlehem*, p. 413.

21. *Ibid.*, p. 424. The Moravians used the term "diacony" to designate financial organizations which maintained separate treasuries and accounts.

22. "Abstract of the rules and regulations agreed upon by the inhabitants of Bethlehem and subscribed to by all housekeepers and masters of trades when the Family Economy ceased, November 21, 1771," MA Beth.

23. For a more detailed analysis of the lease system see Levering, *A History of Bethlehem*, pp. 611–12.

24. Population statistics for this period are to be found in the annual inventories taken by the various choir institutions, as well as the communal authorities, and which were generally recorded in the choir diaries and the Bethlehem diary on the last day of the year.

25. Comments of a visiting Moravian from Lidiŧz, Lidiŧz Congregational Diary, May 16, 1778, MA Beth.

26. Levering, *A History of Bethlehem*, p. 506.

27. *Ibid.*, p. 511.   28. *Ibid.*, p. 609.

29. H. Erbe, *Bethlehem*, p. 155.

30. Quoted in Uttendörfer, *Wirtschaftsgeist*, pp. 377–78.

31. Quoted from the Proceedings of the Synod of 1769, Uttendörfer, *Wirtschaftsgeist*, p. 382.

32. Uttendörfer, *Wirtschaftsgeist*, pp. 393–94.

33. On this point see Dürninger's low esteem of the economic skills of his fellow Brethren; Wagner, *Die Handlung Dürninger*, p. 92.

34. Uttendörfer, *Wirtschaftsgeist*, p. 393.

35. *Ibid.*, pp. 394–95; see also J. T. Hamilton, *A History of the Church*, pp. 548–51.

Conclusion

1. For a summary of major turning points in the patterning of such institutional interdependence see the Dissertation Copy, pp. 572–82.

2. Deets, *The Hutterites: A Study in Social Cohesion*, p. 60.

3. Norman Birnbaum, "Conflicting Interpretations of the Rise of Capitalism: Marx and Weber," *British Journal of Sociology*, IV (1953), 125–41.

4. Bailyn noted a similar development among the Puritan merchants of New England a century earlier: "Economically all-powerful, politically influential but circumscribed, the merchants—willingly or not—were prime movers in a gradual, subtle, but fundamental transformation of New England society. Their involvement in the world of Atlantic commerce committed them to interests and attitudes incompatible with life in the Bible Commonwealths. Most of them did not seek the destruction of the Puritan society; but they could not evade the fact that in many ways commercial success grew in inverse proportion to the social strength of Puritanism." (*The New England Merchants*, p. 105.)

5. "Here is the essential paradox of social action—the 'realization' of values may lead to their renunciation." Robert K. Merton, "The Unanticipated Consequences of Purposive Social Action," *American Sociological Review*, I (1936), 903.

6. Weber appears to have felt that the social actions of the Moravians represented an affectual regression from rational action (*The Protestant Ethic*, pp. 131, 136, 248), whereas in fact they represent a questioning of this very "rationality." The major difficulty with Weber's concept of rational types of action is that he treats the ends of human action as given. But by excluding the objective evaluation of action of ends and taking into account only its subjective meaning to the actor he makes us ignore irrational components of his rational categories as well as rational

aspects of his traditional and affectual types. (See Worsley, *The Trumpet Shall Sound,* p. 272.)

7. Weber, *The Protestant Ethic,* p. 278.

8. Zinzendorf's collected sermons and addresses, December, 1741, MA Hh, quoted in Uttendörfer, *Alt-Herrnhut,* p. 182.

SELECTED BIBLIOGRAPHY

THE VOLUME of literature dealing with the history of the Moravians in the eighteenth and nineteenth centuries is considerable. The bulk of these secondary sources are, however, of limited value to us. Because they are for the most part concerned with descriptions of the religious activities and customs of the Moravians, especially their missionary work, they tell little of the social and economic context within which these religious activities took place. Most of these works, moreover, by Moravians as well as non-Moravians, lack objectivity.

Generally speaking, the history of Herrnhut has been studied in greater detail and with greater scholarship than has that of Bethlehem. Certain institutions of the Moravians have been examined at some length, while others have received scant attention. The disproportionate emphasis on the religious character of this group has already been noted. Their economic arrangements, in particular their attempts to develop a kind of religious communism of property and labor, have also been studied in some detail. Yet their attempt to establish a type of family surrogate, in the form of the choir system, and their use of the lot have to our knowledge never been examined systematically.

It would in any case have been desirable to supplement the secondary accounts with primary source material. Given the limitations of the secondary accounts, it was essential. Fortunately the Moravians were diligent not only in recording important events in the life of their community, but also in preserving these records for posterity. The Archives of the Moravian Church in Bethlehem are filled with personal, choir, and communal diaries, with letters and series of correspondence between Bethlehem and Herrnhut, with brief autobiographical sketches of almost every member of the community, with numerous statements of accounts and other economic transactions, as well as deeds of property and maps of the community at different points in time. It has been estimated that these Archives contain more than a million pages of manuscript, of which at least eighty per cent were written in German. Most of this collection, with the exception of manuscripts dealing with missionary work, has not, as yet, been catalogued. Two excellent guides to these Archives are Kenneth G. Hamilton, "The Resources of the Moravian Church Archives," *Pennsylvania History,* XXVII (1960), 263–72; and William H. Allison, *Inventory and Unpublished Materials for American Religious History,* pp. 147–65.

For Herrnhut we have had to rely mostly on published primary sources to supplement the secondary materials already alluded to. Uttendörfer, who was Chief Archivist of the Herrnhut collection for more than two decades, compiled a number of historical works on Herrnhut which consist primarily of lengthy extracts from manuscripts in the Archives held together by a minimum of personal narrative. (The two works of primary relevance to this study are *Alt-Herrnhut* and *Wirtschaftsgeist und Wirtschaftsorganisation Herrnhuts.*) As literature they make very poor reading; as compilations of historical documents they are excellent and form an important source of data on the community of Herrnhut. Many decisions affecting the fate of Herrnhut were made at Synods of the Moravian Church as a whole, or at meetings of the Unity Elders Conference. Copies of the minutes and resolutions of these conferences were kept in the archives of Bethlehem. Moreover, the *Gemein-Nachrichten,* which consist of extracts from the diaries of Moravian congregations throughout the world transcribed in Germany for the benefit of the Moravian Church as a whole, of which the Bethlehem Archives have an almost complete set, also provide much firsthand information on the community of Herrnhut.

The bibliography which follows contains most of the Moravian materials consulted, as well as some relevant comparative studies of other religious groups. General sociological references have, however, been omitted; specific acknowledgments to such sources are made in footnote citations throughout the book. For a more comprehensive bibliography and more detailed discussion of the sources, the reader may wish to consult the Dissertation Copy.

Manuscript Sources

Amerikanische Provincial Synoden, 1748–1835. 20 vols. Bethlehem Archives MSS. Original Minutes and Documents of the American Church North.

Beckel, Clarence E., ed. Marriage Records of the Bethlehem Congregation, 1742–1892. Unpublished typescript. Bethlehem Archives MSS.

Correspondence with public authorities in America, with the leaders of the Moravian Church in Herrnhut, as well as with private individuals, in particular from such writers as Zinzendorf, Spangenberg, Böhler, Antes, Cammerhoff, and Ettwein. Bethlehem Archives MSS.

Diarium der Gemeine zu Bethlehem, 1742–1850. 30 vols. Bethlehem Archives MSS. Original Minutes of the Proceedings of the Congregation at Bethlehem, with Extracts from the Diaries of other Moravian Congregations in Pennsylvania, and copies of documents, including letters and autobiographies, pertaining to the history of the community.

Diarium der Ledigen Brüder zu Bethlehem, 1742–1817. 5 vols. Bethlehem Archives MSS. A history of outstanding events in the daily life of the Single Brethren's choir.

Diarium der Ledigen Schwestern zu Bethlehem, 1748–1841. 5 vols. Bethlehem Archives MSS. A history of important events in the daily life of the Single Sisters' choir.

Gemeinnachrichten, 1747–1818. 162 vols. Title varies: 1747–1749 Gemein Diarium; 1749–1753 Diarium der Hütten, mit Beylagen; 1756–1760 Jüngerhaus Diarium; 1761–1764 Gemein-Haus Diarium; 1765–1818 Gemeinnachrichten. Indexed by Vernon H. Nelson, Bethlehem Archivist, 1964. Bethlehem Archives MSS. Contains extracts from the official proceedings of the Moravian Church throughout the world as well as information transcribed from the communal diaries of all Moravian congregations.

Levering, J. Mortimer. Notebooks compiled by Levering and his assistants citing specific manuscript materials which were subsequently used in the author's published history of Bethlehem. See in particular the notebooks entitled "Organization and Administration." 1742–1897. Bethlehem Archives MSS.

Monatliche Nachrichten aus der Provincial Helfer Conferenz, 1802–1848. 7 vols. Bethlehem Archives MSS. This conference constituted the government of the Moravian Church in America when the Provincial Synod was not in session.

Monatliche Nachrichten aus der Unitäts Ältesten Conferenz, 1764–1858. 11 vols. Bethlehem Archives MSS. Reports and Proceedings of the Unity Elders Conference, the governing board of the Moravian Church as a whole.

Pennsylvanische Synoden Verlass, 1742–1748. 12 vols. Bethlehem Archives MSS. Reports and Proceedings of Zinzendorf's attempt to unite the German Protestant sects into a single Church.

Plitt, Johannes. Denkwürdigkeiten aus der Geschichte der Brüder Unität, 1841. 3 vols. Unpaginated MS. Bethlehem Archives MSS.

Protocolle der Ältesten Conferenz zu Bethlehem, 1764–1862. 30 vols. Bethlehem Archives MSS. Reports and Proceedings of the Local Elders Conference.

Protocolle des Aufseher Collegium, 1780–1849. 19 vols. Bethlehem Archives MSS. Proceedings of the Supervisory Council of Bethlehem.

Protokolle der Helfers Conferenz, Bethlehem, 1752–1769. Bethlehem Archives MSS. Reports and Proceedings of the Provincial Helpers' Conference in Bethlehem.

Protocolle der Kinder-Conferenz und Kinder-chor Memorabilia, 1752–1762. Bethlehem Archives MSS. Reports and Proceedings of the Children's Conference and the Supervisors of the Children's choir in Bethlehem.

Synodal Verlasz, 1746–1836. 23 vols. Bethlehem Archives MSS. Reports and Proceedings of the General Synods of the Moravian Church.

Printed Primary Sources

Acrelius, Israel. "A Visit by the Reverend Provost Israel Acrelius to the American Cloister at Bethlehem," *A History of New Sweden; or The Settlements on the River Delaware.* Tr. by William M. Reynolds. Philadelphia, The Historical Society of Pennsylvania, 1874, pp. 402–34.

Alter und Neuer Brüder Gesang. 2 parts. London, Moravian Publications Office, 1953–1954.

Büdingische Sammlung Einiger in der Kirchen-Historie Sonderlich Neuerer Schriften. 3 vols. Büdingen, Christian Stöhr, 1742–1745.

Der Brüder Bote. Herrnhut, 1826–1891.

A Collection of Hymns of the Children of God in All Ages . . . Designed Chiefly for the Use of the Congregations in Union with the Brethren's Church. London, 1754.

Dober, Martin. *Beschreibung und zuverlässige Nachricht von Herrnhut.* Leipzig, Samuel Benjamin Walther, 1735.

Frohberger, Christian Gottlieb. *Briefe über Herrnhut und die Brüdergemeine.* Barby, Schöps, 1797.

—— *Reise durch Kursachsen.* Barby, Schöps, 1909.

Goll, Jaroslav. *Quellen und Untersuchungen zur Geschichte der Böhmischen Brüder.* Prague, Vol. I, 1878; Vol. II, 1882.

Great Britain, Parliament, House of Commons. *Report of the Committee on United Moravian Churches.* London, 1749.

Jahrbuch der Brüdergemeine. Vols. I–IV. Herrnhut, 1906–1961.

Kurze zuverlässige Nachricht von der, unter dem Namen der Böhmisch-Mährischen Brüder bekannten Kirche Unitas Fratrum, Herkommen, Lehrbegriff, äussern und innern Kirchenverfassung und Gebräuchen, aus richtigen Urkunden und Erzählungen von einem ihrer Christlich unparteischen Freunde herausgegeben. [n.p.], 1757. Ascribed by Spangenberg to Zinzendorf, by Beyreuther to Cranz.

The Litany Book According to the Manner of Singing at Present Mostly in Use Among the Brethren. London, 1759.

Neisser, Georg. *A History of the Beginnings of the Moravian Work in America.* Tr. by William N. Schwarze and Samuel H. Gapp. Bethlehem, Pa., Archives of the Moravian Church, 1955. No. 1.

Ogden, John Coser. *An Excursion into Bethlehem and Nazareth in Pennsylvania in the Year 1799.* Philadelphia, Pa., 1805.

"Regeln und Ordnungen der Brüder Gemeine in Bethlehem, Pa., 1851," reproduced in *Digest of the Provincial Synod of Salem, N.C., 1856.*

Reincke, Abraham. *A Register of Members of the Moravian Church and of Persons Attached to Said Church in this Country and Abroad, 1727–1754.* Bethlehem, H. T. Clauder, 1873.

Spangenberg, August Gottlieb. *Idea Fidei Fratrum oder kurzer Begrif der Christlichen Lehre in den evangelischen Brüdergemeinen.* Barby, Christian Laux, 1782.

—— "Report to Governor Denny, Bethlehem, November 29, 1756, containing a catalogue of all men, women, and children who for the present belong to the Bethlehem Economy," *Pennsylvania Archives and Colonial Records,* III, 1st series, 1852, pp. 69–75.

Verlässe, und Verhandlungen von, und Mitteilungen aus der Brüder Unität. A printed version of the Gemeinnachrichten. Herrnhut, 1836–1899.

Zinzendorf, Nicholas Ludwig von. *Deutsche Gedichte.* Berlin, 1735.

—— *Maxims, Theological Ideas and Sentences, out of the Present Ordinary of the Brethren's Churches.* Tr. by John Gambold. London, J. Beecroft, 1751.

—— *Peremtorisches Bedencken: His Short and Peremptory Remarks on the Way and Manner Where He has Hitherto been Treated in Contraversies.* Dresden and London, 1753.

Secondary Sources

Addison, William George G. *The Renewed Church of the United Brethren, 1722–1930.* London, Macmillan, 1932.

Aland, Kurt. *Spener Studien.* Berlin, W. de Gruyter, 1943.

Allison, William H. *Inventory and Unpublished Materials for American Religious History in the Protestant Church Archives and Other Repositories* (Carnegie Institution, Publication No. 137, Washington, 1910), pp. 147–65.

Aubert, Vilhelm. "Chance in Social Affairs," *Inquiry,* II (1959), 1–24.

Bailyn, Bernard. *The New England Merchants in the Seventeenth Century.* New York, Harper Torchbooks, 1964.

Banyas, Frank A. "The Moravians in Colonial Pennsylvania." Unpublished Master's thesis, Columbus, Ohio State University, 1940.

Batty, Beatrice. *Moravian Schools and Customs.* London, Swan & Sonnenschein, 1889.

Bechler, Theodor. *Ortsgeschichte von Herrnhut mit besonderer Berücksichtigung der älteren Zeit.* Herrnhut, Verlag der Missionsbuchhandlung, 1922.

—— *Wie es zur Gründung Herrnhuts kam.* Herrnhut, 1922.

Beckel, Clarence E. "Early Marriage Customs of the Moravian Congregation in Bethlehem, Pa.: The Use of the Lot in Relation to Marriage Rites and Description of Some Notable Ceremonies," *Pennsylvania-German Folklore Society*, III (1938), 1–32.

Becker, Bernhard. *Zinzendorf im Verhältniss zu Philosophie und Kirchentum seiner Zeit.* Leipzig, J. C. Hinrisch, 1886.

Bemmann, Herbert. "Die Soziologische Struktur des Herrnhutertums." Unpublished Ph.D. dissertation, University of Heidelberg, Germany, 1921.

Bender, Harold S. *Hutterite Studies: Essays by Robert Friedmann.* Goshen, Ind., Mennonite Historical Society, 1961.

Benner, D. Johann Hermann. *Die gegenwärtige Gestalt der Herrnhuterey in ihrer Schalkheit.* Giesen, 1748.

Bestor, Arthur Eugene. *Backwoods Utopias: The Sectarian and Owenite Phases of Communitarian Socialism in America, 1663–1829.* Philadelphia, University of Pennsylvania Press, 1950.

Betterman, Wilhelm. *Theologie und Sprache bei Zinzendorf.* Gotha, Leopold Klotz, 1935.

Beyreuther, Erich. *Nikolaus Ludwig von Zinzendorf.* (Vol. I, *Der junge Zinzendorf,* 1957; Vol. II, *Zinzendorf und die sich allhier beisammen finden,* 1959; Vol. III, *Zinzendorf und die Christenheit,* 1961.) Marburg an der Lahn, Francke, 1957–1961.

Bining, Arthur Cecil. *Pennsylvania Iron Manufacture in the Eighteenth Century.* Vol. IV. Harrisburg, Pa., Pennsylvania Historical Commission, 1938.

—— *British Regulation of the Colonial Iron Industry.* Philadelphia, University of Pennsylvania Press, 1933.

Binöder, Carl. "Zur soziologischen Bedeutung der Herrnhuter Brüdergemeine." Unpublished Ph.D. dissertation, University of Erlangen, Germany, 1956.

Blanke, Fritz. *Zinzendorf und die Einheit der Kinder Gottes.* Basel, Mojer, 1950.

Bolles, Albert Sidney. *Pennsylvania: Province and State, 1609–1790.* Philadelphia, John Wanamaker, 1899.

Bothen, Heinrich Joachim. *Zuverlässige Beschreibungen des nunmehr ganz entdeckten Herrnhuterischen Ehe-Geheimnisses.* Berlin, 1751.

Bötticher, Walter von. *Geschichte des Oberlausitzer Adels und seiner*

Güter, 1635–1815. 3 vols. Görlitz, Oberlausitzer Gesellschaft der Wissenschaften, 1912.

Böttinger, Karl Wilhelm. *Geschichte des Kurstaates und Königreiches Sachsen.* 2d ed., 4 vols. Gotha, F. A. Perthes, 1867–1873.

Brock, Peter de Beauvoir. *The Political and Social Doctrines of the Unity of the Czech Brethren in the Fifteenth and Early Sixteenth Centuries.* 'S-Gravenhage, Mouton, 1959.

Burkhardt, G. *Die Brüdergemeine.* Parts I and II. Gnadau, Verlag der Unitätsbuchhandlung, 1893, 1897.

Clewell, John Henry. *Historical Outline of the Moravian Seminary and College for Women from 1742 to the Present.* Bethlehem, Pa., Moravian Publications Office, 1911.

Cohen, John. *Chance, Skill and Luck: The Psychology of Guessing & Gambling.* London, Pelican, 1951.

Comenius, Johann Amos. *De Bono Unitatis et Ordinis Disciplinae et Obedientiae.* Amsterdam, Christopheri Cunradi, 1665.

—— *Ratio Disciplinae Ordinisque Ecclesiastici in Unitate Fratrum Bohemorum.* Amsterdam, Christopheri Cunradi, 1660.

Conkin, Paul K. *Two Paths to Utopia: The Hutterites and the Llano Colony.* Lincoln, University of Nebraska Press, 1964.

Cotter, Arundel. *The Story of Bethlehem Steel.* New York, Moody, May & Book, 1916.

Cranz, David. *Alte und neue Brüder-Historie, oder, Kurzgefasste Geschichte der evangelischen Brüderunität in den ältern Zeiten und insbesonderheit in dem gegenwärtigen Jahrhundert.* 2d ed. Barby, C. F. Laux, 1772.

—— *The Ancient and Modern History of the Brethren.* Tr. by La Trobe. London, 1780.

Cröger, E. W. *Geschichte der alten Brüderkirche.* Gnadau, 1854.

—— *Geschichte der erneuerten Brüderkirche.* Gnadau, 1864.

Deets, Lee Emerson. *The Hutterites: A Study in Social Cohesion.* Gettysburg, Pa., Times Publishing Co., 1939.

Dunaway, Wayland Fuller. *A History of Pennsylvania.* 2d ed. Englewood Cliffs, New Jersey, Prentice-Hall, 1948.

Eckstein, Fritz, ed. *Comenius und die Böhmischen Brüder.* Zürich, Insel Bücher, 1939. No. 96.

Erbe, Hans-Walther. "Zinzendorf und der fromme hohe Adel seiner

Zeit." Unpublished Ph.D. dissertation, University of Leipzig, Germany, 1928.

Erbe, Helmuth. *Bethlehem, Pa.: Eine Herrnhuter-Kolonie des 18. Jahrhunderts.* Herrnhut, Gustav Winter, 1929.

Finley, Samuel. *Satan Strip'd of His Angelick Robe; Being the Substance of Several Sermons Preached at Philadelphia, January, 1742–1743 . . . with an Application to the Moravians.* Philadelphia, 1743.

Fries, Adelaide L. *The Moravians in Georgia, 1735–1740.* Raleigh, Edwards & Broughton, 1905.

—— and J. K. Pfohl. *The Moravian Church, Yesterday and Today.* Raleigh, Edwards & Broughton, 1911.

Gataker, Thomas. *Of the Nature and Use of Lots.* London, Griffin, 1619.

Gerth, H. H., and C. Wright Mills. *From Max Weber: Essays in Sociology.* New York, Oxford University Press, 1953.

Görlitz, Industrie und Handelskammer für die preussische Oberlausitz. *Das Wirtschaftliche Werden der preussischen Oberlausitz.* [n.n.], 1926.

Haller, Mabel. *Early Moravian Education in Pennsylvania. Transactions of the Moravian Historical Society,* Vol. XV. Bethlehem, Pa., Times Publishing Company, 1953.

Hamilton, John Taylor. *A History of the Church Known as the Moravian Church or the Unity of the Brethren, During the Eighteenth and Nineteenth Centuries. Transactions of the Moravian Historical Society,* Vol. VI. Bethlehem, Pa., Times Publishing Company, 1900.

—— *A History of the Missions of the Moravian Church, During the Eighteenth and Nineteenth Centuries.* Bethlehem, Pa., Times Publishing Company, 1901.

Hamilton, Kenneth Gardiner. *John Ettwein and the Moravian Church During the Revolutionary Period.* Bethlehem, Pa., Times Publishing Company, 1940.

—— "The Office of the Bishop in the Renewed Moravian Church," *Transactions of the Moravian Historical Society,* Vol. XVI. Bethlehem, Pa., Times Publishing Company, 1953, pp. 30–58.

—— "The Resources of the Moravian Church Archives," *Pennsylvania History,* XXVII (1960), 263–72.

Hammer, Herbert. *Abraham Dürninger, ein Herrnhuter Wirtschaftsmensch des 18. Jahrhunderts.* Berlin, Furche Verlag, 1925.

Haupt-Schlüssel zum Herrnhuterischen Ehe-Sacrament. Frankfurt, 1755.

Hennig, Liemar. *Kirche und Offenbarung bei Zinzendorf.* Zürich, University of Zürich, 1939.

Henry, James. *Sketches of Moravian Life and Character.* Philadelphia, J. B. Lippincott, 1859.

Herpel, Otto. *Zinzendorf über Glaube und Leben.* Berlin, Furche Verlag, 1925.

Hertz, Karl H. "Max Weber and American Puritanism," *Journal for the Scientific Study of Religion,* I (1962), 189–97.

Hirzel, Stephan. *Der Graf und die Brüder: Die Geschichte einer Gemeinschaft.* Gotha, Leopold Klotz, 1935.

Hök, Gösta. *Zinzendorf's Begriff der Religion.* Uppsala, Universitets Arsskrift, 1948.

Holloway, Mark. *Heavens on Earth: Utopian Communities in America, 1680–1880.* New York, Library Publishers, 1951.

Holmes, John B. *History of the Protestant Church of the United Brethren.* London, 1825.

Hostetler, John Andrew. *Amish Society.* Baltimore, Johns Hopkins University Press, 1963.

Huizinga, J. *Homo Ludens.* London, Rutledge and Kegan Paul, 1948.

Hutton, Joseph E. *History of the Moravian Church.* 2d ed. London, Moravian Publications Office, 1909.

—— *A History of the Moravian Missions.* London, Moravian Publications Office, 1923.

Hymnal and Liturgies of the Moravian Church. Bethlehem, Pa., Moravian Publications Office, 1920.

Jecht, Walther. *Untersuchungen zur Gründungsgeschichte der Stadt Görlitz und zur Entstehung des Städtewesens in der Oberlausitz.* Görlitz, 1919.

Jordan, J. W. "Moravian Immigration to Pennsylvania," *Pennsylvania Magazine of History and Biography,* III (1879), 528–37.

Kauffman, Jay Howard. "A Comparative Study of the Traditional and Emergent Family Types Among Midwest Mennonites." Unpublished Ph.D. dissertation, Chicago, University of Chicago, 1960.

Kautsky, Karl. *Communism in Central Europe in the Time of the Reformation.* New York, Russell and Russell, 1910.

Kellenbenz, Hermann. "German Aristocratic Entrepreneurship: Economic Activities of the Holstein Nobility in the Sixteenth and Seventeenth Centuries," *Explorations in Entrepreneurial History,* VI (1953), 103–14.

Knothe, Hermann. *Die Stellung der Gutsuntertanen in der Oberlausitz zu den Gutsherrschaften von der ältesten Zeit bis zu den Ablösungen der Zinsen und Dienste.* Berlin, 1851.

——— *Urkundliche Grundlagen zu einer Rechtsgeschichte der Oberlausitz von der ältesten Zeit bis Mitte des sechzehnten Jahrhunderts.* Berlin, 1872.

Knox, Ronald A. *Enthusiasm: A Chapter in the History of Religion, with Special Reference to the Seventeenth and Eighteenth Centuries.* London, Oxford University Press, 1950.

Kohnova, Marie J. "The Moravians and Their Missionaries, a Problem in Americanization," *Mississippi Valley Historical Review,* XIX (1932), 348–61.

Kölbing, Frederick Ludwig. *Die Gedenktage der alten und der erneuerten Brüderkirche.* Gnadau, Verlag der Missionsbuchhandlung, 1821.

Kölbing, L. W. *Geschichte der Verfassung der evangelischen Brüderunität in Deutschland.* Leipzig, 1906.

Kortz, Edwin W. "The Liturgical Development of the American Moravian Church," *Transactions of the Moravian Historical Society,* Vol. XVIII, Part 2. Nazareth, Pa., Whitefield House, Laros Publishing Co., 1962, pp. 267–382.

Kramer-Wendell, Barlow. "Criteria for the Intentional Community: A Study of the Factors Affecting the Success and Failure in the Planned, Purposeful, Cooperative Community." Unpublished Ph.D. dissertation, New York, New York University, 1955.

Langston, Edward. *History of the Moravian Church, the Story of the First International Protestant Church.* London, George Allen & Unwin, 1951.

Lederhose, Charles T. *The Life of Augustus Gottlieb Spangenberg.* London, William Mallalieu, 1855.

Leibert, Augustus H. "Historical and Statistical Matters Relating to the Widows' Society of Bethlehem," *Transactions of the Moravian Historical Society,* Vol. X. Bethlehem, Pa., Times Publishing Company, 1917, pp. 41–104.

Levering, J. Mortimer. *A History of Bethlehem, Pennsylvania, 1741–1892, with Some Account of Its Founders and Their Early Activity.* Bethlehem, Times Publishing Company, 1903.

Lohmann, Martin. *Die Bedeutung der deutschen Ansiedlungen in Pennsylvanien.* Stuttgart, 1923.

Martin, John Hill. *Historical Sketch of Bethlehem, Pa.* Philadelphia, Lippincott, 1869.

Meyer, Henry Herman. *Child Nature and Nurture According to Nicholas Ludwig von Zinzendorf.* London, Abingdon Press, 1928.

Moravian Church Southern Province of North America, Provincial Synod. *Guide to the Manuscripts in the Archives of the Moravian Church in America, Southern Province.* (Historical Records Survey, North Carolina.) Raleigh, N.C., 1942.

Mortimer, Charlotte B. *Marrying by Lot: A Tale of the Primitive Moravians.* New York, Putnam, 1868.

———— *Bethlehem and Bethlehem School.* New York, Stanford and Delisser, 1858.

Müller, Joseph Theodor. *Geschichte der Böhmischen Brüder.* 3 vols. Herrnhut, Missionsbuchhandlung, 1922–1931.

———— *Zinzendorf als Erneuerer der Brüderkirche.* Leipzig, Friedrich Jansa, 1900.

Myers, Elizabeth Fetter. *A Century of Moravian Sisters: A Record of Christian Community Life.* New York, Revell, 1918.

Nitsche, Elsa Koenig. *Marriage by Lot, a Novel Based on Moravian History.* Allentown, Pa., Pennsylvania-German Folklore Society, 1958.

Oppen, Dietrich von. "Die Säkularisierung als soziologisches Problem," *Diakonie zwischen Kirche und Welt.* Hamburg, Furche Verlag, [n.d.], pp. 37–58.

Pescheck, C. A. *Geschichte der Industrie und des Handels in der Oberlausitz.* Leipzig, 1921.

Peters, Victor. *All Things Common: The Hutterian Way of Life.* Minneapolis, The University of Minnesota Press, 1965.

Pfister, Oskar. *Die Frömmigkeit des Grafen Ludwig von Zinzendorf: Ein Psychoanalytischer Beitrag zur Erkenntnis der religiösen Sublimierungsprozesse und zur Erklärung des Pietismus.* Wien, Franz Deutiche, 1910.

Pinson, Koppel S. *Pietism as a Factor in the Rise of German Nationalism.* New York, Columbia University Press, 1934.

Plitt, Hermann. *Zinzendorf's Theologie.* 3 vols. Gotha, Friedrich Andreas Perthes, 1869–1874.

Redlich, Fritz. "European Aristocracy and Economic Development," *Explorations in Entrepreneurial History*, VI (1953), 78–91.

—— *Iron and Steel*. Vol. I of *History of American Business Leaders*. Ann Arbor, Michigan, Edwards, 1940.

Reichel, Gerhard. *Die Anfänge Herrnhuts*. Herrnhut, Verlag der Missionsbuchhandlung, 1922.

—— *August Gottlieb Spangenberg, Bischof der Brüderkirchen*. Tübingen, J. C. B. Mohr, 1906.

—— *Zinzendorf's Frömmigkeit im Lichte der Psychoanalyse. Eine kritische Prüfung des Buch von Dr. Oskar Pfister*. Tübingen, J. C. B. Mohr, 1911.

Reichel, Levin Theodore. *The Early History of the Church of the United Brethren, Commonly Called Moravians, in North America, A.D. 1734–1748. Transactions of the Moravian Historical Society*, Vol. III. Nazareth, Pa., Whitefield House, 1888.

Reichel, Samuel Hartley. *The Lot as at Present Used in the Moravian Church*. Leominster, Orphan Press, 1889.

Reichel, William Cornelius. *A History of the Crown Inn*. Philadelphia, Lippincott, 1872.

—— *A History of the Rise, Progress and Present Condition of the Moravian Seminary for Young Ladies, at Bethlehem, Pa., with a Catalogue of Its Pupils, 1785–1870*. Philadelphia, Lippincott, 1870.

—— *Memorials of the Renewed Moravian Church*. Philadelphia, Lippincott, 1870.

Reichman, Felix, and Eugene Edgar Doll. *Ephrata as Seen by Contemporaries*. Allentown, Pa., Pennsylvania-German Folklore Society, 1954.

Renkewitz, Heinz. *Die Brüdergemeine: Ihr Auftrag und ihre Gestalt*. Stuttgart, 1949.

—— *Zinzendorf*. Herrnhut, Verlag der Missionsbuchhandlung, 1935.

Richter, Paul Emil, ed. *Literatur der Landes-und Volkskunde des Königreichs Sachsen*. Dresden, A. Huhle, 1919.

Rimius, Henry. *A Candid Narrative of the Rise and Progress of the Herrnhuters Commonly Called Moravians or Unitas Fratrum*. London, 1753.

Ritschl, Albrecht. *Geschichte des Pietismus*. 3 vols. Bonn, Adolph Marcus, 1886.

Ritter, Abraham. *History of the Moravian Church in Philadelphia*. Philadelphia, Hayes and Zell, 1857.

Rondthaler, Edward. "The Use of the Lot in the Moravian Church." Paper read before the Wachovia Historical Society, 1901. Copy in Bethlehem Archives.

Rothermund, Dietmar. "Denominations and Political Behaviour in Colonial Pennsylvania, 1740–1770." Unpublished Ph.D. dissertation, Philadelphia, University of Pennsylvania, 1959.

Roucek, Joseph S. "The Moravian Brethren in America," *Social Studies*, XLIII (1959), 58–61.

Sachse, Julius Friedrich. *The German Sectarians of the Province of Pennsylvania: A Critical and Legendary History of the Ephrata Cloister and the Dunkers*. Philadelphia, 1900.

Sawyer, Edwin Albert. *The Religious Experience of the Colonial American Moravians. Transactions of the Moravian Historical Society*, Vol. XVIII, Part 1. Nazareth, Laros Publishing Company, 1961. (Footnote page references refer to the original Ph.D. dissertation of the same title, New York, Columbia University, 1956.)

Schultze, Augustus. "A Brief History of the Widows' Society of Bethlehem Compiled from Minutes of the Society," *Transactions of the Moravian Historical Society*, Vol. II. Nazareth, Pa., Whitefield House, 1884, pp. 49–124.

Schunke, Siegfried. "Beziehungen der Herrnhuter Brüdergemeine zur Grafschaft Mark." Unpublished Ph.D. dissertation, Münster Westfählische Landes Universität, Germany, 1949.

Schwarze, William N. *John Hus*. New York, Revell, 1915.

De Schweinitz, Edmund Alexander. *The Financial History of the American Province of the Unitas Fratrum and of Its Sustenation Fund*. Bethlehem, Pa., Moravian Publications Office, 1877.

—— *The History of the Church Known as the Unitas Fratrum, or the Unity of the Brethren, Founded by the Followers of John Hus, the Bohemian Reformer and Martyr*. Bethlehem, Pa., Moravian Publications Office, 1885.

—— *The Moravian Manual, Containing an Account of the Protestant Church of the Moravian United Brethren or Unitas Fratrum*. Philadelphia, Lindsey & Blakiston, 1859.

Sessler, Jacob John. *Communal Pietism Among Early American Moravians.* New York, Holt, 1933.

Spangenberg, August Gottlieb. *Das Leben des Herrn Grafen Nickolaus Ludwig von Zinzendorf und Pottendorf.* 3 vols. Herrnhut, Verlag der Brüdergemeine, 1772–1775.

Stocker, Henry Emilius. *Moravian Customs.* Bethlehem, Pa., Times Publishing Company, 1918.

Talmon, Yonina. "Pursuit of the Millennium: The Relation Between Religion and Social Change," *Archives Européenes de Sociologie,* III (1962), 125–48.

Transactions of the Moravian Historical Society. 21 vols. Nazareth, Pa., Whitefield House, Laros Publishing Company, and Bethlehem, Pa., Times Publishing Company, 1876–1966. (Name and place of publication varies.)

Uttendörfer, Otto. *Alt-Herrnhut: Wirtschaftsgeschichte und Religionssoziologie Herrnhuts während seiner ersten zwanzig Jahre, 1722–1742.* Herrnhut, Verlag der Missionsbuchhandlung, 1925.

—— *Das Erziehungswesen Zinzendorfs und der Brüdergemeine in seinen Anfängen.* Berlin, Weidmann, 1912.

—— *Wirtschaftsgeist und Wirtschaftsorganisation Herrnhuts und der Brüdergemeine von 1743 bis zum Ende des Jahrhunderts.* Herrnhut, Verlag der Missionsbuchhandlung, 1926.

—— *Zinzendorf's Christliches Lebensideal.* Gnadau, Unitätsbuchhandlung, 1940.

—— *Zinzendorf's Gedanken über den Gottesdienst.* Herrnhut, Gustav Winter, 1931.

—— *Zinzendorf und die Jugend: Die Erziehungsgrundsätze Zinzendorf's und der Brüdergemeine.* Berlin, Furche Verlag, 1923.

—— *Zinzendorf und die Mystik.* Berlin, Christlicher Zeitschrift Verlag, [n.d.].

—— *Zinzendorf's religiöse Grundgedanken.* Herrnhut, Verlag der Missionsbuchhandlung, 1935.

—— *Zinzendorf's Weltbetrachtung: eine systematische Darstellung der Gedankenwelt des Begründers der Brüdergemeine.* Berlin, Furche Verlag, 1929.

—— and Walther E. Schmidt. *Die Brüder: Aus Vergangenheit und*

Gegenwart der Brüdergemeine. Gnadau, Verlag der Unitätsbuch-handlung, 1914.

Vallier, Ivan. "Production Imperatives in Communal Systems: A Comparative Study with Special Reference to the Kibbutz." Unpublished Ph.D. dissertation, Harvard University, Cambridge, Mass., 1958.

Wagner, Hans. *Die Handlung Abraham Dürninger und Co. in den Jahren, 1747–1833.* Herrnhut, Gustav Winter, 1934.

Webber, Everett. *Escape to Utopia: The Communal Movement in America.* New York, Hastings House, 1959.

Weber, Max. *The Protestant Ethic and the Spirit of Capitalism.* Tr. by T. Parsons. New York, Scribner's, 1930.

—— *Gesammelte Aufsätze zur Religionssoziologie.* 2 vols. Tübingen, J. C. B. Mohr, 1947.

Westphal, Milton C. "Early Moravian Pietism," *Pennsylvania History,* III (1936), 164–81.

Williams, Henry L. "The Development of the Moravian Hymnal," *Transactions of the Moravian Historical Society,* Vol. XVIII, Part 2. Nazareth, Pa., Whitefield House, Laros Publishing Company, 1962, pp. 239–66.

Wilson, William E. *The Angel and the Serpent.* Bloomington, Indiana University Press, 1964.

Worsley, Peter. *The Trumpet Shall Sound: A Study of Cargo Cults in Melanesia.* London, MacGibbon & Kee, 1957.

INDEX